IMAGES
of America

Southern Adirondack Foothills Fishing, Hunting, and Trapping

On the Cover: Helen Plete Wood was the daughter of Anna Harvey Plete and Adirondack guide Philip "Bill" Plete. She and her father are pictured in his boat with two lake trout after an early season fishing day. Helen was born in 1937. She married Ernest Wood in 1963. She died in 2012 at age 74. (Author's collection.)

IMAGES
of America

Southern Adirondack Foothills Fishing, Hunting, and Trapping

Megan Plete Postol

ARCADIA
PUBLISHING

ISBN 978-1-4671-2881-0

Published by Arcadia Publishing
Charleston, South Carolina

Printed in the United States of America

Library of Congress Control Number: 2017963182

For all general information, please contact Arcadia Publishing:
Telephone 843-853-2070
Fax 843-853-0044
E-mail sales@arcadiapublishing.com
For customer service and orders:
Toll-Free 1-888-313-2665

Visit us on the Internet at www.arcadiapublishing.com

This work is dedicated to the Plete men:
my brother, my dad, my grandpa, and my great-grandfather.
Their passion for the outdoors is my inspiration.

Contents

Acknowledgments

I am full of gratitude for the many people who shared their stories, photos, and memories with me in the course of this project: Steve and Ronna Hitchcock, Iona Rieck Trussell, Charlie Appleton, Chris Graves, Greg Baker, Ron Plete, Bill Plete, Tom McDonald, Jeff Evans, Wendy and Bryan Postol, Michael Schauer, Tom Murphy, and Shawn Horstman. Their generosity brought this book to life. Thank you again goes to my husband and my family for patience and encouragement as I worked on this project.

Introduction

The biography *Adirondack French Louie* by Harvey Dunham was published in 1953 and focused on the hermit Louis Seymour, or "French Louie." Dunham wrote about Seymour's life in the deep mountain forests of the Adirondacks. Seymour fished, hunted, and trapped the game of the woods to sustain his way of life:

> It is not a story of the achievement of great fame or riches . . . it's merely a homely narrative about a remarkable old character in his way and the simple life in our own North woods . . . French Louie! Every neck of the woods had its French Louie, each well known in his immediate locality. The Fulton Chain region had a French Louie at Rondaxe Lake, the Morehouseville section had one; at Tupper Lake Junction a French Louie "lived in a log cabin and froze to death in a snowbank"; there was one at Northville and there was a French Louie around Cranberry Lake. The woods were full of them; but the greatest of them all, known from Boonville to North Creek, was French Louie of the West Canada Lakes.

Adirondack French Louie is a regional classic. It was an early title in the long list of thousands of books that have been written that celebrate the Adirondack Park and the intriguing people who inhabit it.

French Louie lives on in all of those who retreat to the mountains in the search for freedom and challenge or in the journey to find rest from a spiraling world.

Even Harvey Dunham, the author who penned French Louie's biography only four years before his own death, found that these mountains made him feel more grounded and more alive. He spent as much time as he could there, tromping through old back-country trails and collecting the region's folklore.

"Harve loved the woods more than any man I ever knew," Lloyd Blankman is quoted saying in *Adirondack Adventures: Bob Gillespie and Harvey Dunham on French Louie's Trail.*

It was Dunham who was responsible for the preservation of French Louie's original fireplace on West Lake. He publicly protested the state's plan for the demolition of the hermit's fireplace in 1938 by submitting letters to the New York State Conservation Department and encouraging others to do the same. His appeal worked, the state backed down, and the fireplace stills stands today, over 100 years past the death of its constructor.

It is in the spirit of Dunham and "ol' Louie" that many Adirondack sportsmen pursue the outdoors today. That timeless, unrelenting pull for wildness is human nature, and the Adirondacks serve as a haven for those in tune with it. It is a place to escape the confines of "civilized" society. In these hills, man is a part of nature, not separate from it. He becomes enmeshed into the wild; he is of it, not master of it.

The Southern foothills region of New York's Adirondack Mountains is a quiet but lively gem. There are fewer developed areas there than in other parts of the park. Less commercial than the High Peaks region and just as beautiful, the area boasts of an abundance of wild game that attracts sportsmen of many kinds to visit or to stay and to etch out a life among the pines.

This region has changed along with history. Just like the building and eventual closing of the Erie Canal (south of the Adirondacks) changed New York State, its feeder, the Black River Canal's construction, and eventual closing changed the face of Forestport and nearby settlements, many of which are mentioned in this book. Woodgate, McKeever, Remsen, Boonville, Wilmurt, Piseco, Speculator, and other settlements once bustled with activity. Each community had businesses and a variety of industries. Logging was the dominant economic engine. The locals often worked winters in the logging camps and summers as guides to city-bred visitors. As early as the 1800s, tourists traveled to the area to fish and hunt. A guide's job was to bring the "sports" safely into the wilderness and back out again, help them harvest game, feed them, and provide shelter. Most guides tossed in the bonus of telling long-winded tall tales after suppertime.

Strong and sturdy like the rough country they inhabited, the guide became a symbol of the Adirondacks.

These foothills echo with the memories of all of those who have passed through the ages. Many of these once-busy places have been abandoned. Old foundations lay under overgrown brush, and graveyards, full of untold stories, sit silently in the mountain shade. Yet time goes on, and the region continues to evolve.

These cold, clean waters flow full of fish, the riverbanks are matted down with the footsteps of many critters, and the glorious wooded forest with its carpet of green moss and pine needles is home to both big and small game.

This area beckons adventurers. Adirondack adventures not only test and nourish sportsmen physically, but also emotionally and spiritually. Within these hills and valleys, people discover their potential and challenge their capabilities. The sense of accomplishment a hunter feels when he finally harvests a giant buck he's been tracking, or a fisherman when he reels in a big heavy trout they've been after, or a trapper when he walks up to a silky, prime-furred fisher in a well-made set is unmatched.

The people who lived, fished, hunted, and trapped (and continue to) in the region are a varied bag of personalities. Some are plain, some are as peculiar as they are charming, and some have the spirit of an independent old hermit suited to a life unbothered by peers. It takes a certain spirit of resilience to take on the challenges of this untamable country. The area exemplifies the pioneering and persevering spirit that our country was built on and continues to operate with today.

The Southern Adirondack Foothills are the backdrop for life for many of these hearty folks. Artists, tradesmen, entrepreneurs, preachers, sportsmen, laborers, housewives, businesspeople, authors, and so many more have come to this land to engage in the age-old tradition of harvesting wild animals.

The triumphs and misadventures of these colorful characters play out here in vintage photographs chronicling their pursuit of fish, feather, and fur.

One

Hunting the North Woods

Native Americans used the Adirondacks as seasonal hunting grounds long before any portion of the region was permanently settled. America's long heritage of hunting accounts for the preservation of wildlife and the continued conservation of the wild places it inhabits, such as the Adirondack foothills. The popularity of hunting these mountains peaked around the turn of the century, in the era of the Adirondack guide, but nonetheless, the tradition continues.

The Southern Adirondack foothills region still draws sportsmen from all over the world. The rugged terrain provides a challenge for the hearty sportsman willing to push himself to the limit.

Whitetail deer, black bear, coyote, wild turkey, snowshoe rabbit, and more fills the north country region with a lot of variety and a lot of opportunity, but being successful in the Adirondacks is not guaranteed. Many hunters head to the mountains every year, but very few of them go home with a filled tag. Still, the challenge and exhilaration this region provides seems to be enough to keep sportsmen coming back for more.

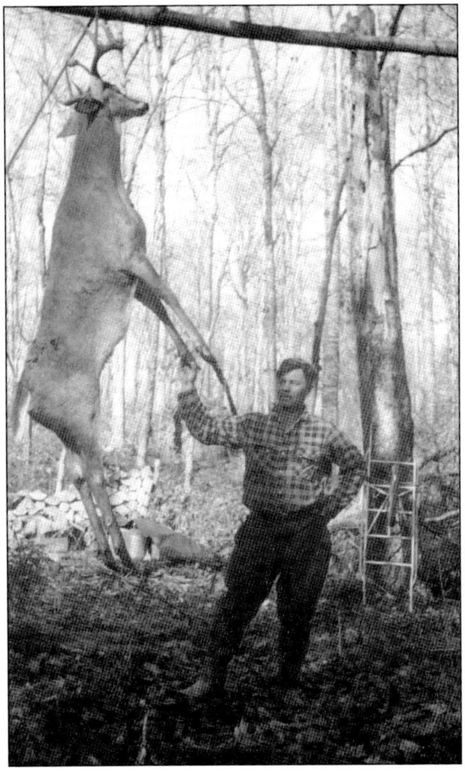

Joe Pomitcher Sr. stands next to his nice buck at the Perkins Clearing camp on International Paper land near Speculator approximately 1950. It used to be common practice for hunters and trappers to put up camps on land they did not own. Pomitcher made his home in the Grant area of Herkimer County. (Author's collection.)

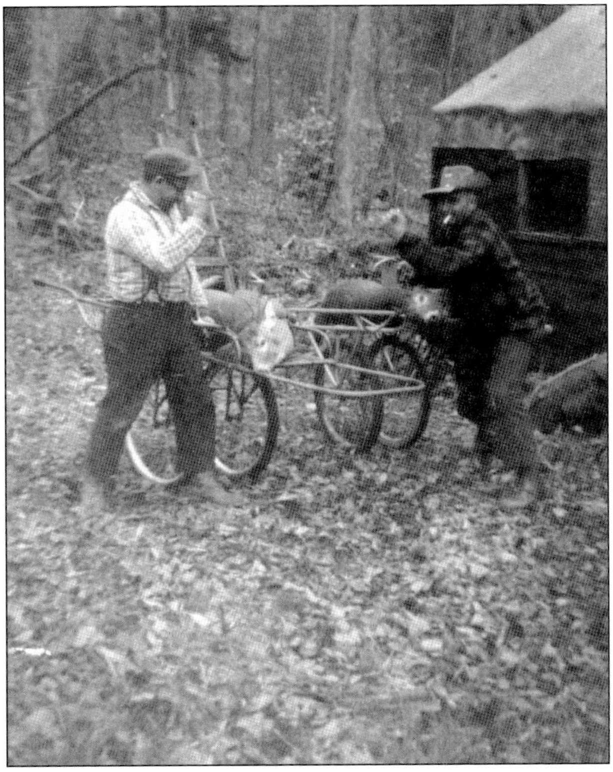

Nick Barley and Philip "Bill" Plete strike a silly pose for the camera with their bucks at the Perkins Clearing camp in the 1960s. The bucks were hauled out on homemade handcarts constructed from recycled bicycle wheels and other leftover parts. (Author's collection.)

Successful hunter Joe Pomitcher stands near his 10-point buck, which is tied to the roof of his 1950 Ford car with rope. The homemade cart that was used in hauling the deer out of the woods is also strapped to the top of the automobile. (Author's collection.)

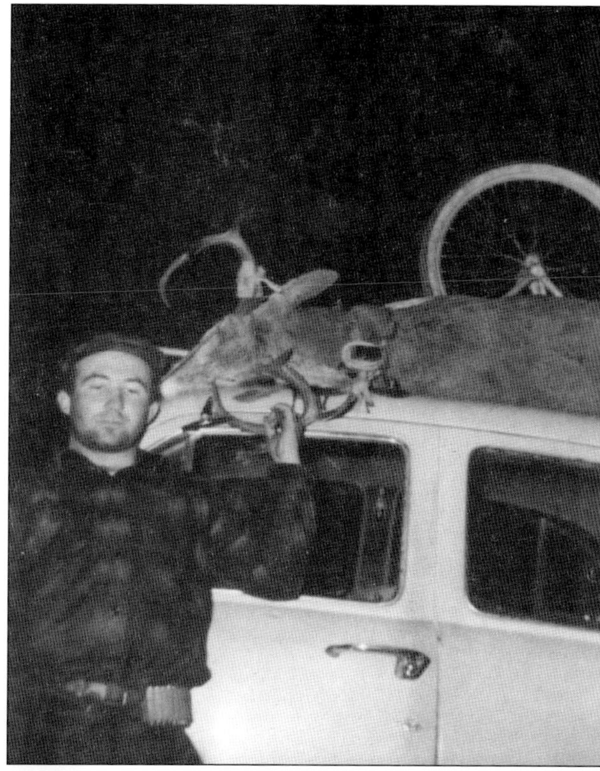

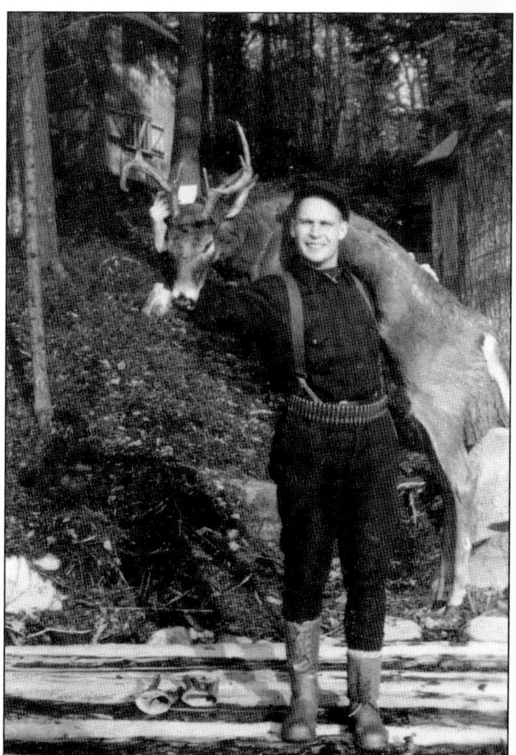

Fred Decker triumphantly shoulders his eight-point buck on November 15, 1950, in a show of victory at deer camp in the Piseco Lake area of the Adirondacks. This area is well known as a fishing destination. Nearby lakes are full of trout, walleye, bass, perch, and other varieties of fish. (Author's collection.)

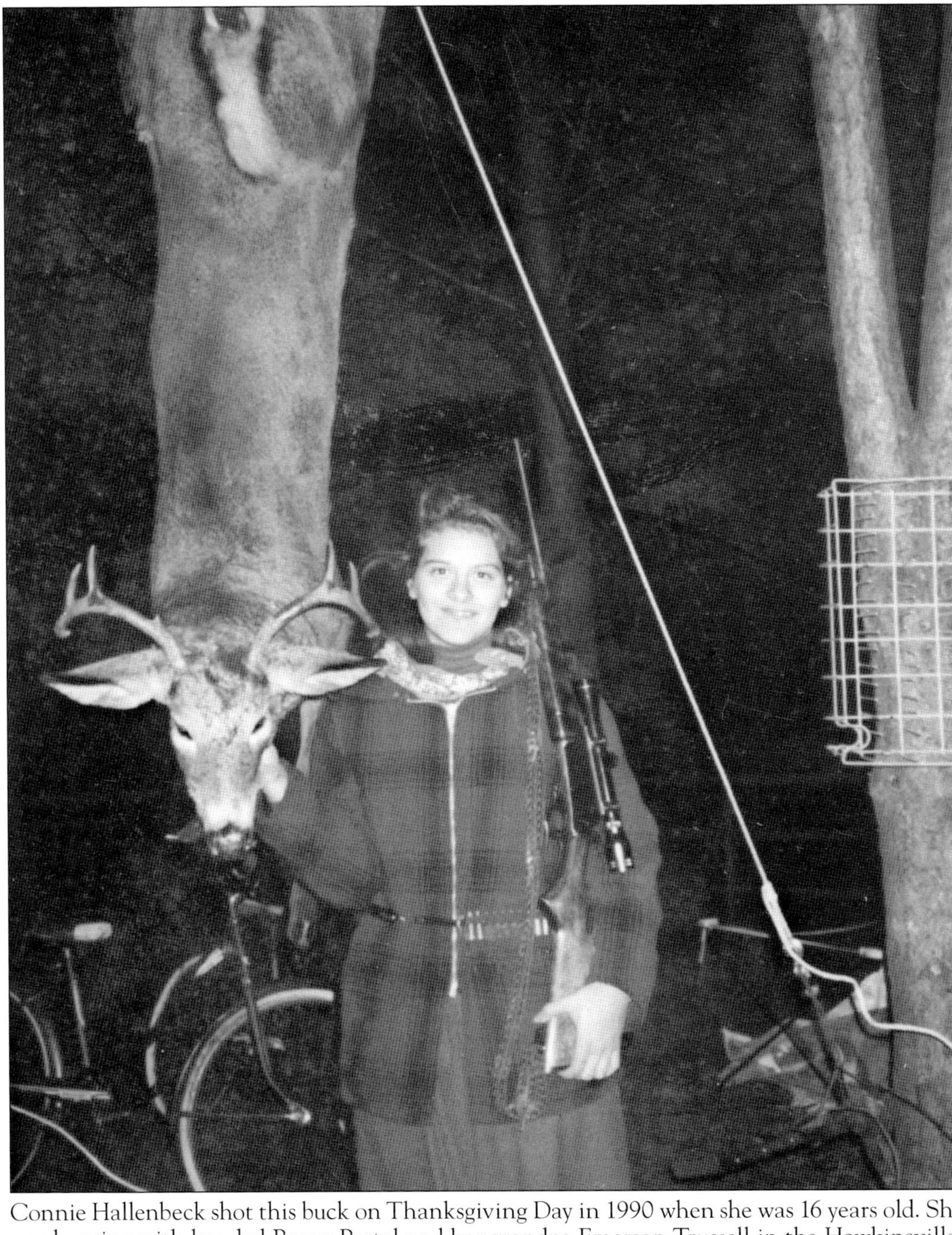

Connie Hallenbeck shot this buck on Thanksgiving Day in 1990 when she was 16 years old. She was hunting with her dad Bryan Postol and her grandpa Emerson Trussell in the Hawkinsville/ Boonville area on the Postol homestead, called "Wilderness Acres." They had gotten her set up on a ridge near a sandpit, told her they would be back to get her later, and then continued on to their spots. "It was getting late and I was worried they had forgotten about me," she said. "I was getting bored so I decided to chew some pink bubble gum. I had just started blowing bubbles when I heard footsteps and thought it was grandpa coming to get me. I turned to the side and it was this buck. I shot it and it only went a little way." (Courtesy of Wendy and Bryan Postol.)

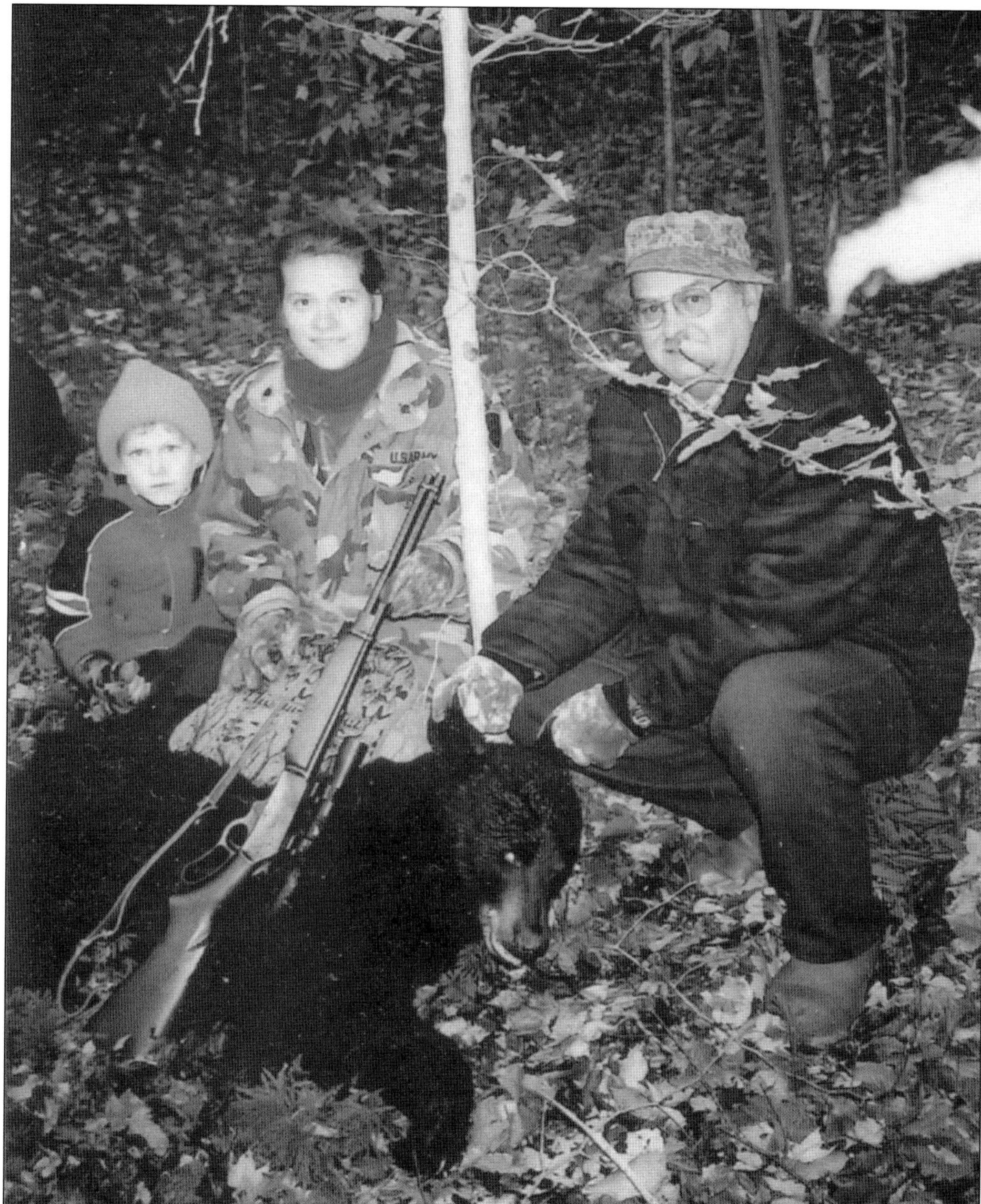

Black bear sightings during deer season are not uncommon in the Adirondack foothills. Connie Hallenbeck was deer hunting in October 2005 when she shot this bear. She was sitting in her dad's hunting blind on a Y in the road waiting for a buck to come when she noticed movement coming out of the nearby swamp. Her young son Doug was sleeping next to her in the blind. She recalls, "The funny thing was I had always prayed, 'God please don't send a bear my way unless I can kill it.' I debated whether to shoot it or not because I didn't want to scare Doug. I decided to (shoot it) and he slept through the whole thing! I had to wake him up to tell him I had shot a bear." (Courtesy of Wendy and Bryan Postol.)

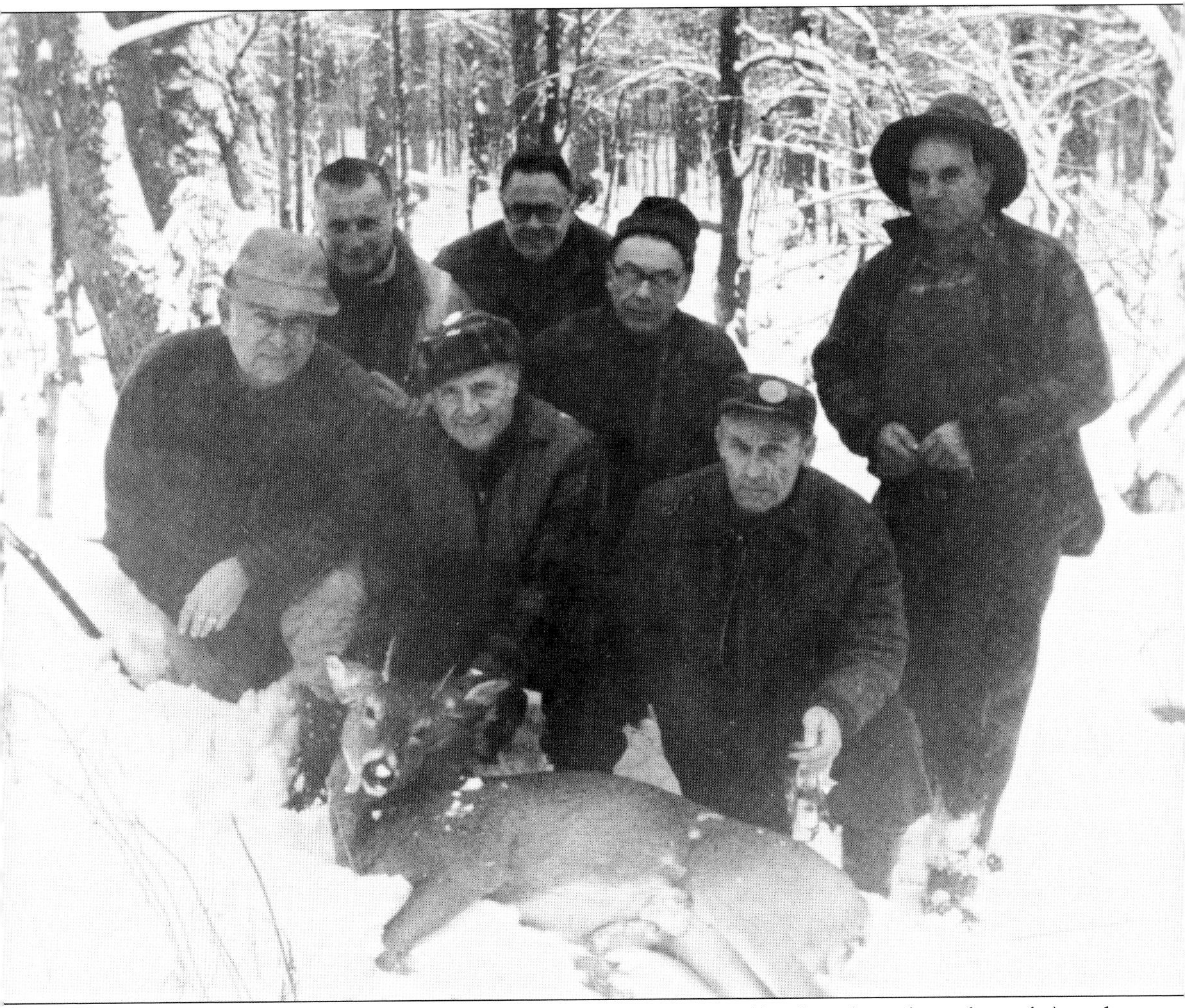

Pictured here in 1974 are local Adirondack guides Philip "Bill" Plete (standing, far right) and Art Baker (kneeling, right) with a group of sports from the Adirondack League Club, a private organization that was formed by wealthy families in 1890 that still exists today. Concerned with the destruction of the forests and the yearly decrease of lake water due to the Erie Canal, the group decided that the 100,000-acre Anson Blake Tract, also known as Honnedaga, would make them a suitable hunting and fishing preserve. In 1890, they incorporated as the Adirondack League Club and offered 500 membership shares for sale. Between 1890 and 1894, the club purchased 20,000 additional acres and leased 71,000 acres. In 1893, the Adirondack League Club merged with the Bisby Club, an earlier-established group that owned and leased land around the group of lakes known as Bisby. The Adirondack League Club currently controls approximately 53,000 acres around the Old Forge area, making it the largest privately owned preserve in the Adirondacks. The club is known for the efforts of its members in conservation; the club's logging methods of selective cutting and reforestation were adopted by the state, and it was in part responsible for state game law changes that included outlawing deer jacking and hounding. (Author's collection.)

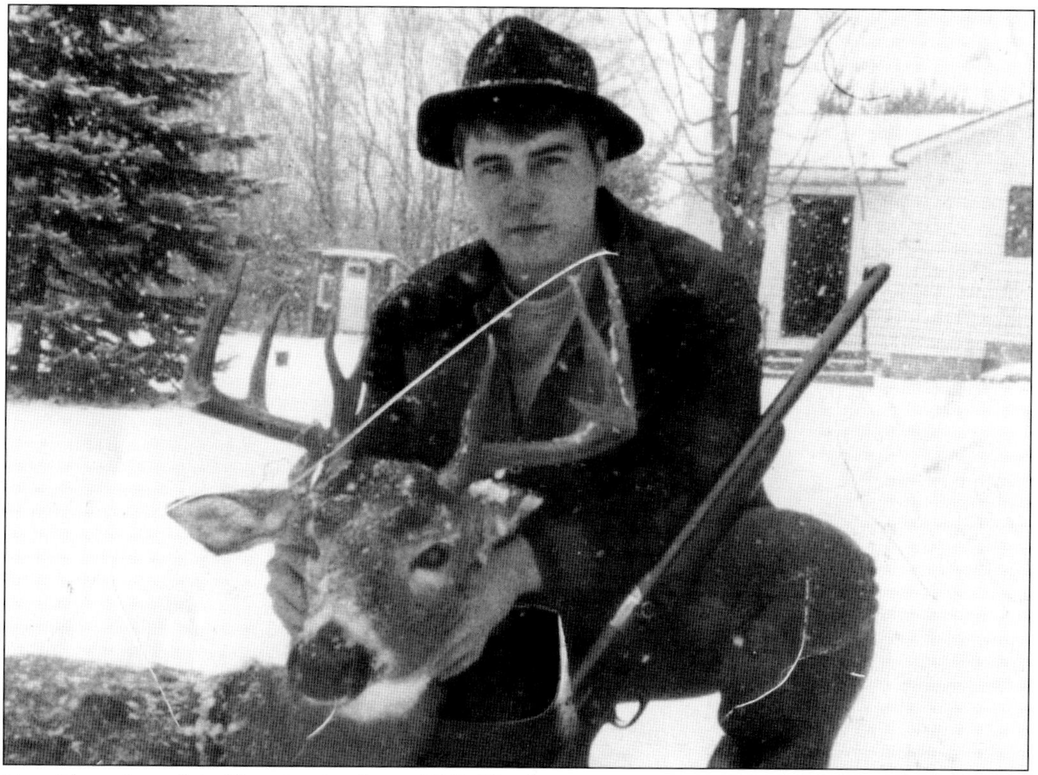

Ron Plete shot this 12-point buck in 1987. The hunting party was made up of him, Bill Plete (Ron's father), Brian Countryman, Art Johnson, and Joe Johnson. Bill, Brian, and Joe went up ahead. Ron and Art started walking to set up a drive. According to Ron, "Art went further in, I stayed in the thicker stuff. On the way in, Art said, 'Pay attention, there's a buck been around here somewhere.' I heard a noise, tearing from where Art was, sounded like a freight train coming. Here comes a doe about 20 yards from me, running as fast as she could. Then I looked and saw big antlers coming at me. The buck came running about 40 yards from me. I just pulled up and started flinging lead at it." The obsolete ammunition he was using in his rifle misfired a few times before he actually killed the deer. It was entered in the Stinger's Bar big buck contest that year and won. Above is Ron with his buck. Below are, from left to right, Joe, Brian, Ron, Bill, and Art. (Both, courtesy of Ron Plete.)

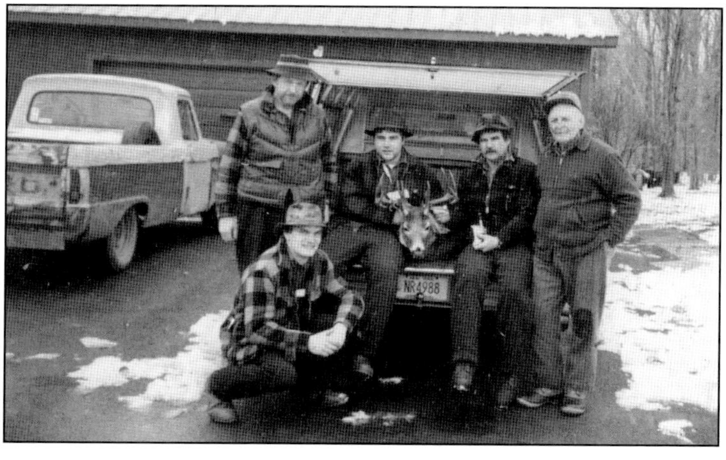

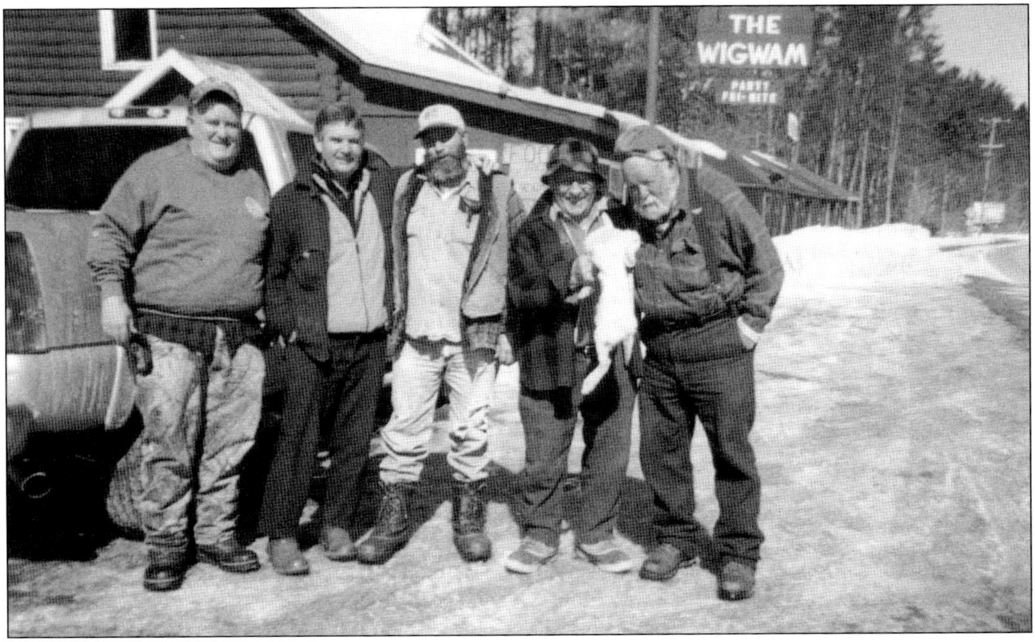

A rowdy group of snowshoe hare hunters poses in front of the Wigwam tavern on Route 28 in Forestport before heading inside for some warm food and cold beer. From left to right are George (last name unknown), Bernard "Bill" Plete of Remsen, Johnny Muncko, Henry Krupa, and Lenny Bull of Connecticut. (Author's collection)

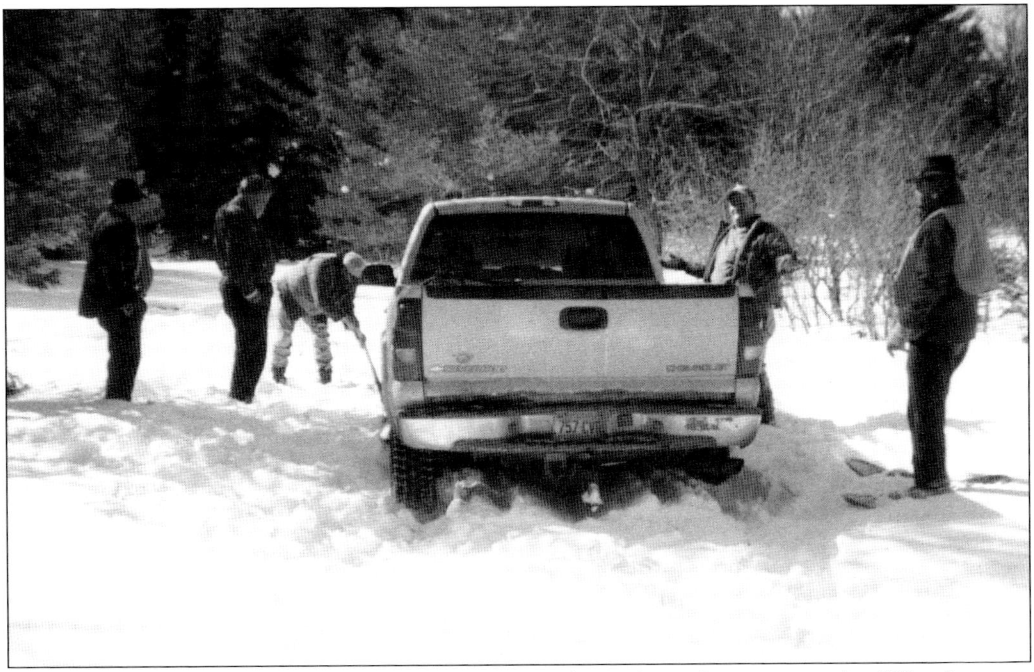
This group of rabbit hunters is dealing with a truck stuck in the snow in the Wheelertown wilderness. If they spend enough time outdoors, eventually, a person will find themselves in a debacle or two. It is days like these out in the elements when a sense of humor goes a long way. (Courtesy of Ron Plete.)

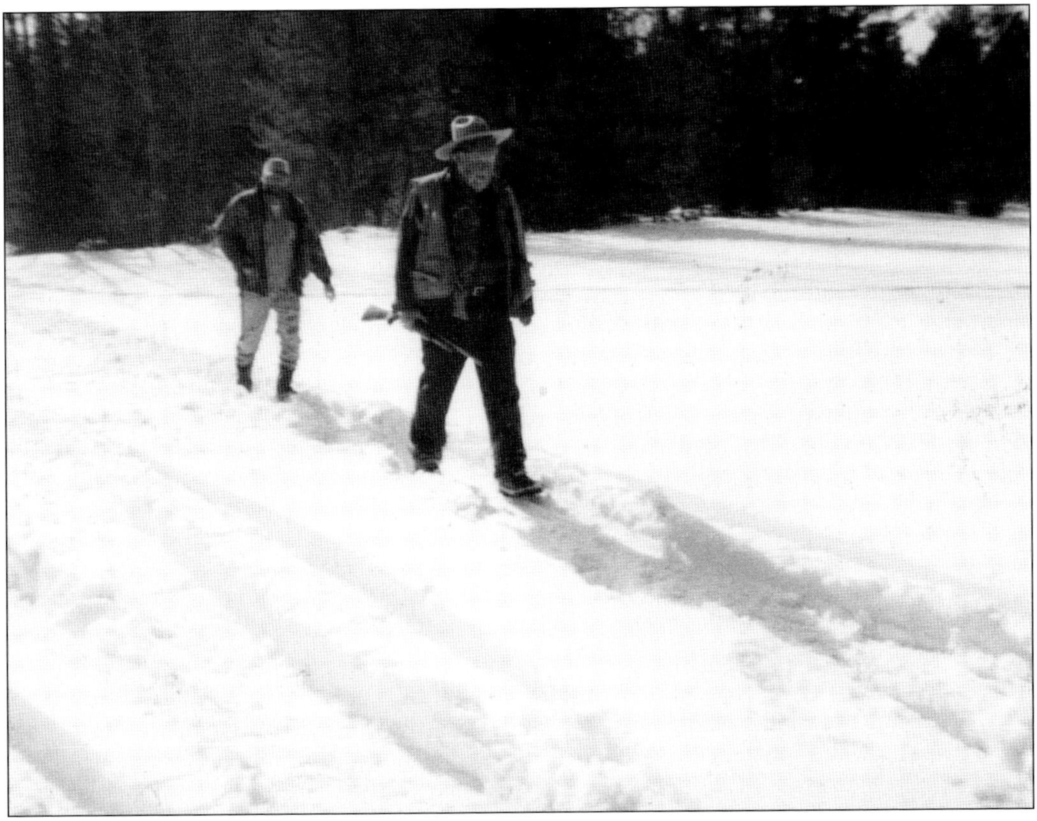

Lenny Bull (in front with the wide-brimmed hat) and a friend are walking in the snow while rabbit hunting. This photograph was taken the same day they got the truck stuck in the snow. A trip to the Wigwam was in order after that fiasco. (Courtesy of Ron Plete.)

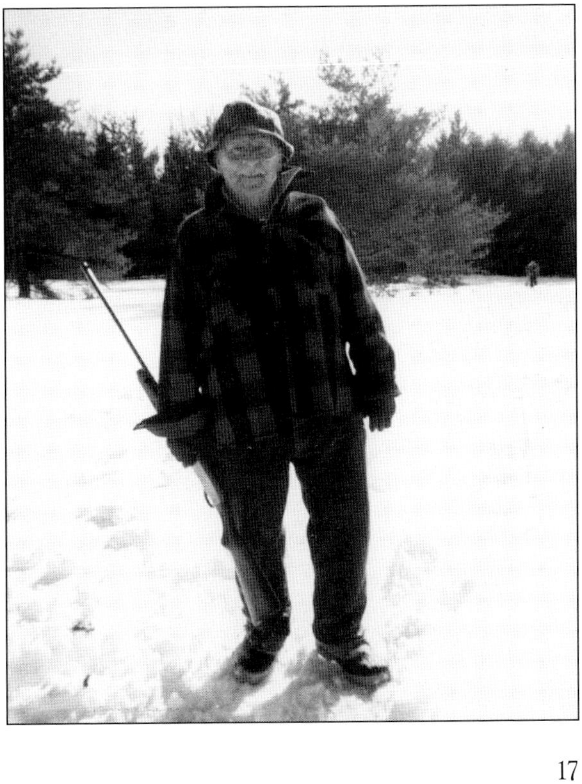

Henry "Boss Man" Krupa frequently traveled from his home in Sharon, Connecticut, to hunt for snowshoe rabbits and white-tailed deer in the foothills of the Adirondack Mountains. He frequently made the drive alone, even in his 90s. He was a D-Day veteran of the US Navy. Krupa died at the age of 96. (Courtesy of Ron Plete.)

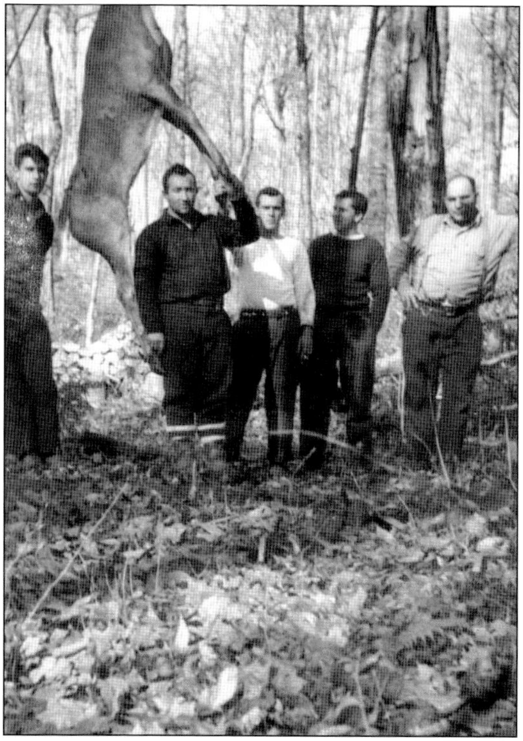

This photograph depicts proud hunter Joe Pomitcher, surrounded by friends, showing off his buck at a hunting camp in the Speculator area wilderness. Deer were more plentiful in upstate New York during the last century, and a diligent hunter had a good chance of filling his or her tag. Notice the chopped firewood stacked in the background. (Author's collection.)

Beginning around or before the 1950s and continuing until the early 1990s, a group of hunters made their hunting camp in the area of Wheelertown Road in Herkimer County. More specifically, near the north branch of the Little Black Creek. It could be quite a hike in, covering steep hills while carrying gear and crossing the creek, which, at times, had a significant current. They usually parked at the Stanley Postol homestead, which now belongs to Stanley's granddaughter Connie and her husband, Dennis Hallenbeck. (Courtesy of Charlie Appleton.)

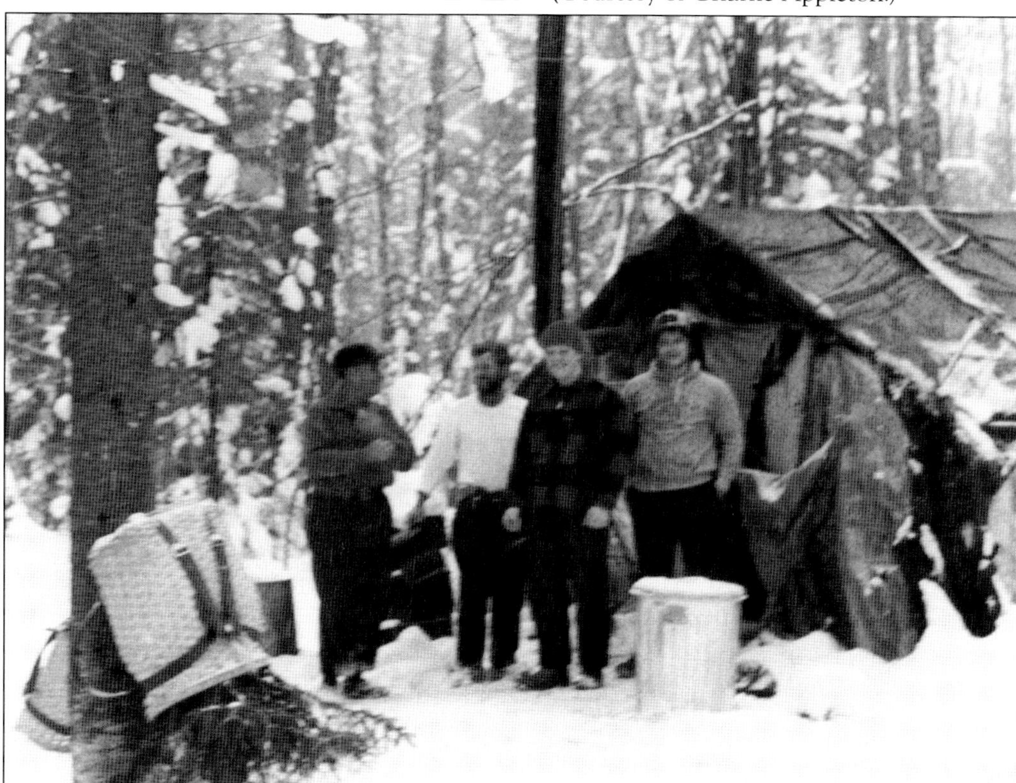

Many good times hunting white-tailed deer were shared at the hunting camp near Little Black Creek. Pictured (in no particular order) are George Briggs, Charlie Appleton Sr., Darrin Appleton, and Charlie Appleton Jr. The younger Charlie killed his first buck at the camp at age 14 in 1979. (Courtesy of Charlie Appleton.)

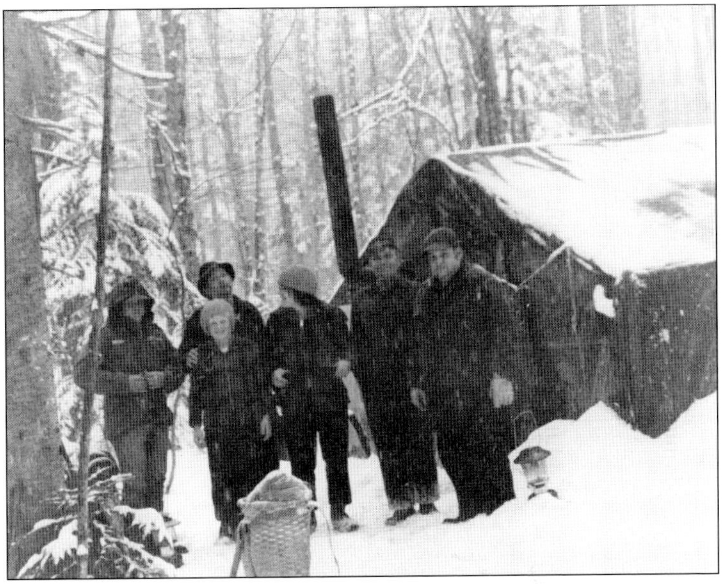

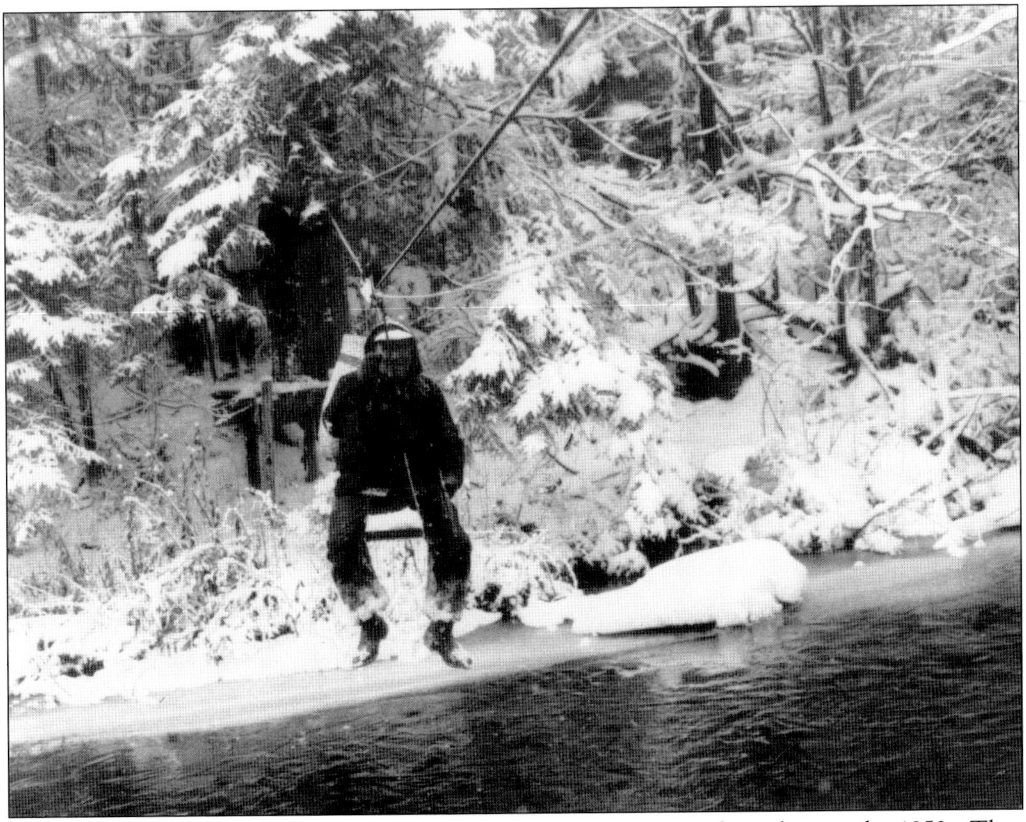

Pete Briggs is shown crossing the Little Black Creek on a homemade zip line in the 1950s. That zip line still stands today, and although a bit worn and creaky, it still functions. Briggs was a hunting guide in the Southern Adirondack foothills for many years. He was the son of William and Charlotte (Wandover) Briggs. He lived to be 96 years old, passing in 2010. (Courtesy of Charlie Appleton.)

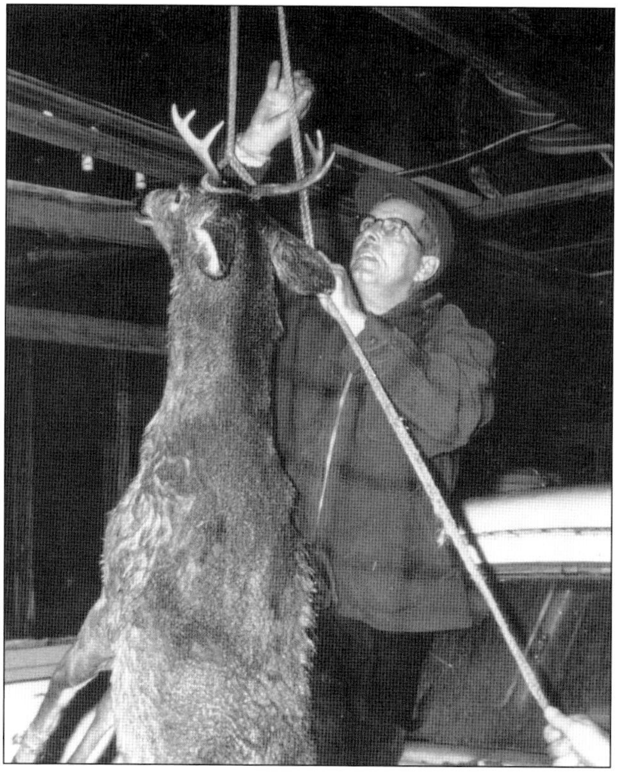

Charles H. Rieck, photographed in 1962, strings up the six-point buck he harvested off the "Frontier" property. He is pictured in the Craeg Manor Farm in Barneveld, where Emerson and Iona Trussell and family lived at the time. Charles was Iona's father. The hand in the bottom-right corner belongs to David W. Rieck, Iona's brother. (Courtesy of Iona Trussell Isbell.)

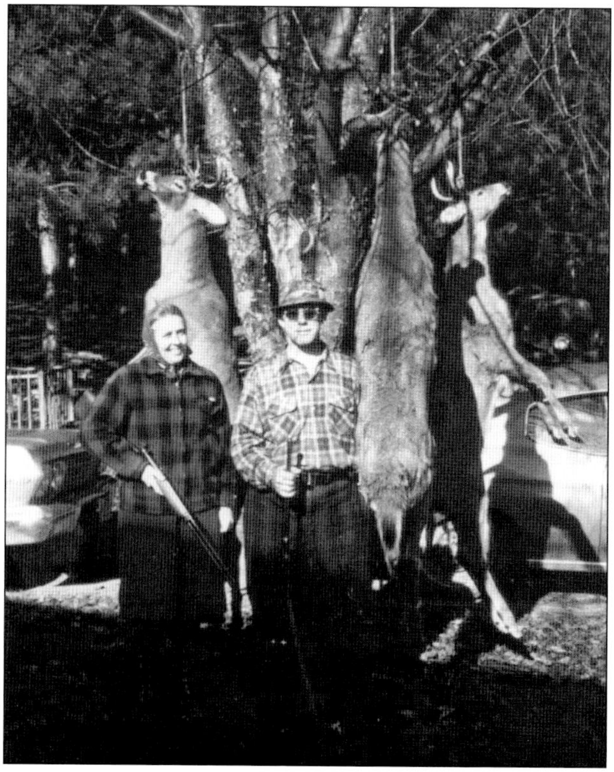

In this November 1974 photo, husband and wife Emerson and Iona Rieck Trussell show off the triple they harvested that morning on the Frontier homestead property between Boonville and Forestport. Emerson shot two spike horns around 9:30 a.m., and Iona shot her five-point earlier, around 8:30 a.m. (Courtesy of Iona Trussell Isbell.)

Iona Rieck Trussell, again pictured at the Frontier property, stands in front of the cabin on the west end and proudly displays the snowshoe rabbit she shot with her Winchester Model 94 30-30. Notice the lack of snow on the ground, a rarity during rabbit season in the Northeast. (Courtesy of Iona Trussell Isbell.)

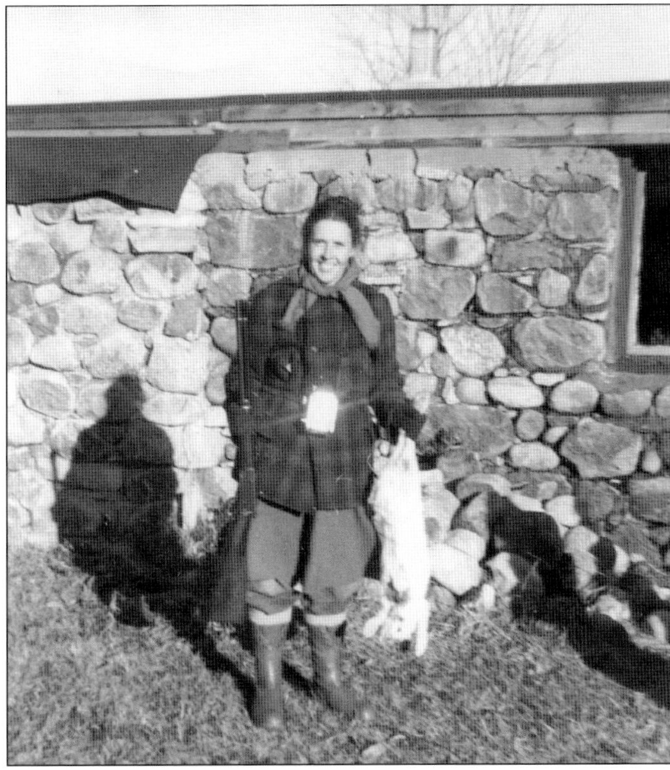

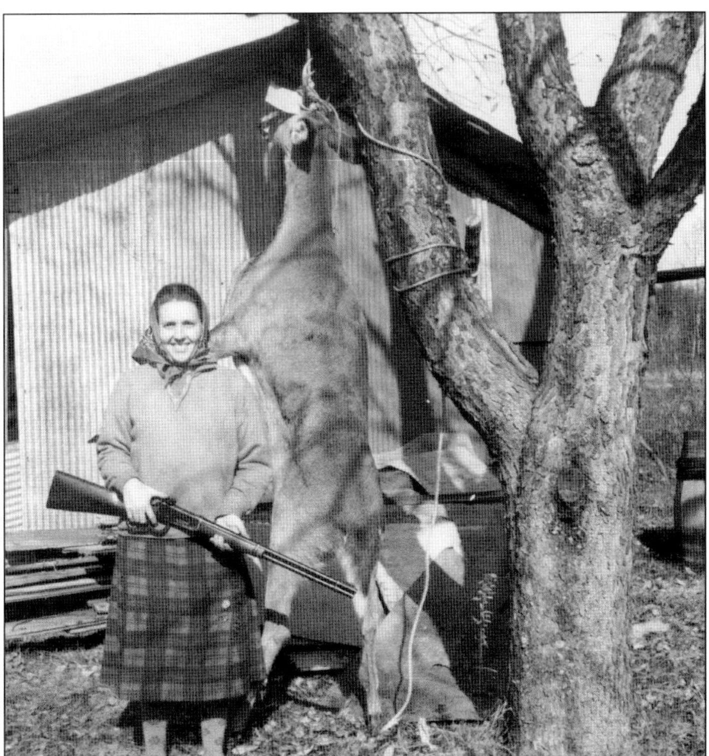

Iona Ruth Rieck Trussell took down this six-point buck with one shot to the neck on October 25, 1966. She was sitting on a ridge near the family homestead, called the Frontier (the old Scanlan farm), between Boonville and Forestport, New York. (Courtesy of Iona Trussell Isbell.)

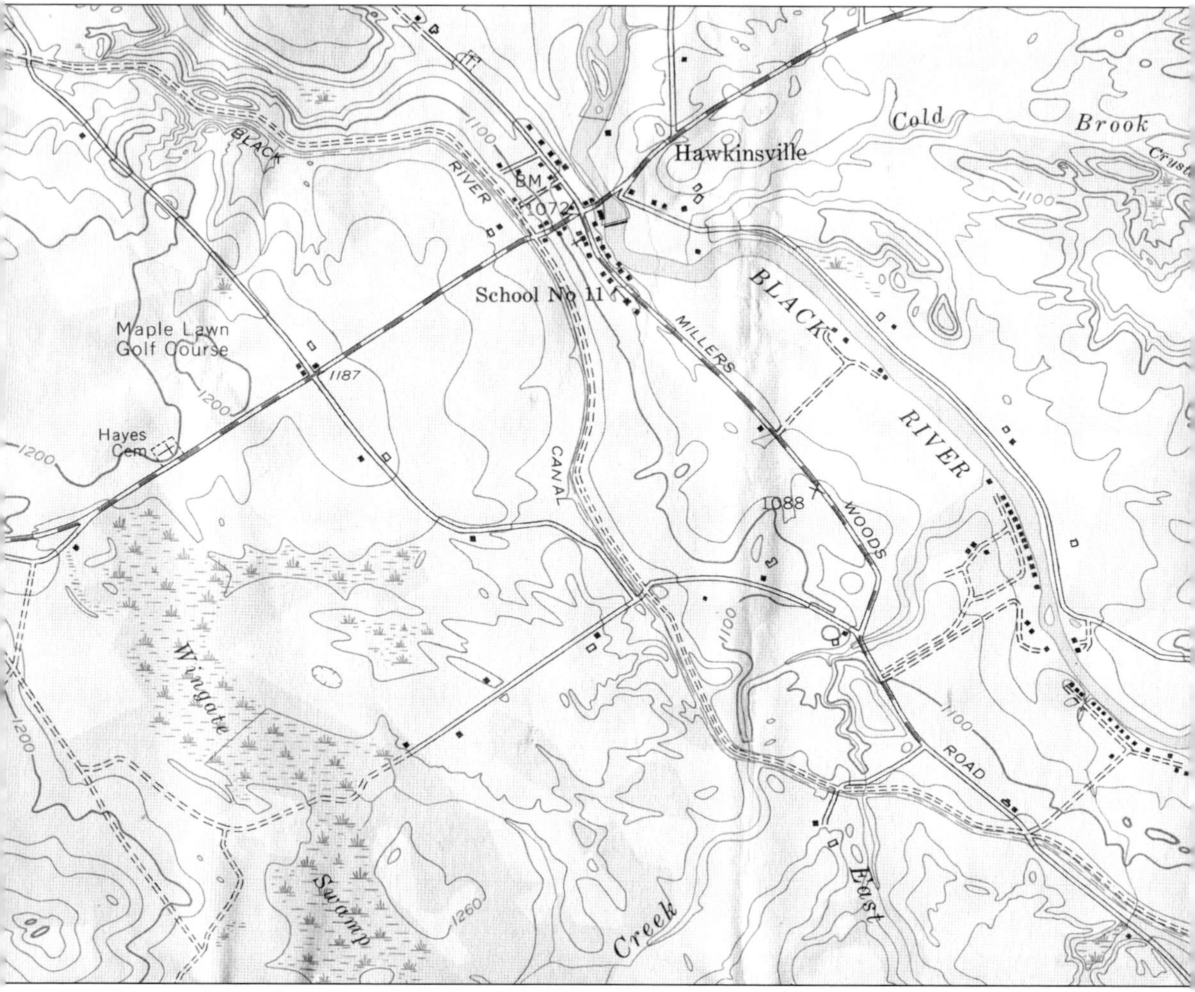

This Hawkinsville map includes a portion of the Black River. Hawkinsville is a small hamlet east of Boonville. During the heyday of the Black River Canal, Hawkinsville was a busy little place. In 1862, Hawkinsville had two churches (German Lutheran and Catholic), a tannery, a carding mill, a gristmill, a chair factory, and about 300 inhabitants. Hawkinsville Road, the main thoroughfare that cuts directly through the hamlet, runs from Boonville to Woodgate, terminating at the blinking caution light on Route 28. (Author's collection.)

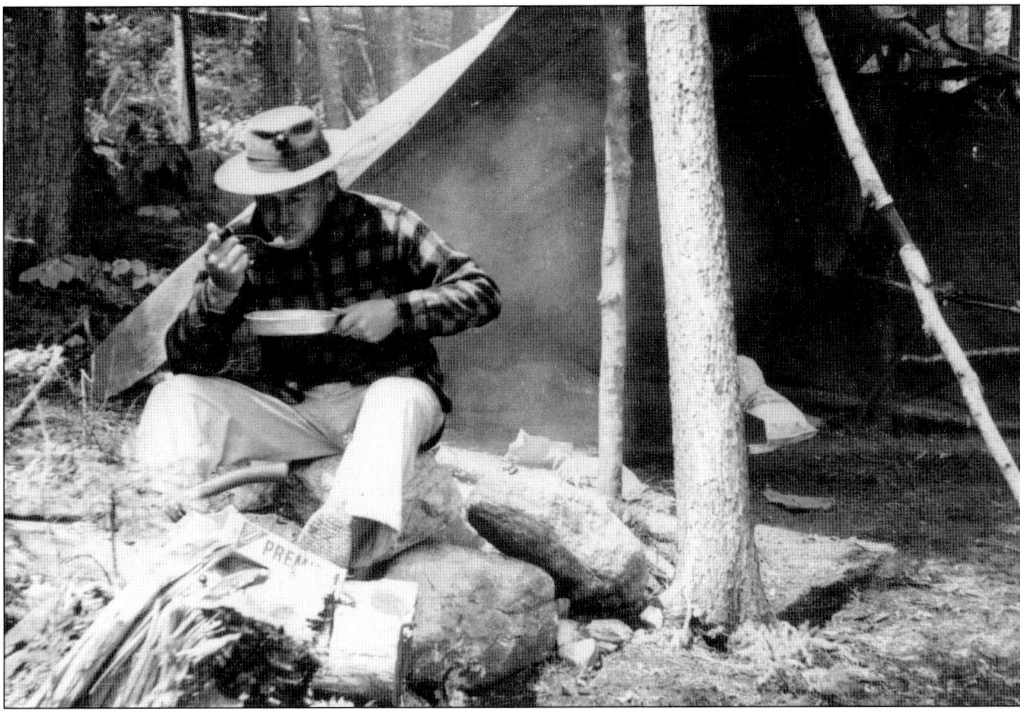

Outdoorsman Nelson Folts stops for a bite to eat in a temporary base camp. He is sitting in front of the campfire, most likely used for cooking and comfort. Notice the cracker boxes on the fire, his blankets laid out on the dirt floor, and chopped limbs used as support beams. (Author's collection.)

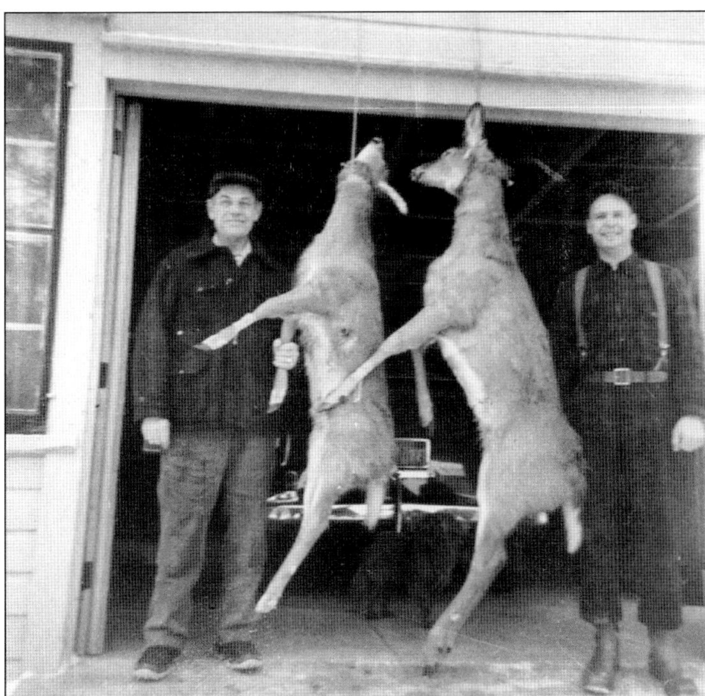

Many sportsmen did, and still do, hunt to provide healthy meat for their families. Venison is lean and can substitute for beef in any recipe. Two unidentified hunters smile proudly for the camera with their deer. (Author's collection.)

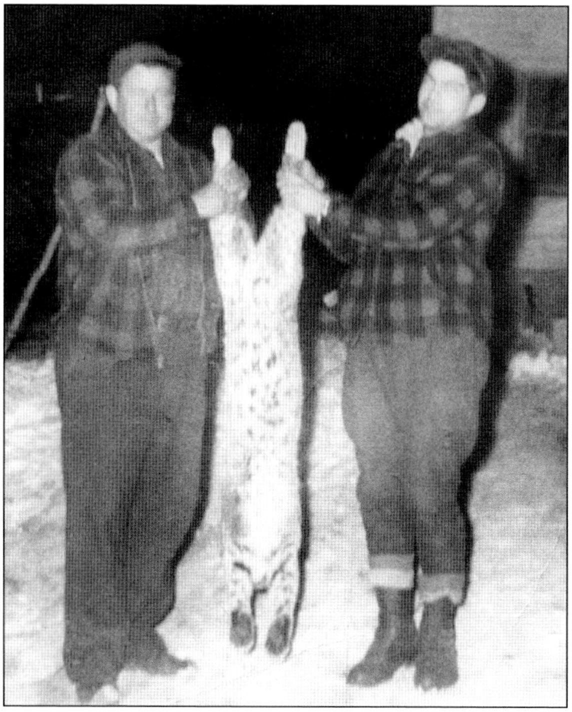

This large bobcat was hunted in the Grant area of Herkimer County. In an amusing coincidence, it was shot in 1953 and weighed 53 pounds. Notice the wool jackets the two men are wearing. Before camouflage, many North Country hunters wore wool; many still do. Wool is warm and breathable and stands up to a lot of wear and tear. (Courtesy of Chris Graves.)

Seven bobcats are strung up at the Williams family farm on the Fairchild Road in Remsen after a bobcat hunt in the 1950s. Some of the men who used to go on these hunts were Tom Williams, Roger Williams, Trevor Williams, Tuck Allen, Neil Shufelt, Ralph Carmen, Otto Koenig, and more. (Courtesy of Chris Graves.)

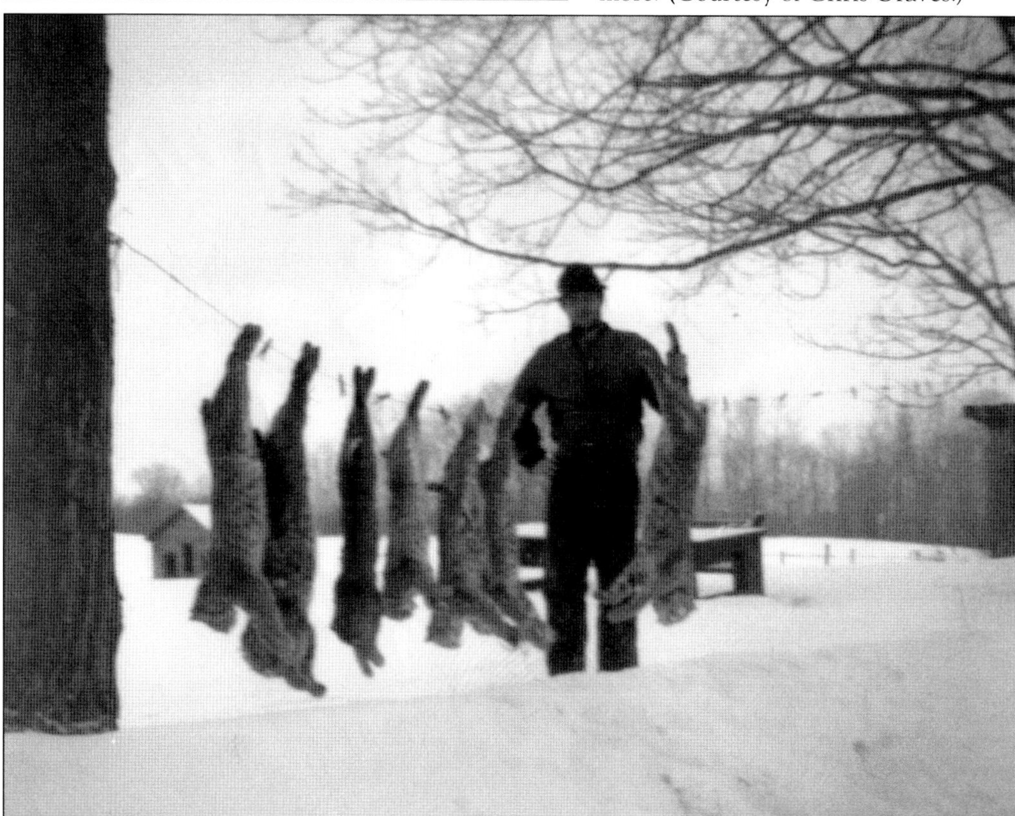

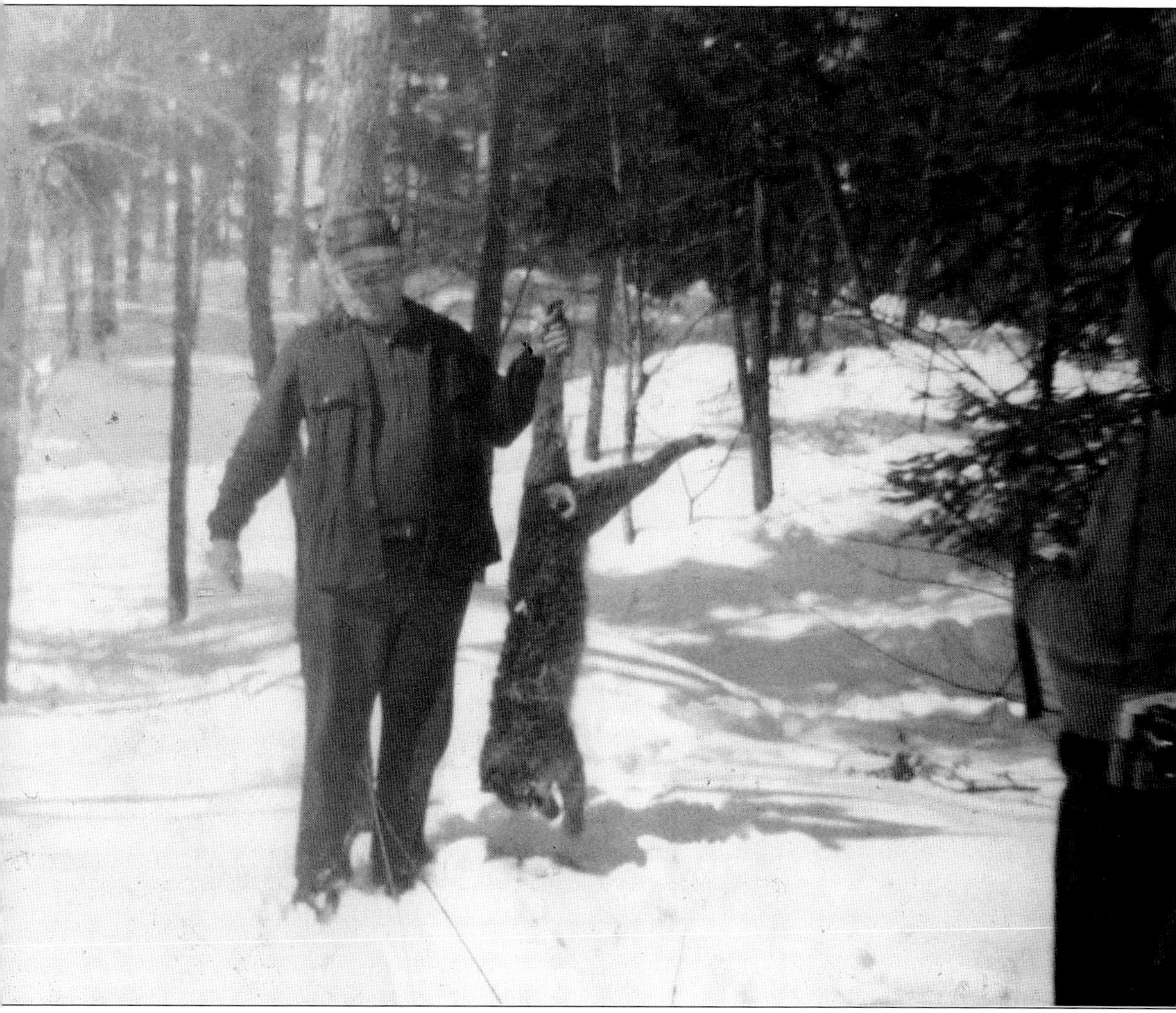

The Williams family did a lot of bobcat hunting in the Southern Adirondacks. Up until 1971, there was a bounty on bobcats in New York State. Bobcat can be found all over the state, but population cluster in three areas: the Adirondack Mountains, the Catskill Mountains, and the Taconic Mountain region. Bobcats like habitats that are isolated from human interference. Bobcats often use rocky ledges, rock piles, brush piles, hollow trees, fallen logs, and even evergreen bogs and swamps for shelter. They create dens for raising young in these places. The New York State Department of Conservation estimates that there are currently about 5,000 bobcats living in the state. (Courtesy of Chris Graves.)

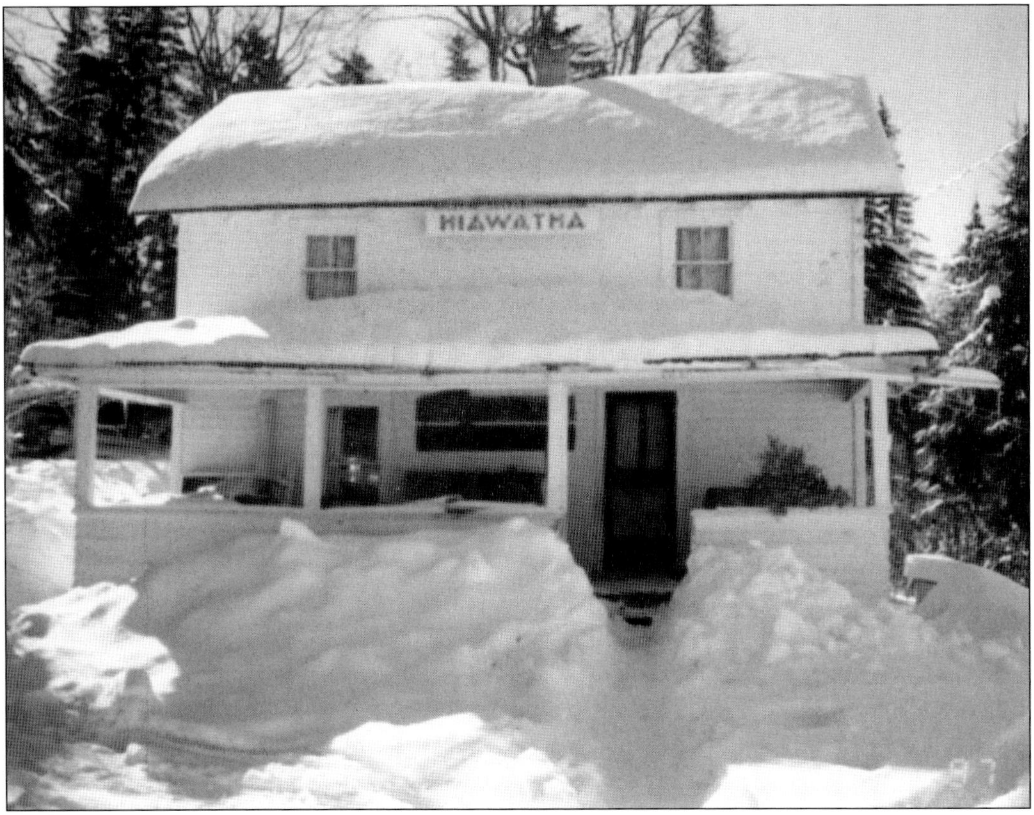

The family camp, "Hiawatha," was located in Big Moose. Chris Graves's grandfather bought the camp in the 1950s. Many fun and successful white-tailed deer and bobcat hunting trips were spent here. The whitetail deer numbers dropped off in the 1970s and 1980s. The grandchildren used to spend summers in the Adirondacks at the camp. (Courtesy of Chris Graves.)

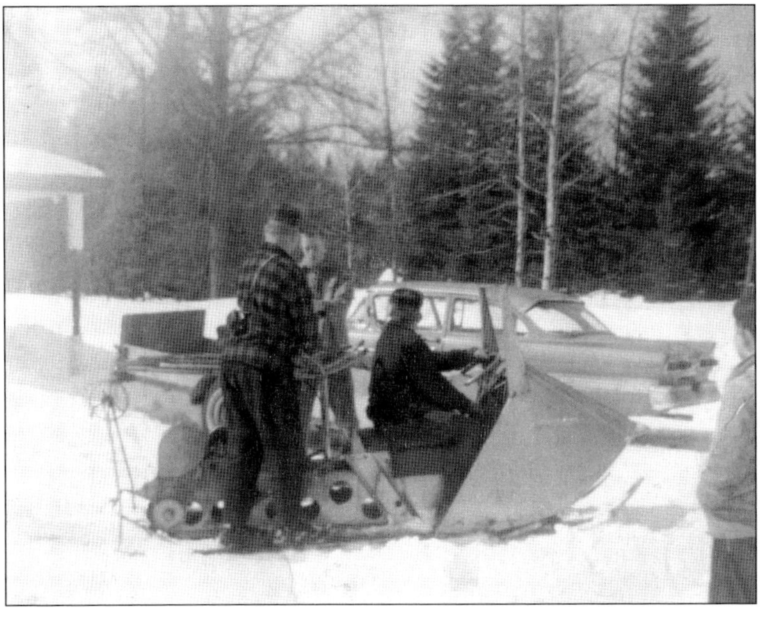

This photograph was taken at the camp Hiawatha sometime in the 1950s or 1960s. The snowmobile was used in hunting trips to navigate the deep Adirondack snow. The snowmobile was a Polaris Sno-Traveler. (Courtesy of Chris Graves.)

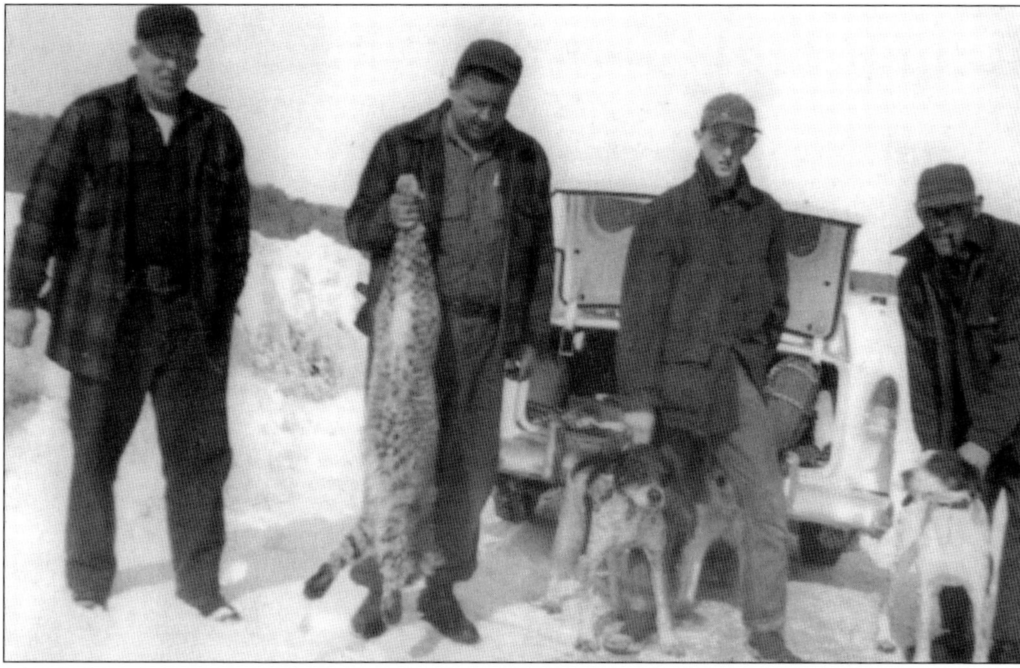

This bobcat hunting party had some luck at North Lake. In this photograph, holding the bobcat is Trevor Williams, the two men with the hounds are Roger Williams and Tom Williams (far right), and the fourth man is unidentified. Bobcats are not uncommon in New York, but they are stealthy and elusive, so sightings are infrequent. An average male is about 25 pounds and usually around 34 inches in length, while a female is usually closer to 15 pounds and about 30 inches long. Both sexes can sometimes exceed 30 pounds, however. Bobcats get their name from their relatively short "bobbed" tail. Their population numbers have remained stable in the state and beyond for many decades. (Both, courtesy of Chris Graves.)

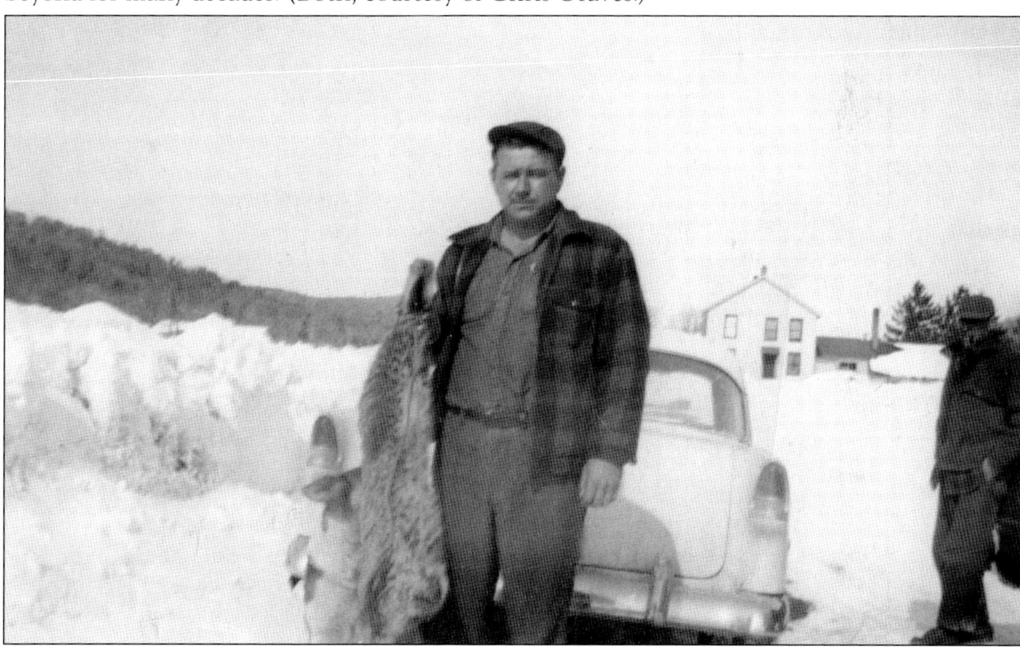

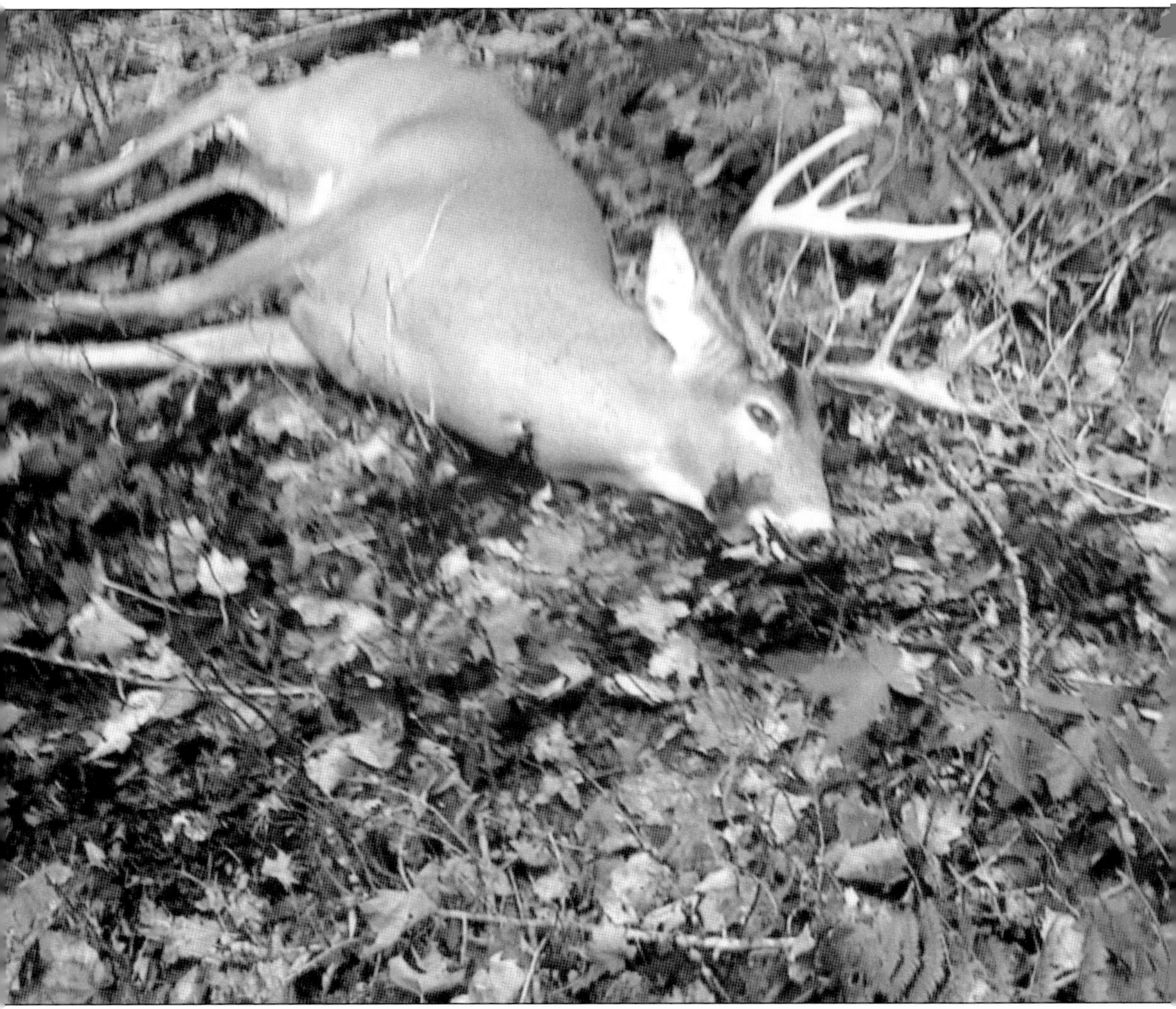

Jeff Evans got his "Phone Call Buck" on Welsh District Road in the town of Remsen. It was the Sunday after Thanksgiving, and as he left for hunting, he told his wife, Sandi, that he was not coming home until he got a buck. On the walk in, he startled a group of five or six deer. When he arrived at the spot he usually hunts, he settled in for a long sit. Then his phone vibrated at about 10:00 a.m. He listened to the voicemail, and it was his buddy calling to break his chops because Jeff had not yet gotten a deer that season. "Just as I was about to move spots, a doe came running in with the ten point on her tail," he said. "I missed the first shot and the doe went back the other way. He stopped and I jumped to shoot again and he dropped in his tracks." Right after that, he was trying to text Sandi about the deer, and his buddy called again so this time he answered it. That's how this deer earned the title the "Phone Call Buck." (Courtesy of Jeff Evans.)

Bryan Postol shot this six-point, 185-pound buck in 1997. For many years, Bryan was the manager of the NAPA store in Remsen. Bryan grew up in a large family. His parents were Lilly and Stanley Postol, and he made his home in the Hawkinsville area. (Courtesy of Bryan and Wendy Postol.)

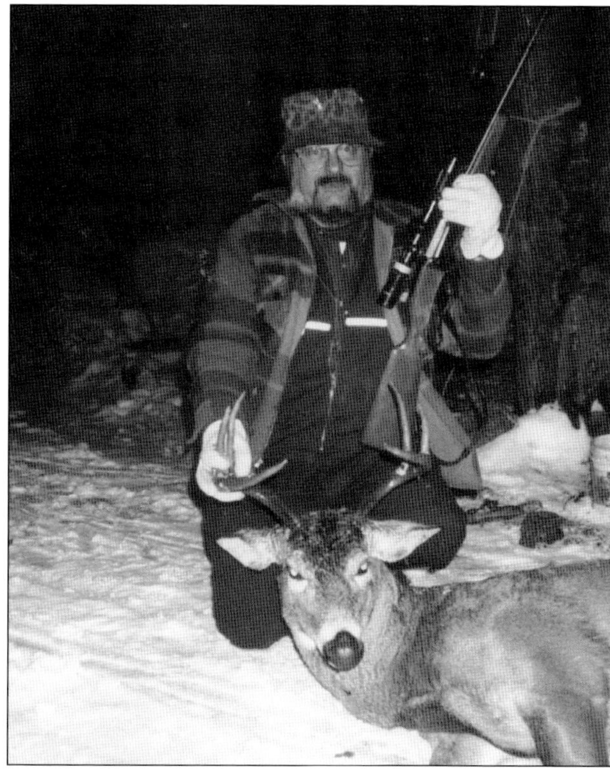

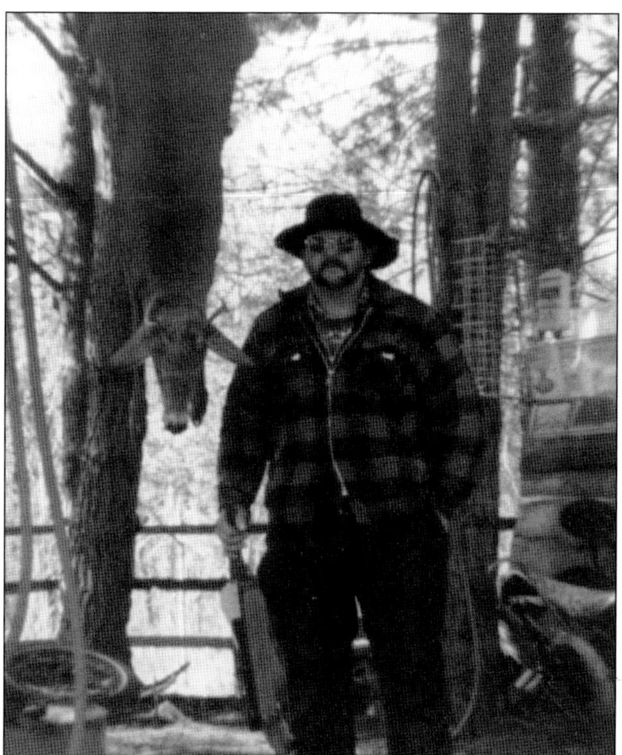

Stanley "Jim" Postol shot this four-point buck on November 25, 1988, from the "McHale" tree stand in Hawkinsville while hunting with his brother Bryan Postol. He grew up on the family homestead in Wheelertown and settled outside of Poland in Herkimer County. (Courtesy of Bryan and Wendy Postol.)

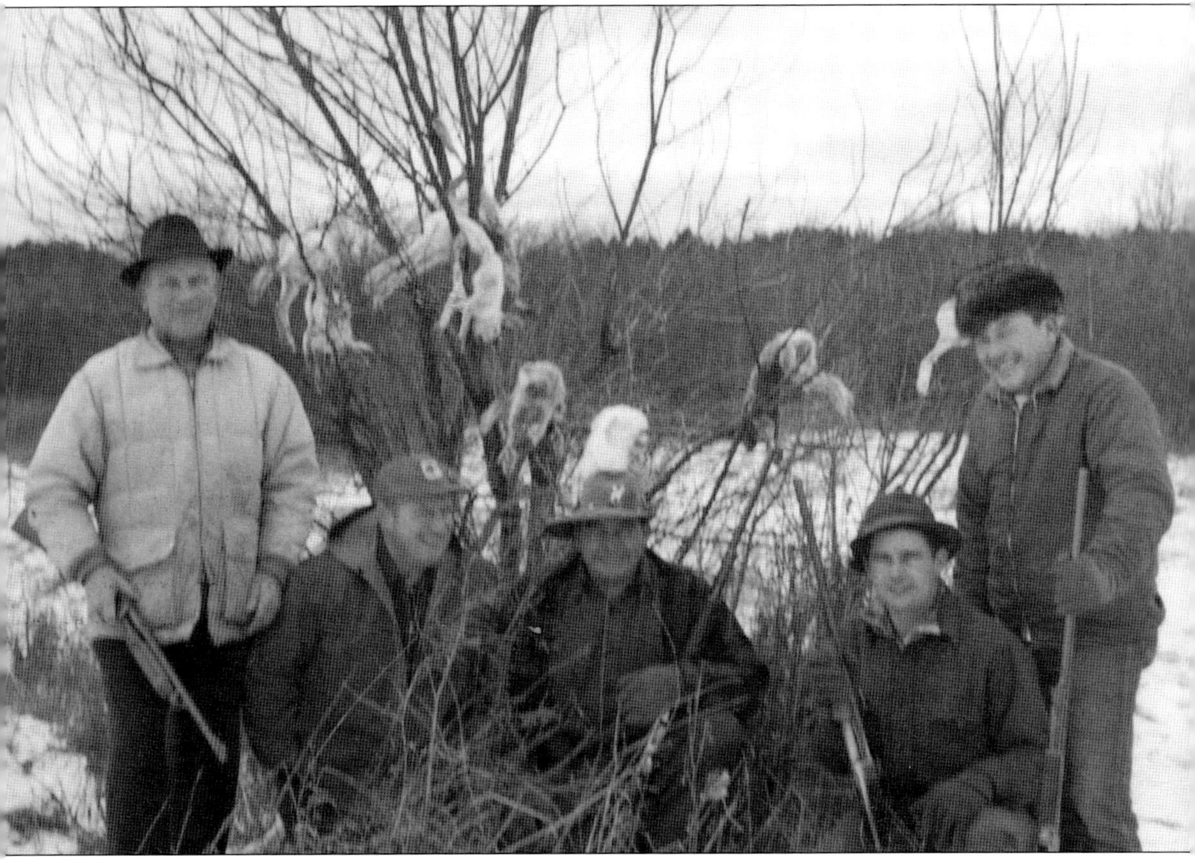

This rabbit-hunting party, photographed in the 1950s, looks mighty pleased with the bounty of bunnies they got that day. That same decade, the *Utica Observer Dispatch* reported that Jerome Darrow of Cold Brook shot a pure black snowshoe hare near the Black Creek. It was believed to be the first of its kind in the region. The black color phase is a rare anomaly. Throughout the winter, the hare usually sports a predominantly white outer coat with black rims around the ears. The underfur is typically a gray or brownish color. Its summer coat is a light- to medium-brown hue. The seasonal color change is a result of molting and takes place over a span of around two months. The snowshoe hare is plentiful in the Adirondacks and inhabits most of the mountainous region. (Author's collection.)

Philip, or the older "Bill," Plete lifts a heavy buck onto his shoulders for the camera. He was a busy man, always hunting, fishing, trapping, socializing, or working. Bill had many friendships that lasted throughout his lifetime. He was an able woodsman and seemed to find joy in whatever he was doing. (Author's collection.)

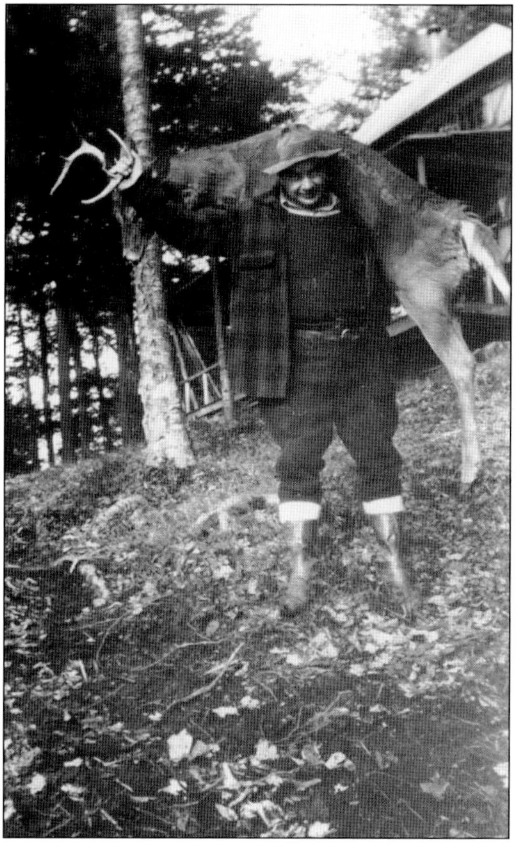

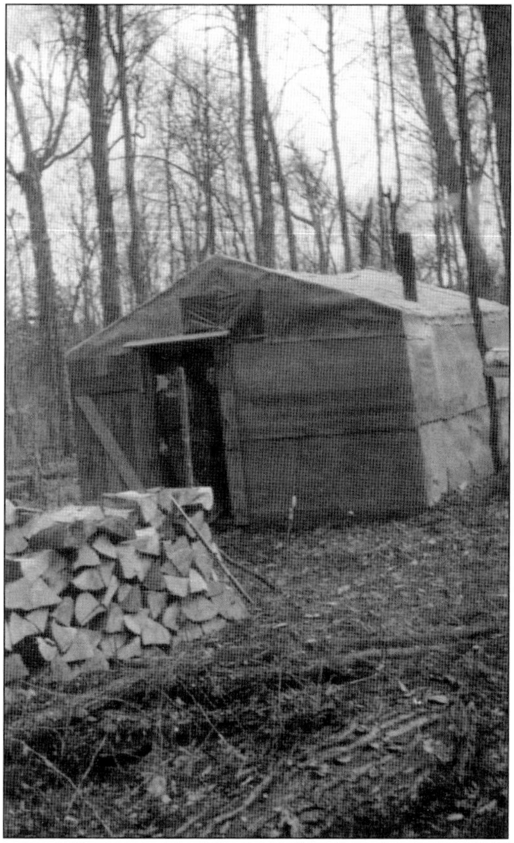

This is a typical example of the kind of tarp deer camps hunters would construct for trips in the Adirondacks. All materials would be hauled in. Tarp camps like these provided good wind cover and made for suitable temporary living quarters. (Author's collection.)

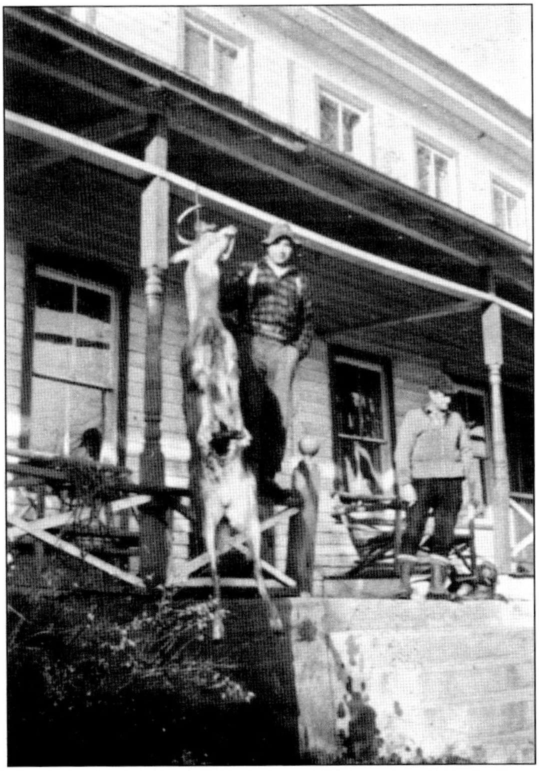

This photograph shows a buck strung up on the front porch of the Grant Hotel. This was a common practice in the past. Many old Adirondack images and postcards depict scenes quite similar to this. (Author's collection.)

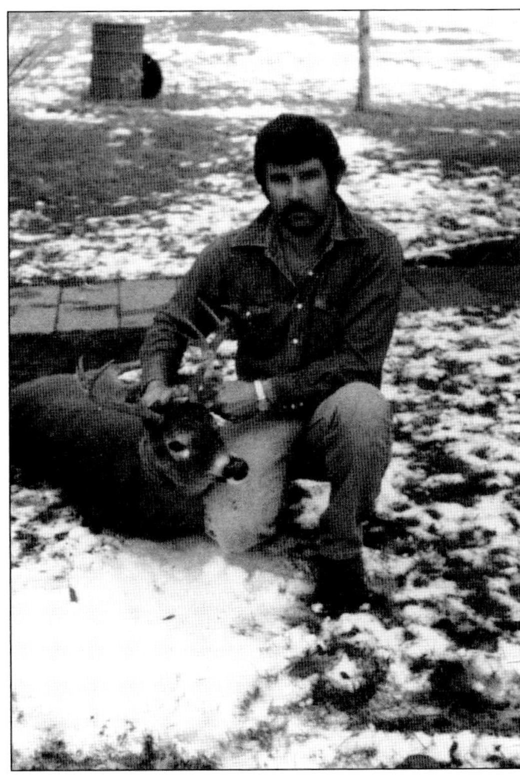

Bernard "Bill" Plete, son of Philip and Anna, crouches in the snow with a buck he shot in the 1970s. He was an avid white-tailed deer hunter his whole life. (Author's collection.)

This guide probably worked for the wealthy gentlemen who had a role in founding the early Rome Fish and Game Club. These sportsmen from the city of Rome, on the Southwestern side outside the park, frequently visited the Adirondacks. (Courtesy of the Rome Historical Society.)

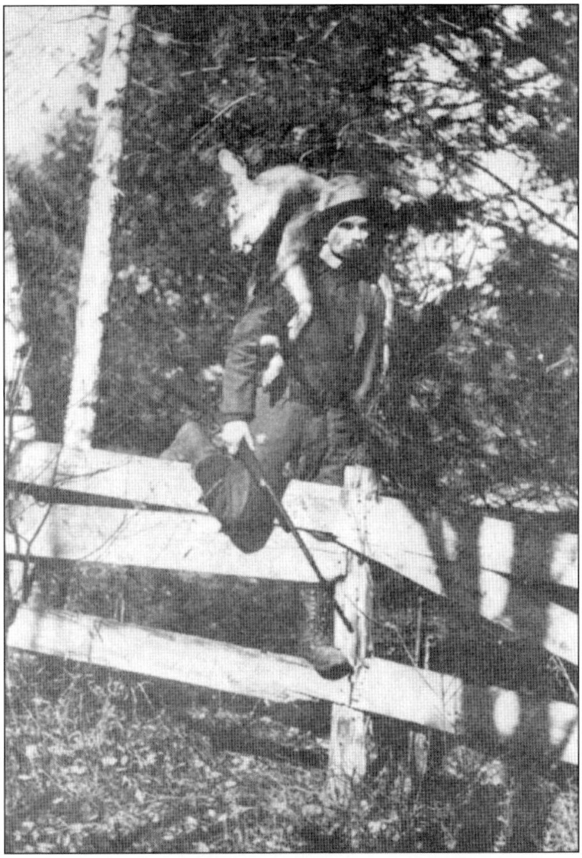

"The fresh and crisp air of the country reminds us that our blood surges from of the natural world and how tied we are to the sprung rhythms of earth and sky, weather and season," Kilroy J. Oldster said. Hunting is an activity that ties humans to their ancestral past. (Courtesy of the Rome Historical Society.)

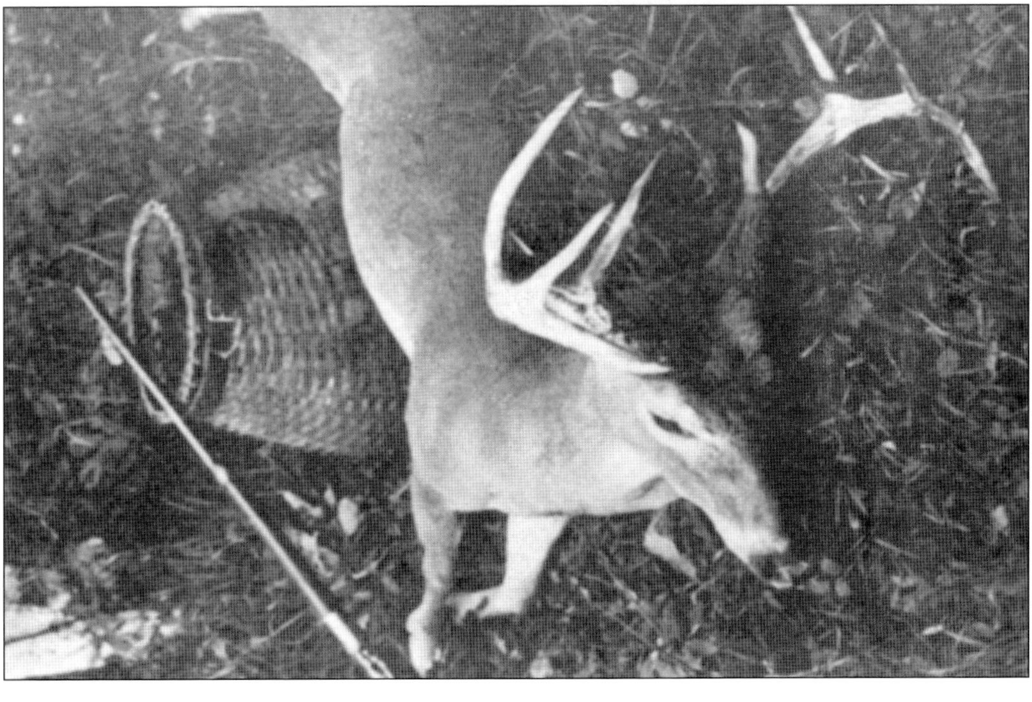

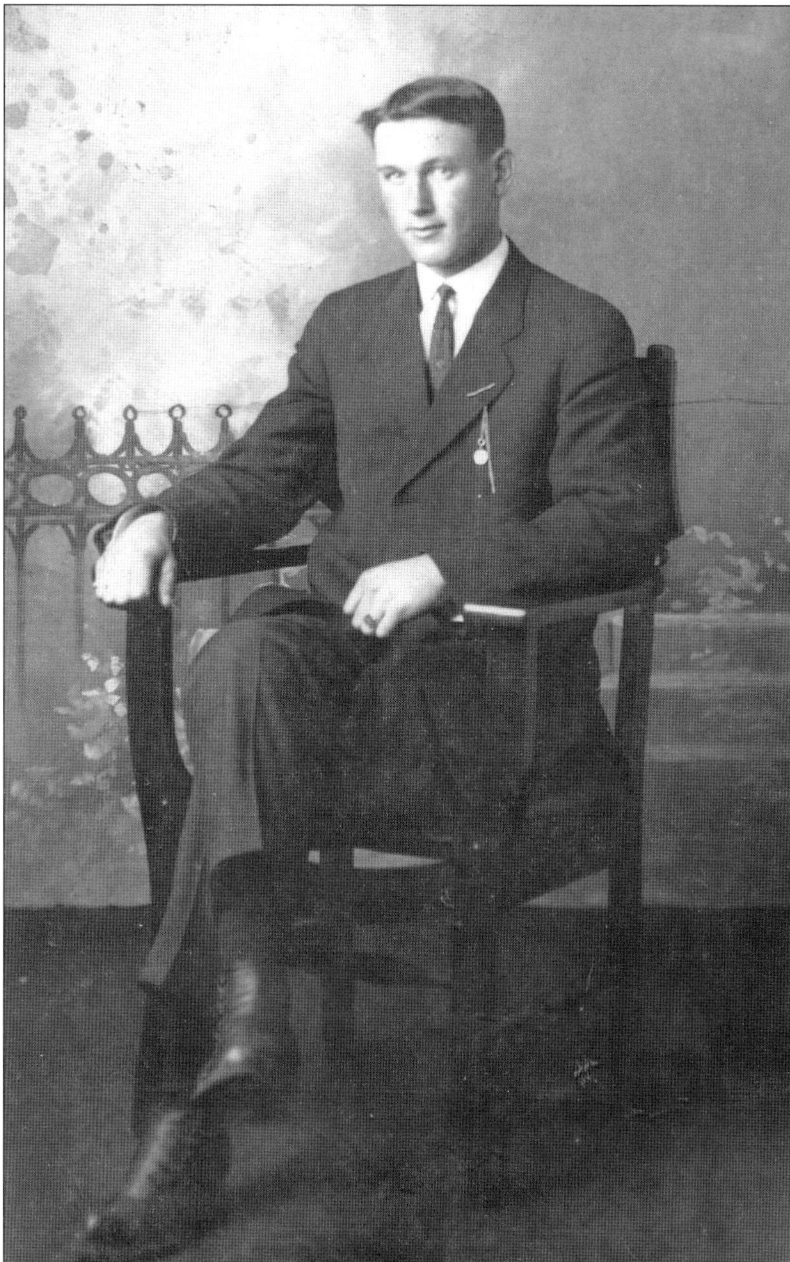

A skillful, dependable guide was highly revered. Visitors relied on their guides to keep them safe, provide or build shelter, cook food, carry supplies, and to lead them to wild game. The guide here, Harold "Dick" Harvey, is all cleaned up for a professional photograph. Harvey was the son of William "Bill" Harvey and Ann Clancy Harvey. He was one of several siblings. He was a popular guide in the West Canada headwaters area and the Black River wilderness area around Nobleboro. Harvey also worked in lumber camps. He settled in the town of Wilmurt, which has since been dissolved and absorbed into the town of Ohio. The Harvey family homestead was located on Dagenkolb Road. His wife, Helen, died at age 29 during the birth of their second child on February 17, 1920. (Author's collection.)

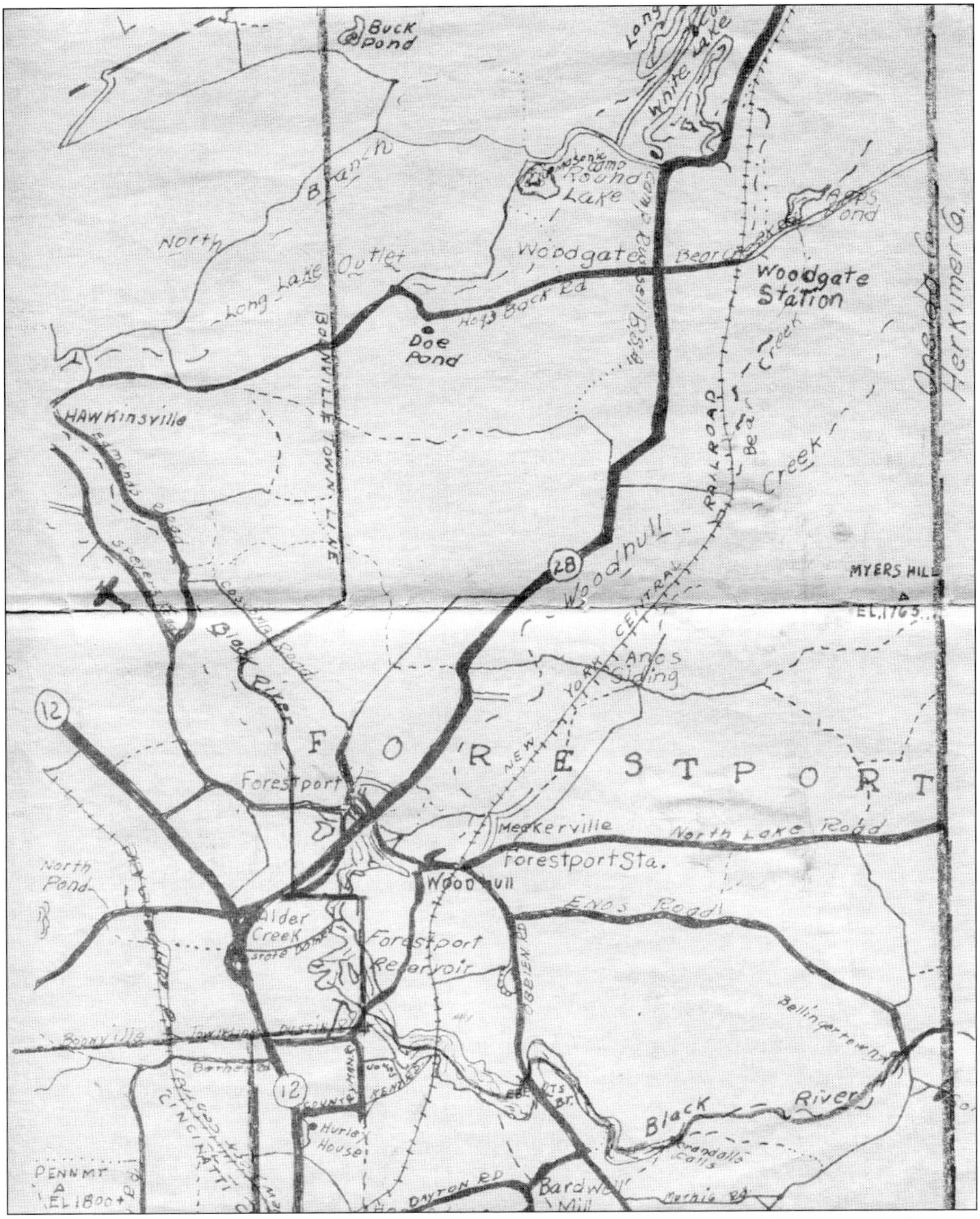

This hand-drawn map of a portion of the town of Forestport was prepared by A.J. Hanschen on October 22, 1960. Certain communities seemed to have clusters of rowdier, rugged types, and Forestport fit that bill. A town known for its high density of outlaws, the saying there was "no law north of Remsen." Forestport was the place where villagers masterminded "the Forestport Breaks" along the Black River feeder canal. The damage created a need for repairs to the canal, therefore funneling more work into the area. This map shows New York State Route 12 and New York State Route 28 where they split at Alder Creek. Route 12 continues north toward Boonville and the Tug Hill. Route 28 meanders northwest through Forestport and on toward the Central Adirondack region. (Author's collection.)

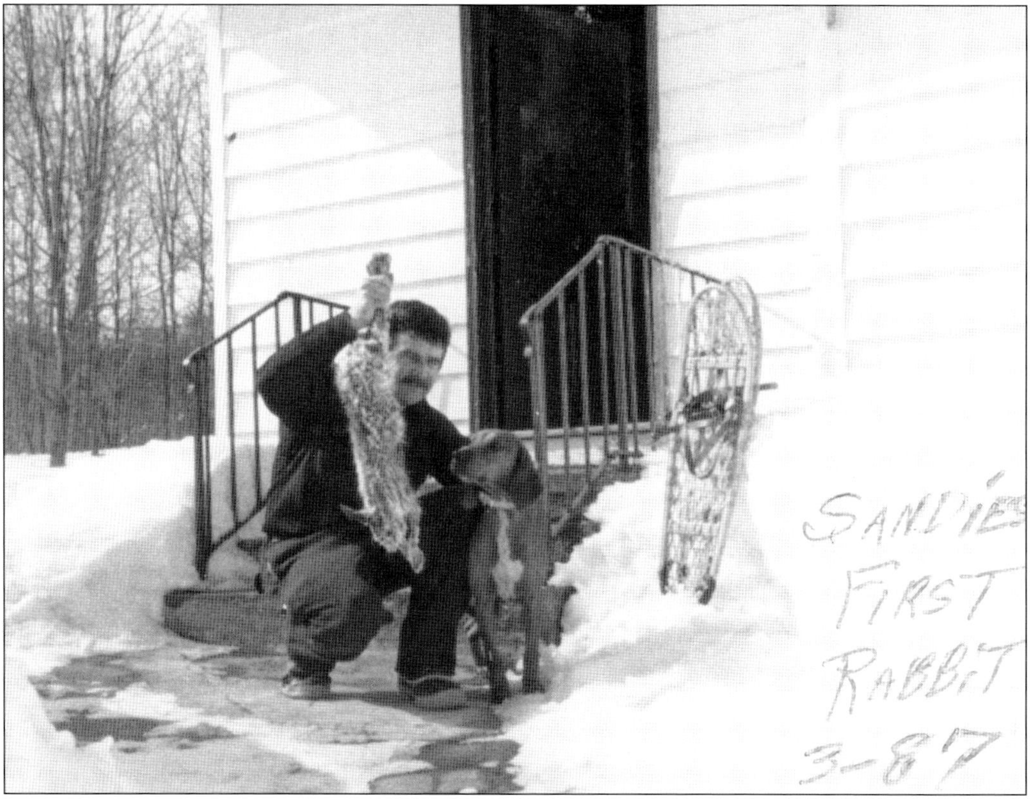

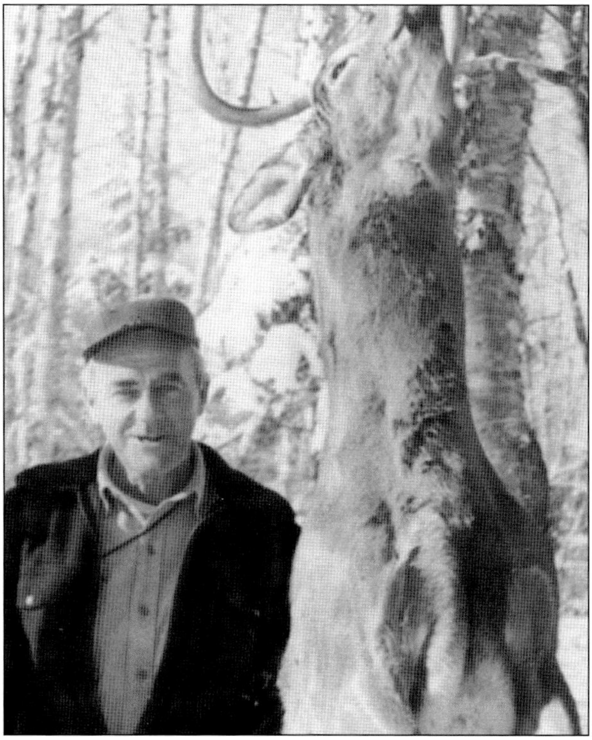

Bernard "Bill" Plete with his rabbit-hunting dog Sandie proudly boast Sandie's first rabbit in March 1987. Historically, purebred beagles have been the most popular breed for hunting rabbits, but other kinds have and can be used. Sandie was a hound mix, and she did a fine job. (Author's collection.)

Art Baker, a guide for the Adirondack League Club, stands next to a nice North Country buck in 1971. Hunting, fishing, and trapping forces those who engage in it to forge an understanding of the natural world. This is why sportsmen are often a leading force in conservation efforts. Millions of dollars paid by sportsmen for their licenses has gone directly into wildlife conservation. (Author's collection.)

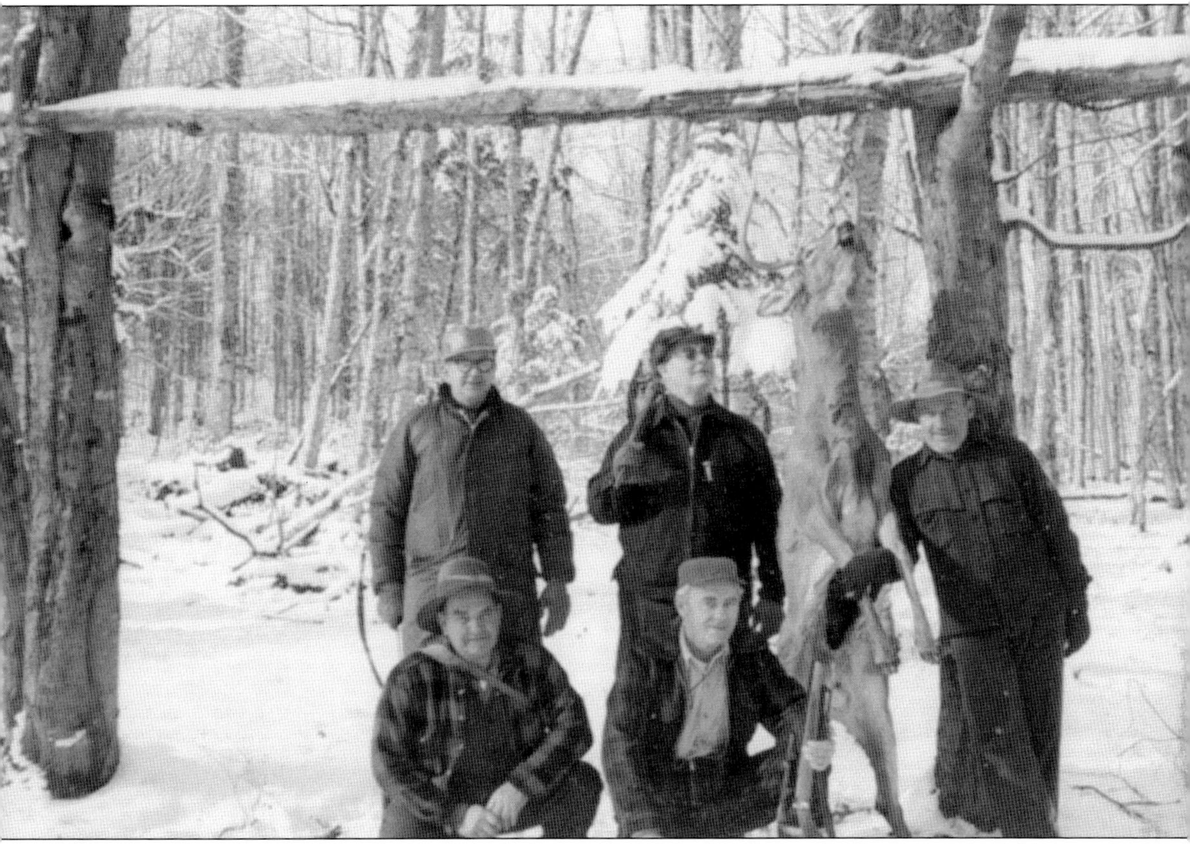

These cheerful Adirondack League Club sports posed for a photograph after a successful hunt with a big buck and their guides, Bill Plete (left) and Art Baker (right), who are kneeling in front. The Adirondack League Club's main objectives were, and still are, "to preserve the forests in a wild condition, to protect the game and fish . . . assist in strictly enforcing the game laws of the State, and promote such legislation as will further protect the North Woods from destruction." (Author's collection.)

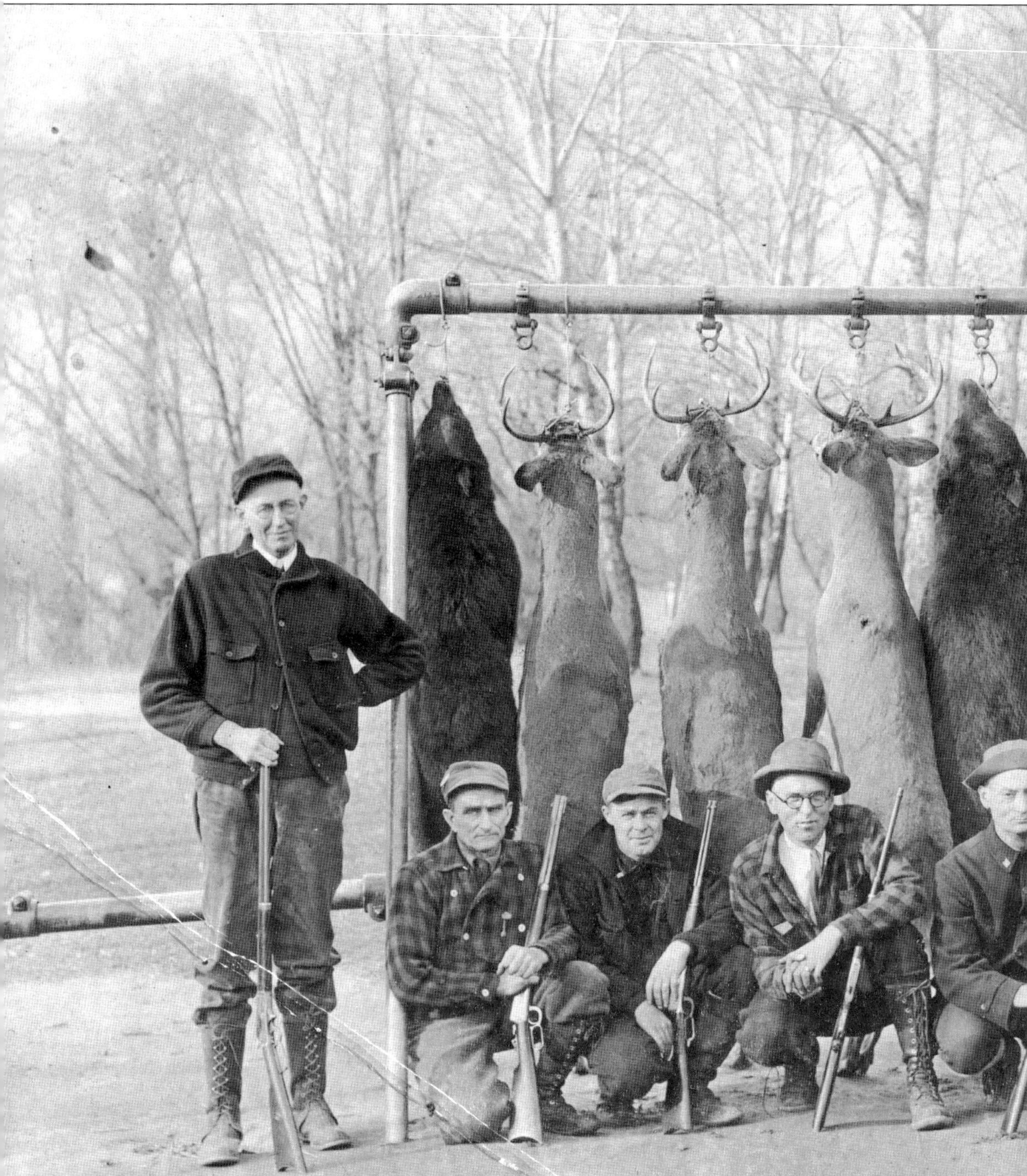

Deer populations in not only the state, but the country, have undergone fluctuations over time. The first big decline in white-tailed deer numbers was tied to the fur trade. In the early 1800s, due to a decline in fur sales and the natural expansion of deer into new habitats, populations were on the rise again, but that did not last. Rampant market hunting in the late-1800s reduced the white-tailed deer population to an all-time low. Then conservation legislation helped the deer numbers to increase again. In 1900, the Lacy Act, the first federal wildlife law, was enacted.

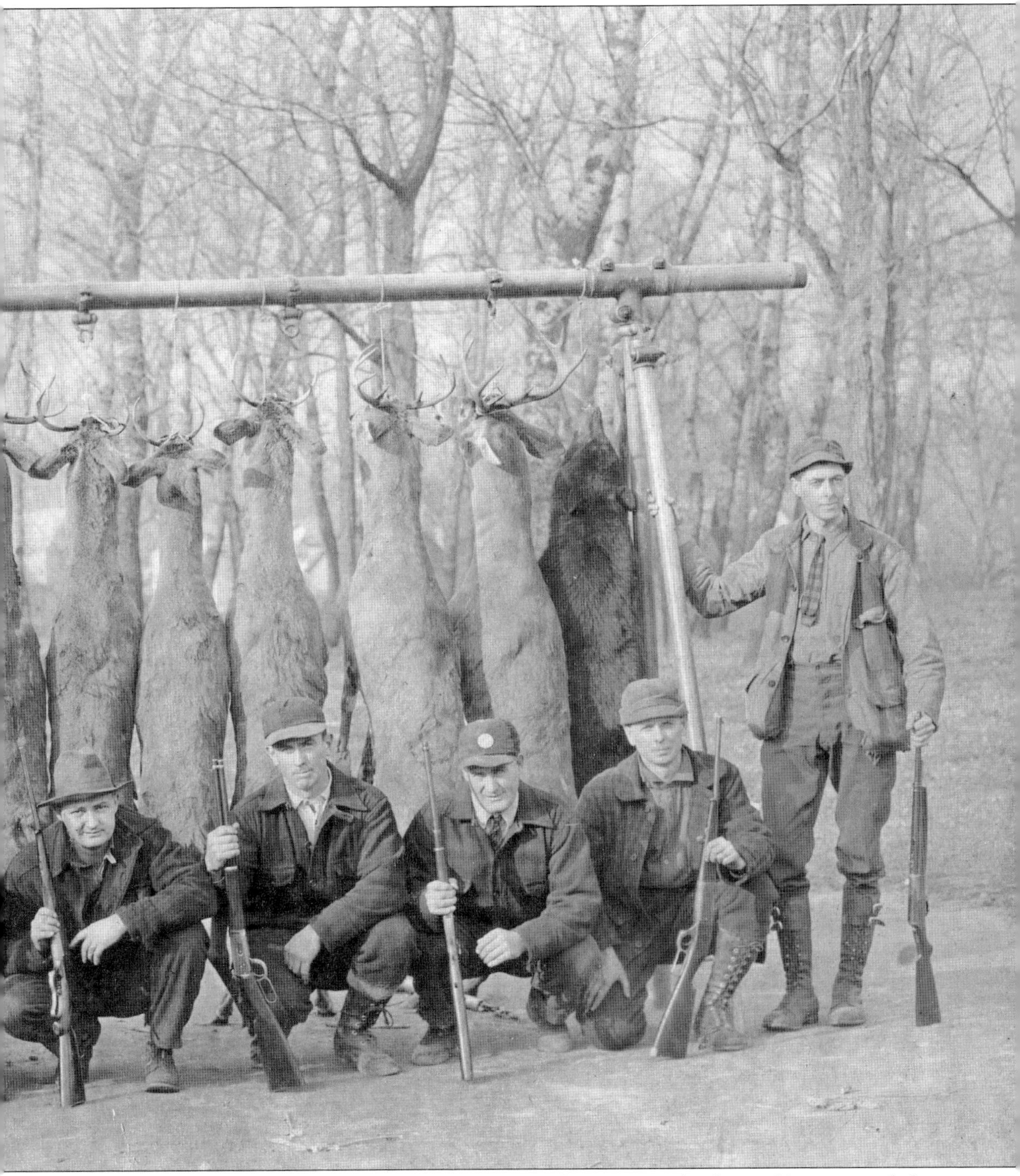

The Lacy Act prohibited the interstate trafficking of venison and other wild game, and the exploitation of white-tailed deer began to slow. In 1908, a total of 41 states established departments of conservation, furthering the protection of deer. Later, the Great Depression settled in, and Americans suffered, but white-tailed deer began to thrive. People relocated from the country to work in cities, and abandoned farms and home sites grew over with brush, grass, and saplings. This changing habitat was good for growing numbers of deer. (Author's collection.)

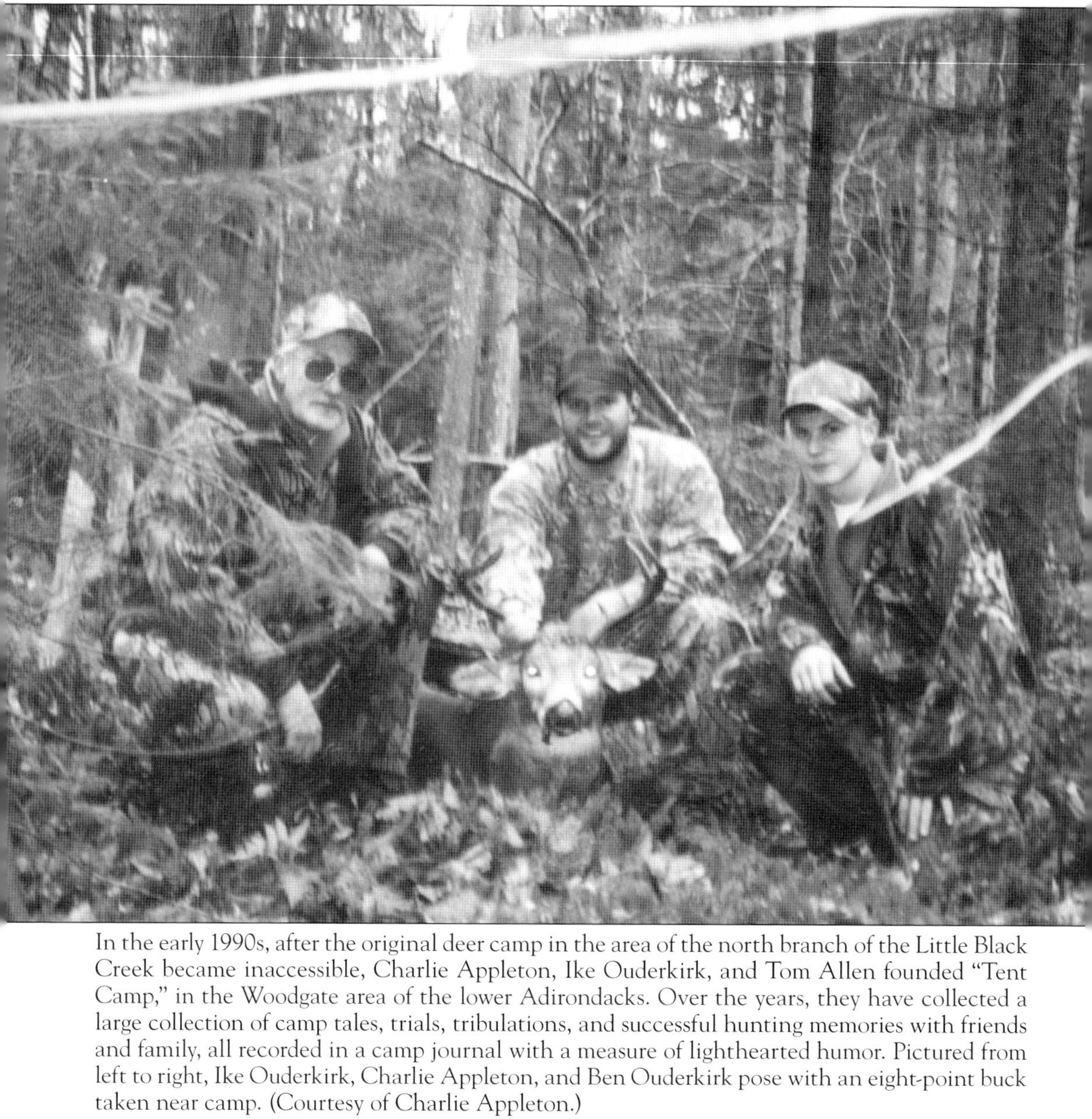

In the early 1990s, after the original deer camp in the area of the north branch of the Little Black Creek became inaccessible, Charlie Appleton, Ike Ouderkirk, and Tom Allen founded "Tent Camp," in the Woodgate area of the lower Adirondacks. Over the years, they have collected a large collection of camp tales, trials, tribulations, and successful hunting memories with friends and family, all recorded in a camp journal with a measure of lighthearted humor. Pictured from left to right, Ike Ouderkirk, Charlie Appleton, and Ben Ouderkirk pose with an eight-point buck taken near camp. (Courtesy of Charlie Appleton.)

From the Tent Camp ledger: "John spotted a deer up ahead feeding on the Witch Hobble. He thought he saw horns but the deer stopped with its head behind a tree. He got himself ready, and when the horn showed beyond the tree he let loose with the 30-06. He watched the deer stumble across Mill Brook and followed up with another round. John soon located him; a seven point." (Courtesy of Charlie Appleton.)

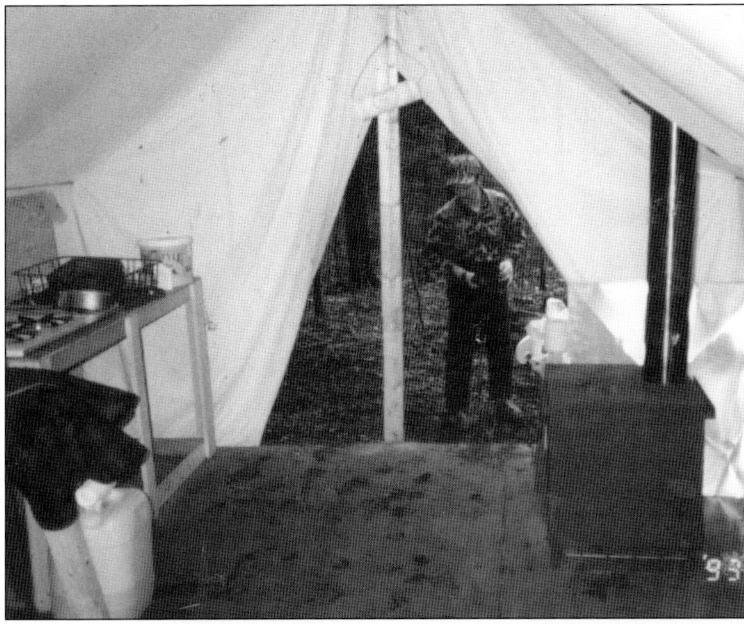

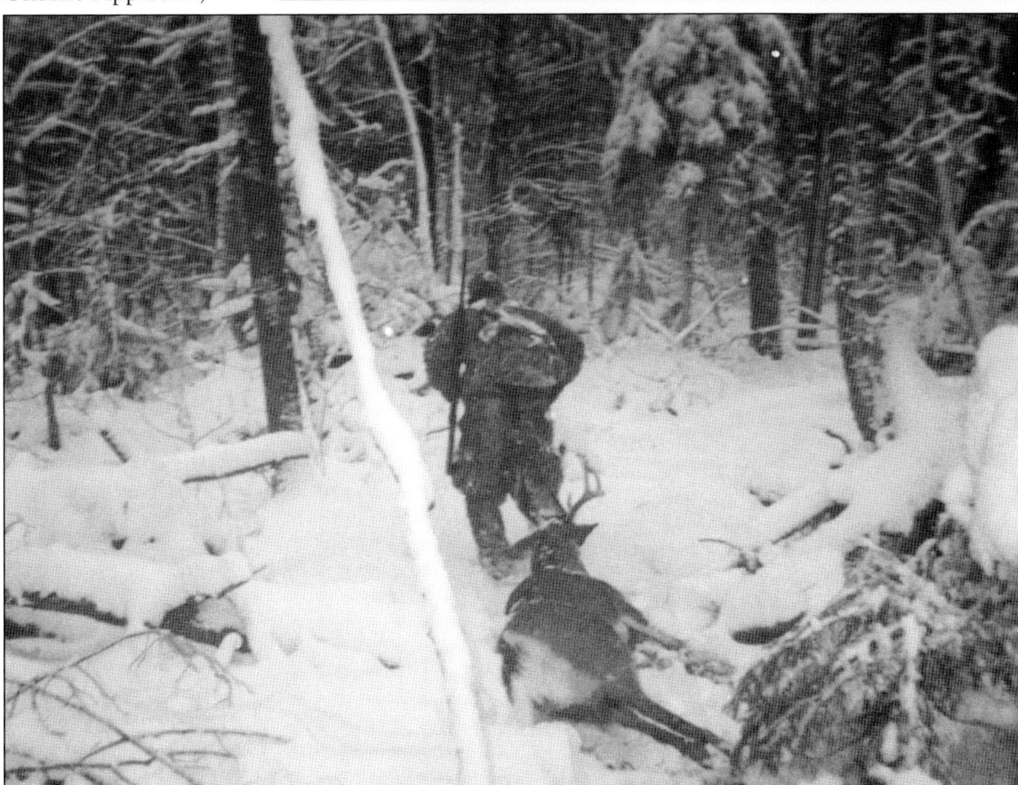

Hunters know that the real work starts after the trigger is pulled. Tracking and getting the deer out of the woods over uneven terrain can be a difficult and grueling process. Charlie Appleton is shown dragging his heavy Adirondack buck over the snow through the forest. (Courtesy of Charlie Appleton.)

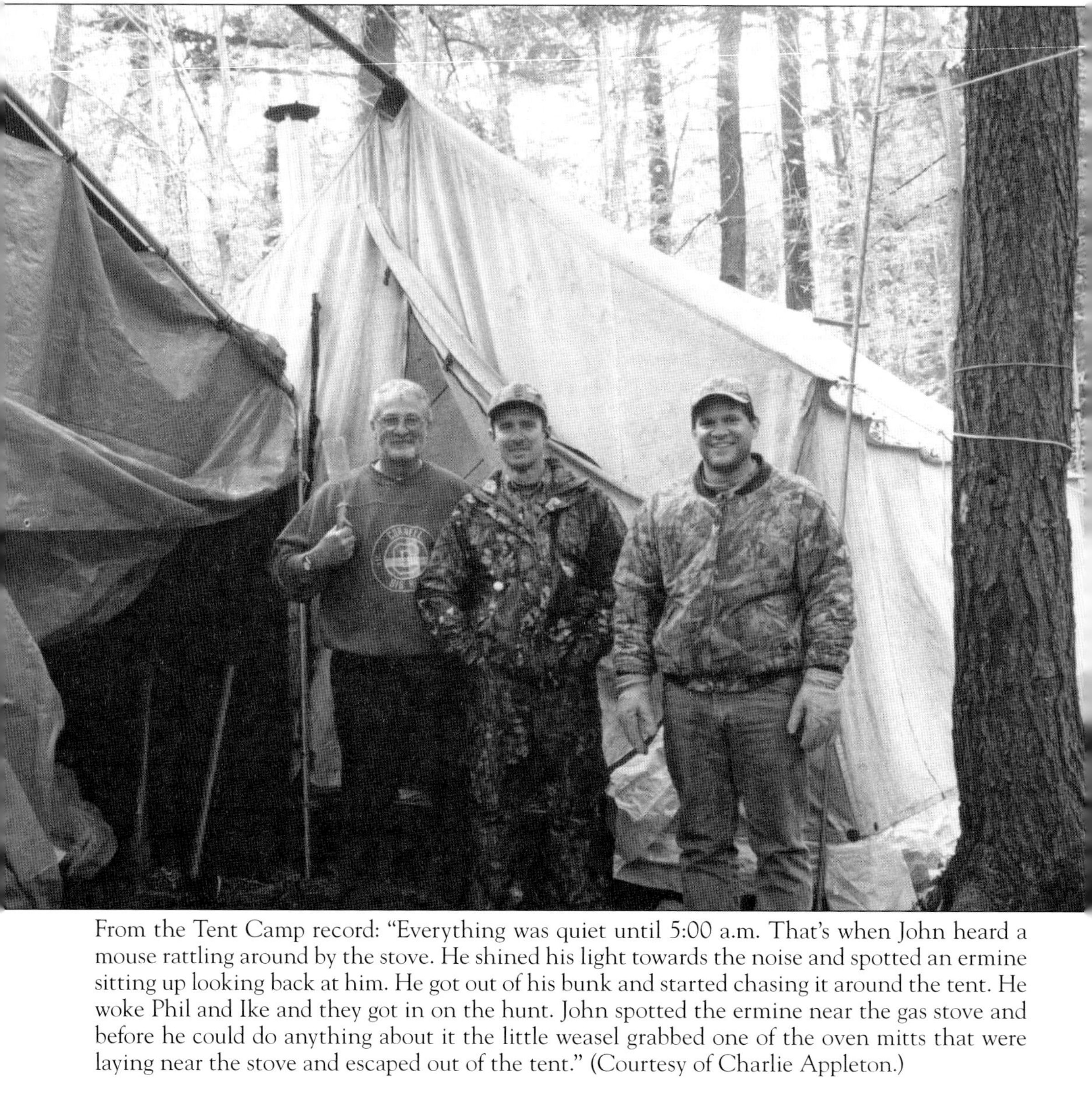

From the Tent Camp record: "Everything was quiet until 5:00 a.m. That's when John heard a mouse rattling around by the stove. He shined his light towards the noise and spotted an ermine sitting up looking back at him. He got out of his bunk and started chasing it around the tent. He woke Phil and Ike and they got in on the hunt. John spotted the ermine near the gas stove and before he could do anything about it the little weasel grabbed one of the oven mitts that were laying near the stove and escaped out of the tent." (Courtesy of Charlie Appleton.)

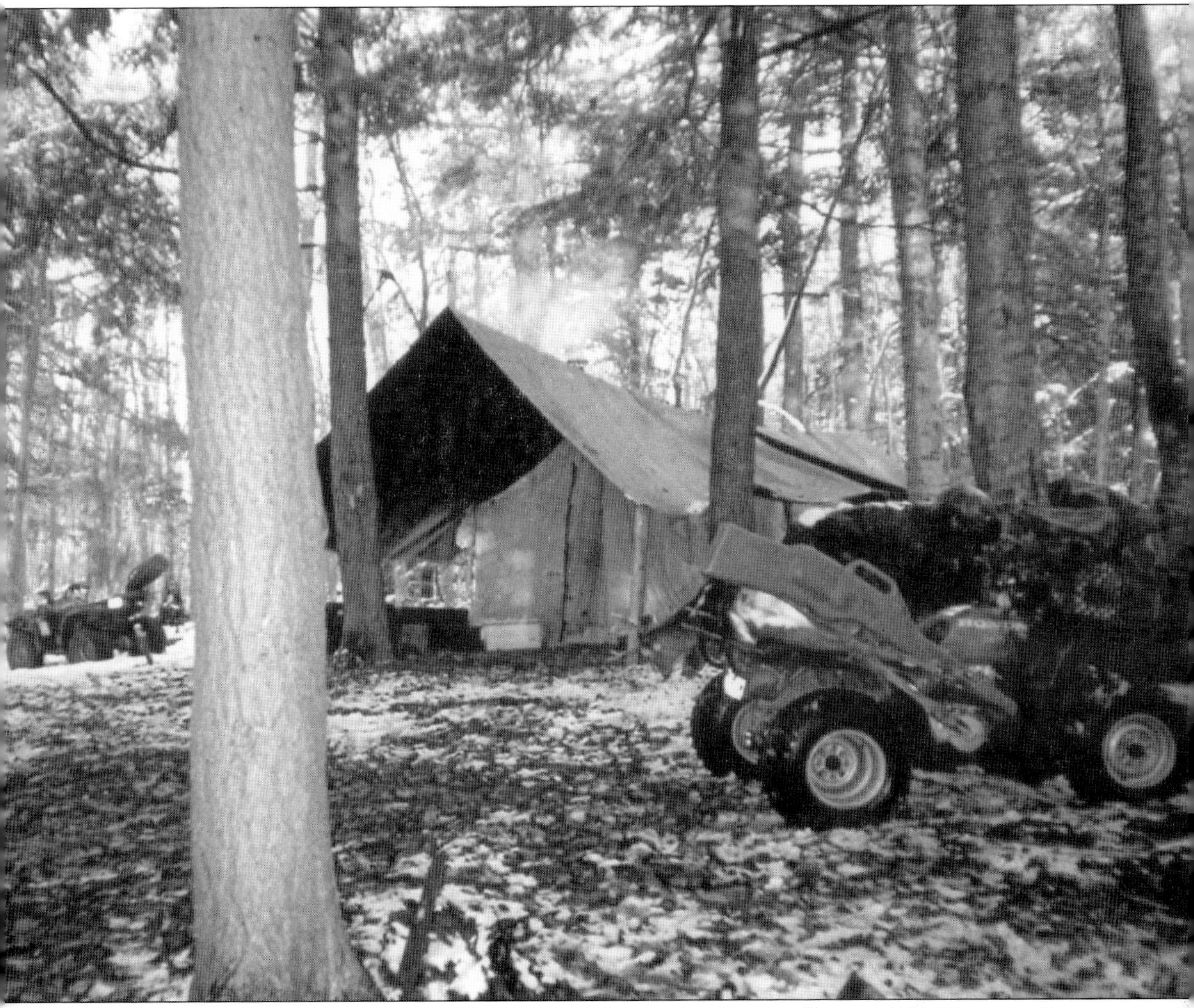

The Tent Camp record continues: "We sat around tent drinking coffee until 11:30 a.m. telling stories about the deer and the weasel. We had to settle for apple pie for breakfast because Ike wasn't in much of a cooking mood. When we did get out we hunted down between the trails. There wasn't much sign. Came back around 2:00 p.m. John is splitting wood and looking for the stolen oven mitts and Phil's having a Labatt Blue lunch to go along with the apple pie breakfast. It doesn't get much better than this!" (Courtesy of Charlie Appleton.)

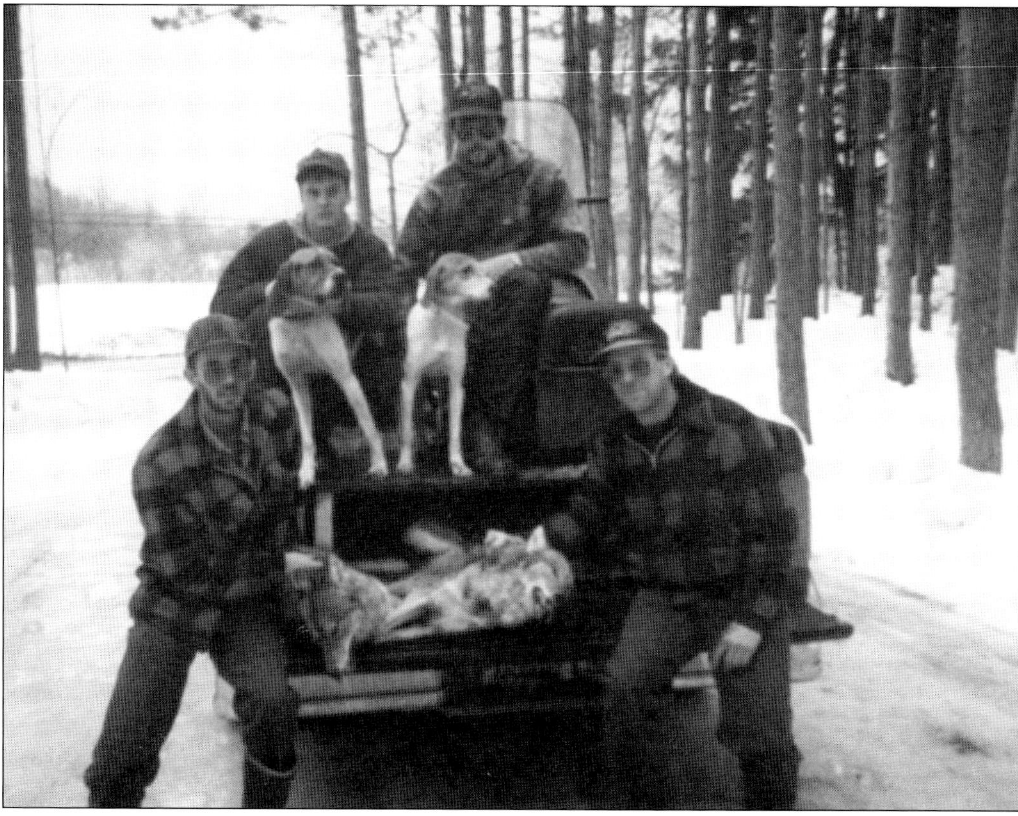

Pictured from left to right, Tim Shew, Jonathan Hill, Chris Graves, and Scott Cook show off two coyotes at the end of the day's hunting. The hounds are Buck and Annie. They are parked in Chris Graves's driveway, with Fairchild Road in Remsen in the background. (Courtesy of Chris Graves.)

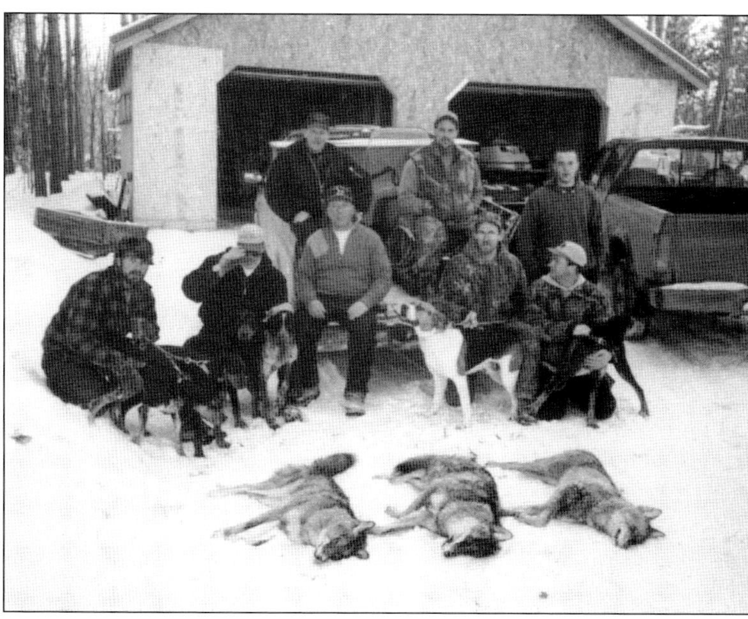

This successful coyote hunting party was photographed in the mid-1990s. In the photograph, from left to right, are (first row) Brian Hill, Blake Yutzler, Perry Piaciento, Jim Murphy, and Jonathan Hill; (second row) Scott Burdick, Jeff Nadeau, and Dick Lehman. Among the hound dogs are Gus, Millie, Buck, Luke, and two unidentified. (Courtesy of Chris Graves.)

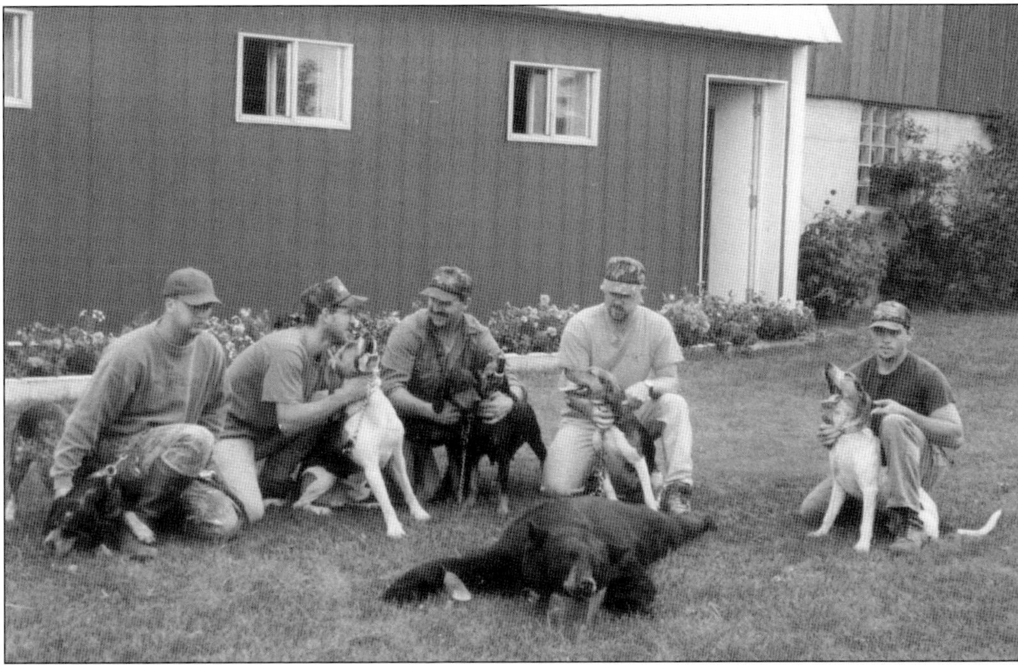

Bear hunting is a centuries-old tradition. Black bear is the only breed of bear to hunt in the Adirondacks. In New York State, there are estimated to be about 6,000–8,000 black bears in areas open to hunting. Approximately 50 to 60 percent of that population is in the Adirondacks. The rest of that population is dispersed with about 30 to 35 percent in the Catskill Mountains, and the other 10 to 15 percent in Central and Western New York. This nuisance bear was shot on the Jones property. In the photograph above, from left to right, are Jon Hill, Tom Murphy, Brian Hill, Jim Murphy, and Josh Graves. In the photograph below are Brian Hill (standing, with two hounds), Jim Murphy (standing, right), and Josh Graves) kneeling, with a hound). (Above, courtesy of Tom Murphy; below, courtesy of Chris Graves.)

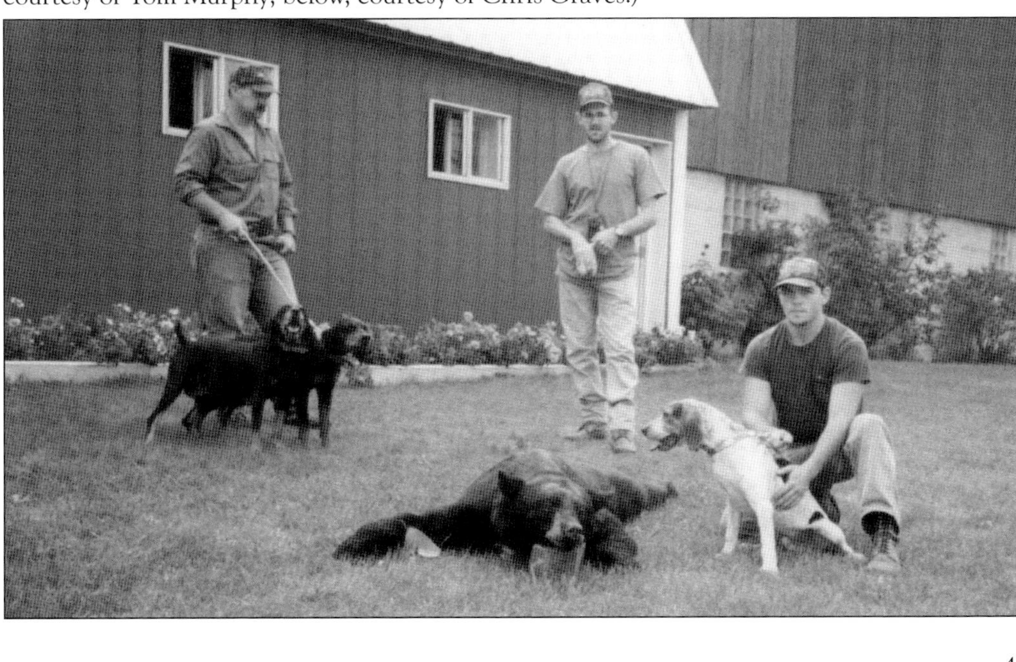

TROPHY HUNTING 39

WHITETAIL and COUES DEER

KIND of DEER

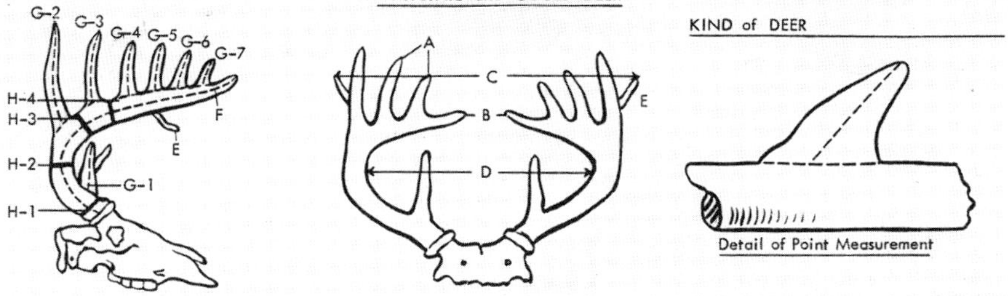

See Other Side for Instructions	Supplementary Data		Column 1	Column 2	Column 3	Column 4
A. Number of Points on Each Antler	R.	L.	Spread Credit	Right Antler	Left Antler	Difference
B. Tip to Tip Spread						
C. Greatest Spread						
D. Inside Spread of Main Beams — Spread credit may equal but not exceed length of longer antler						
If Inside Spread of Main Beams exceeds longer antler length, enter difference						
E. Total of Lengths of all Abnormal Points						
F. Length of Main Beam						
G-1 Length of First Point, if present						
G-2 Length of Second Point						
G-3 Length of Third Point						
G-4 Length of Fourth Point, if present						
G-5 Length of Fifth Point, if present						
G-6 Length of Sixth Point, if present						
G-7 Length of Seventh Point, if present						
H-1 Circumference at Smallest Place Between Burr and First Point						
H-2 Circumference at Smallest Place Between First and Second Points						
H-3 Circumference at Smallest Place Between Second and Third Points						
H-4 Circumference at Smallest Place between Third and Fourth Points or halfway between Third Point and Beam Tip if Fourth Point is missing						
Totals						

Add	Column 1		Exact Locality where killed
	Column 2		Date Killed — By whom killed
	Column 3		Present owner
Total			Address
Subtract Column 4			Guide's Name and Address
Final Score			Remarks: (Mention any abnormalities)

Courtesy Boone and Crockett Club.

Official scoring system for North American big-game trophies—whitetail and coues deer.

This trophy hunting scoring system provided by the Boone and Crockett Club was featured in one of the group's publications in the 1970s. The Boone and Crockett Club is North America's oldest wildlife and habitat conservation organization, founded in the United States in 1887 by Theodore Roosevelt and a few like-minded associates. The group was organized to address the decline in wildlife populations on a national scale and was the first hunter-conservationist organization in North America. The Boone and Crockett Club still operates as a nonprofit organization dedicated to hunter and conservation ethics, education, and demonstration. The group had helped establish a conservation model in the United States that has replenished populations of game species and ensured hunting opportunities for future generations. The North American Model of Wildlife Conservation is based upon the sustainable use of natural resources and ensuring the long-term health of the environment. (Author's collection.)

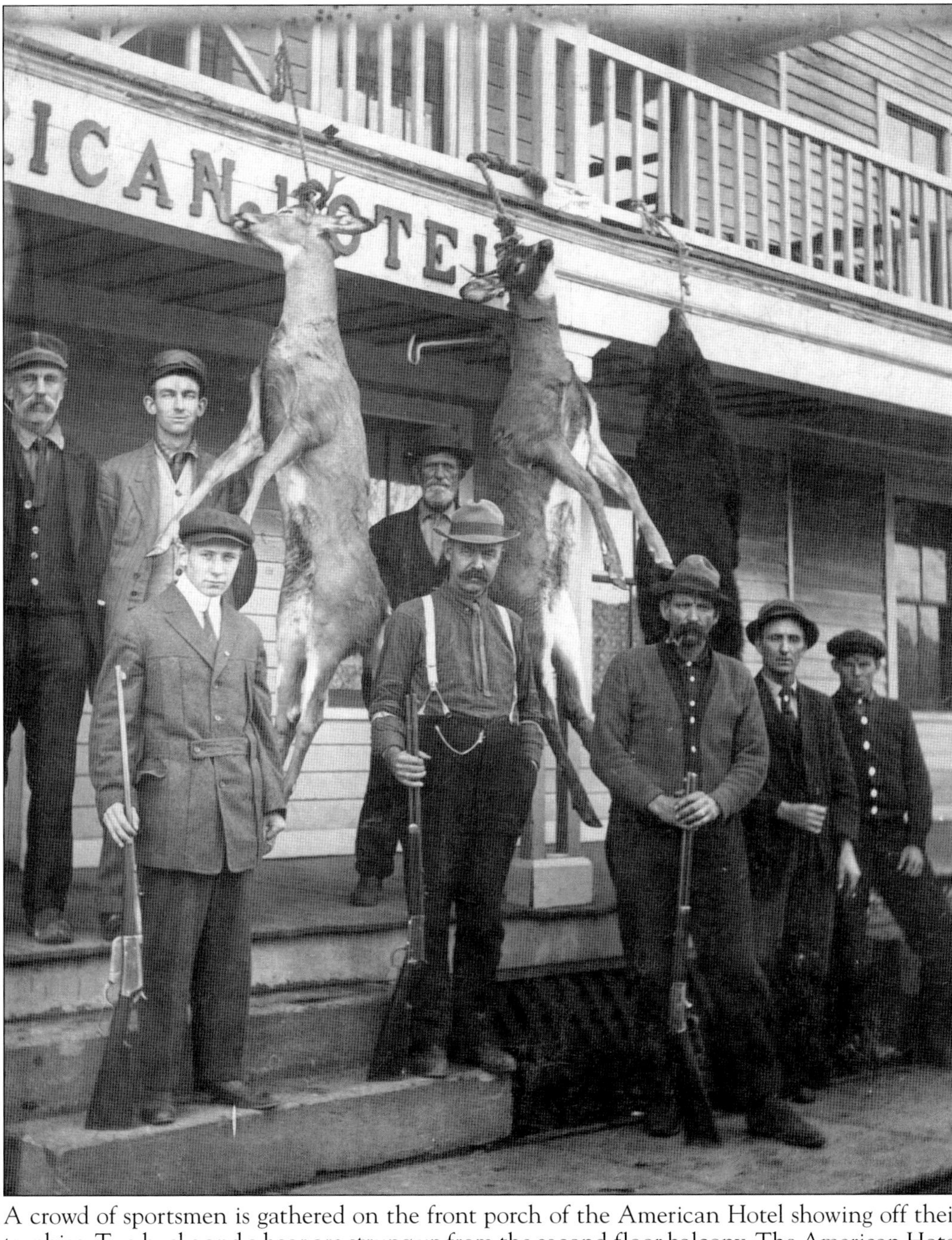

A crowd of sportsmen is gathered on the front porch of the American Hotel showing off their trophies. Two bucks and a bear are strung up from the second-floor balcony. The American Hotel was a popular gathering place for locals and travelers alike. The American Hotel, also known as the American House, operated for 30 years in Grant. It was a large three-story structure with a two-story porch. The third floor housed a ballroom. The hotel burned down in 1915. A handyman was rescued from the blaze, only to die a few days later. Hotels, like the American Hotel, were often the heartbeat of little communities scattered all throughout the Adirondacks. They served as gathering places. Few still stand. Many, like the American Hotel, have burned, collapsed, or have had to be torn down. (Photograph by Henry Beach, author's collection.)

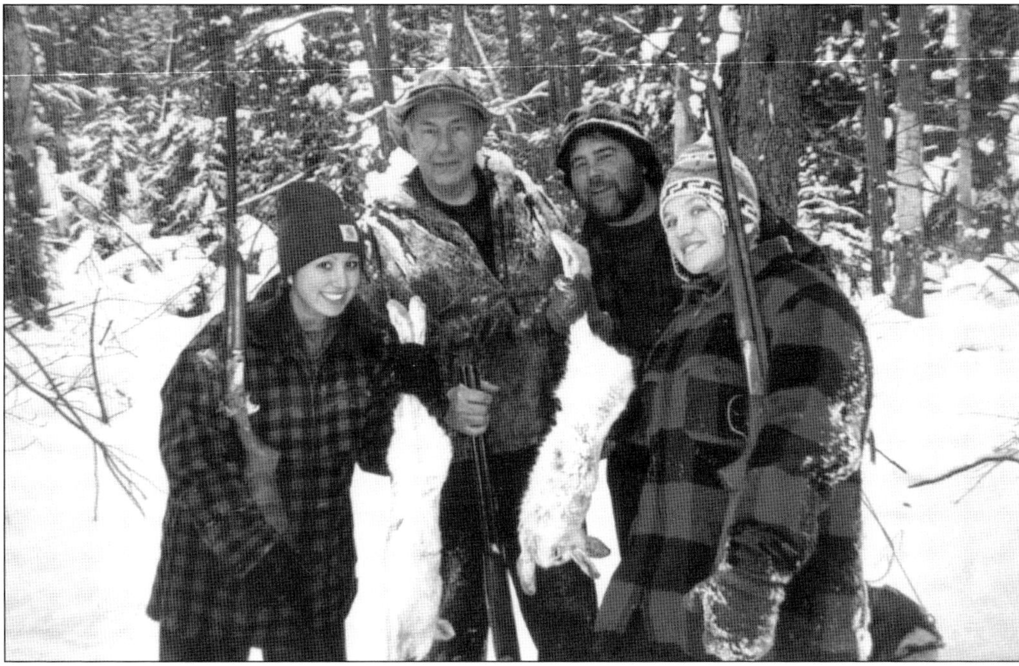

Bob Crochetiere (second from left) from Connecticut poses for a photograph with Ron Plete (third from left), Lindsay Maida (right), and author Megan Plete Postol (left), all from Remsen, after a day of rabbit hunting in the lower foothills of Herkimer County in the Southern Adirondacks, just inside the Blue Line. The hunting party built a campfire and roasted hot dogs in the snow that day. The beagle hound that accompanied the crew was named Barney. (Author's collection.)

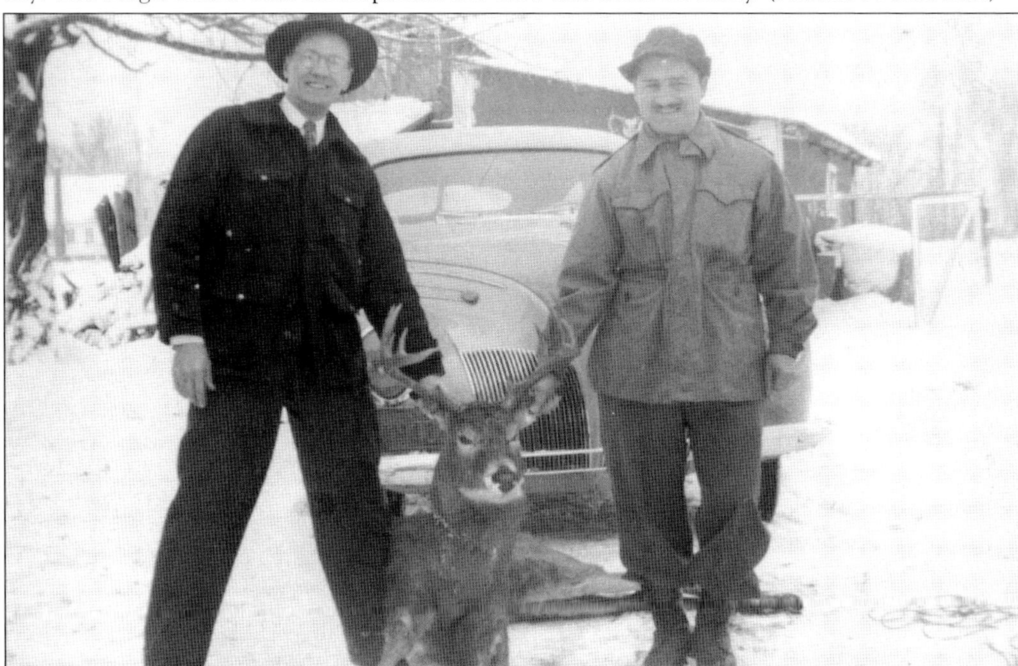

In this photograph, two gentlemen hold up a nice buck. (Author's collection.)

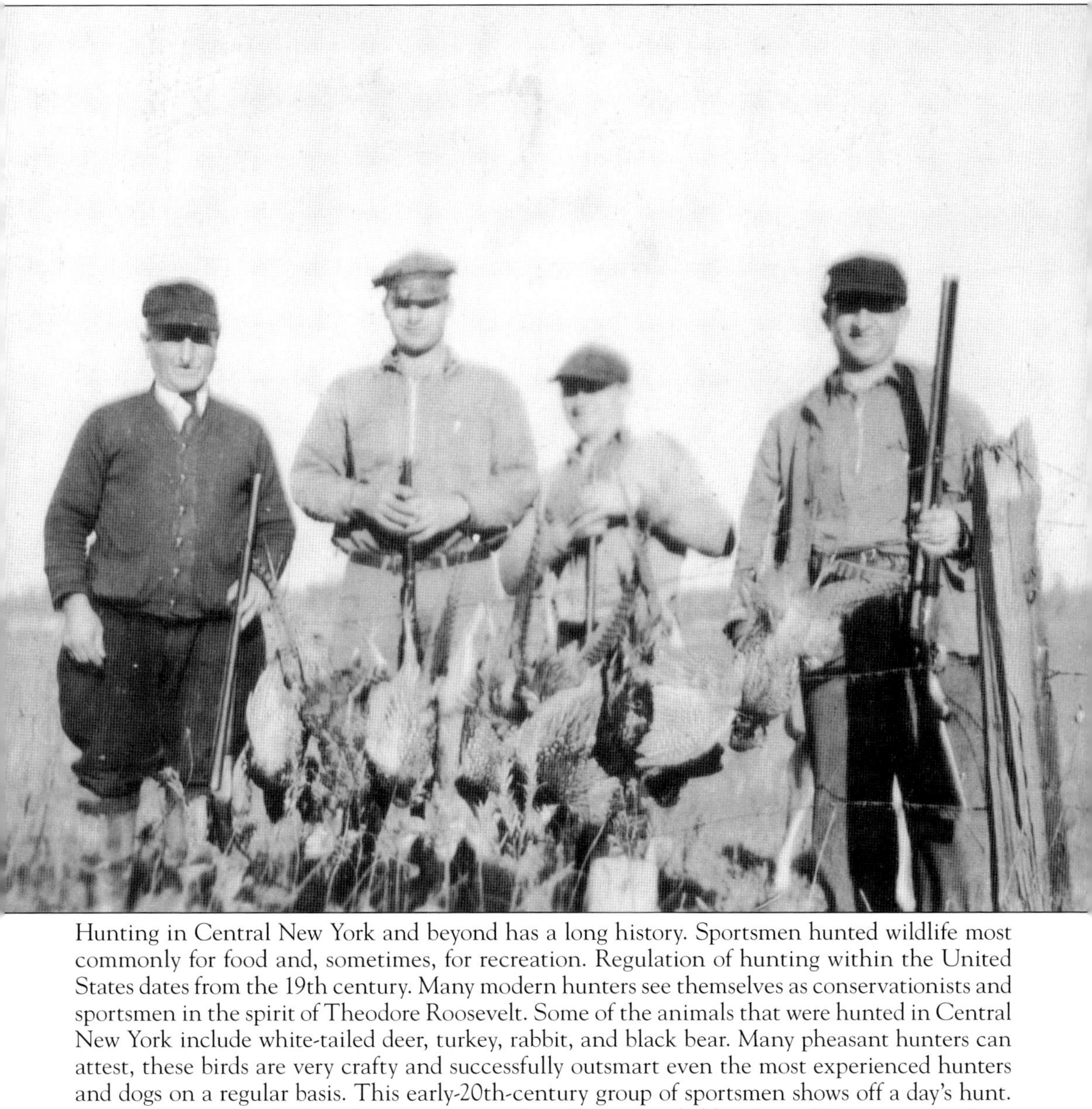

Hunting in Central New York and beyond has a long history. Sportsmen hunted wildlife most commonly for food and, sometimes, for recreation. Regulation of hunting within the United States dates from the 19th century. Many modern hunters see themselves as conservationists and sportsmen in the spirit of Theodore Roosevelt. Some of the animals that were hunted in Central New York include white-tailed deer, turkey, rabbit, and black bear. Many pheasant hunters can attest, these birds are very crafty and successfully outsmart even the most experienced hunters and dogs on a regular basis. This early-20th-century group of sportsmen shows off a day's hunt. Notice the man on the far left is wearing a necktie. He was probably a "sport." Sports were visitors that contracted local guides to lead them on hunting, fishing, and hiking trips. The men in the photograph are unidentified. (Author's collection.)

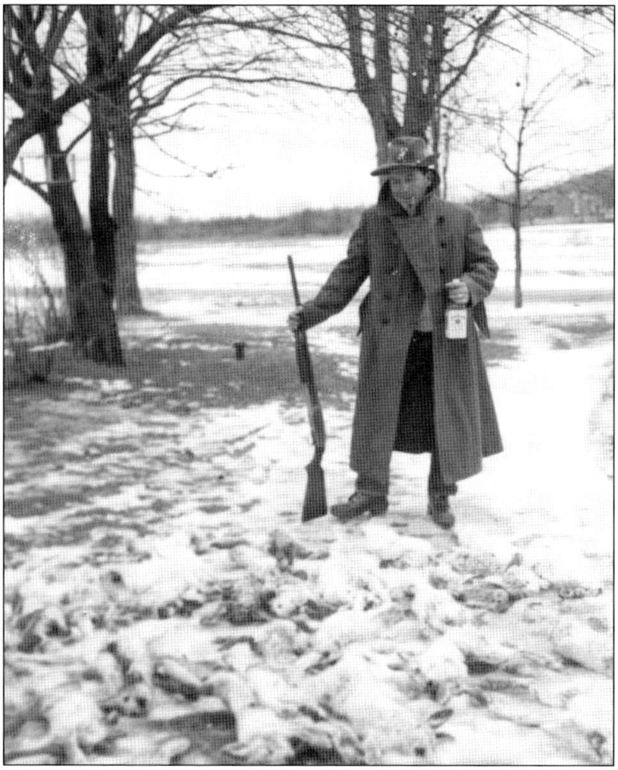

Cheerful hunter Jim Arute poses for a photograph while goofing around and celebrating the successful rabbit hunt with a bottle of Jim Beam, a tobacco pipe stuck in his mouth, and his shotgun. Notice the pile of harvested rabbits in the foreground. (Author's collection.)

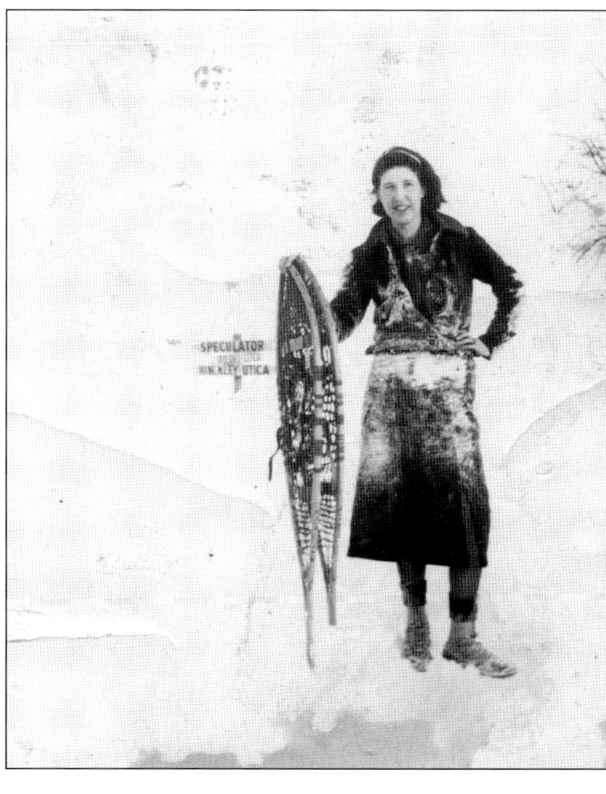

Trappers and hunters utilized snowshoes to trek long distances through deep snow cover in the forests. Winters in upstate New York were harsh and snow often accumulated as high as the rooftops. Many people besides trappers and hunters used snowshoes because it made walking in the wintertime on the snow easier. The woman pictured, posing next to the directional sign, is Anna Harvey Plete. (Author's collection.)

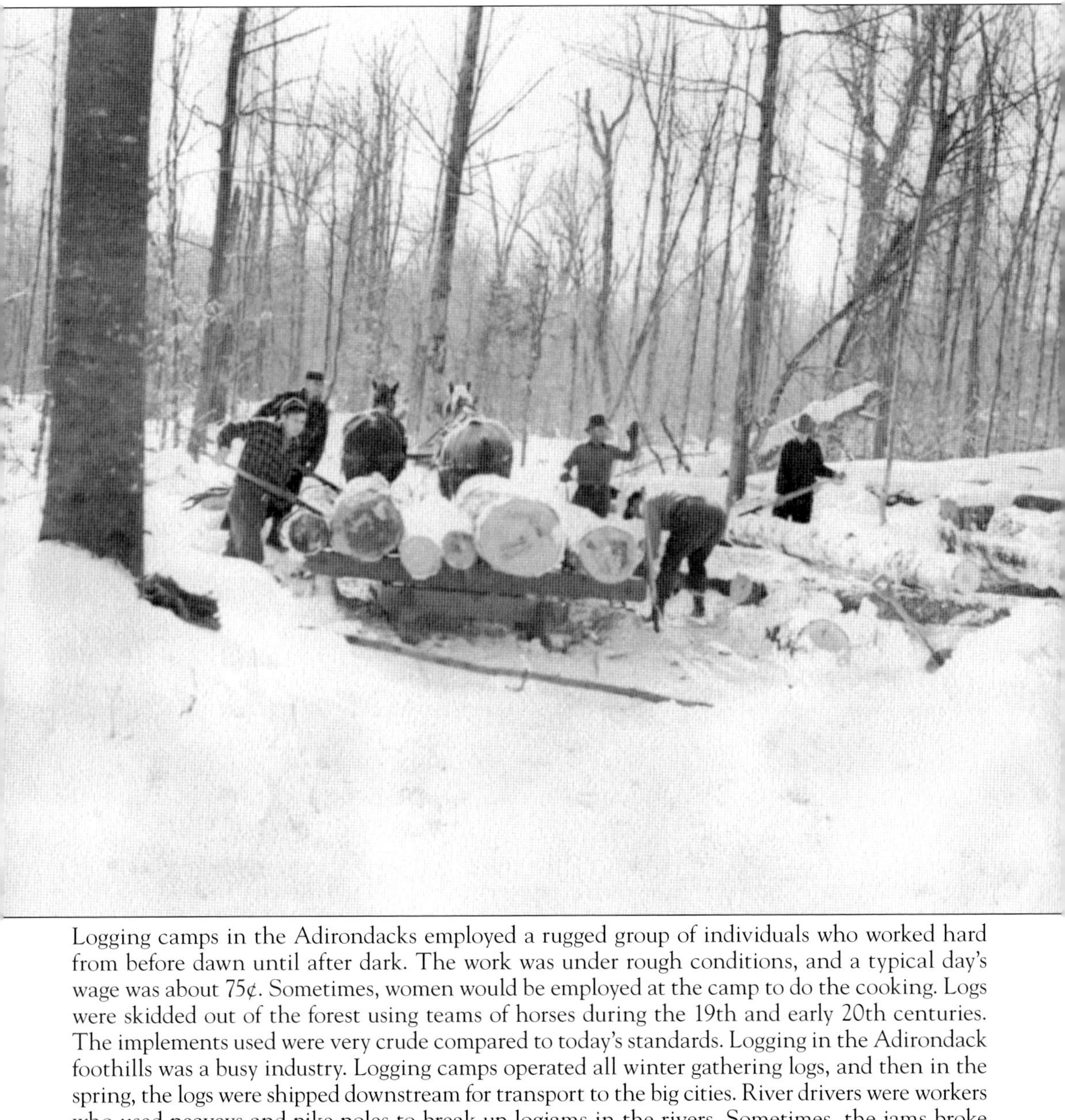

Logging camps in the Adirondacks employed a rugged group of individuals who worked hard from before dawn until after dark. The work was under rough conditions, and a typical day's wage was about 75¢. Sometimes, women would be employed at the camp to do the cooking. Logs were skidded out of the forest using teams of horses during the 19th and early 20th centuries. The implements used were very crude compared to today's standards. Logging in the Adirondack foothills was a busy industry. Logging camps operated all winter gathering logs, and then in the spring, the logs were shipped downstream for transport to the big cities. River drivers were workers who used peaveys and pike poles to break up logjams in the rivers. Sometimes, the jams broke suddenly and forcefully, swallowing the river driver up within it. Breaking up jams killed many good river drivers. (Author's collection.)

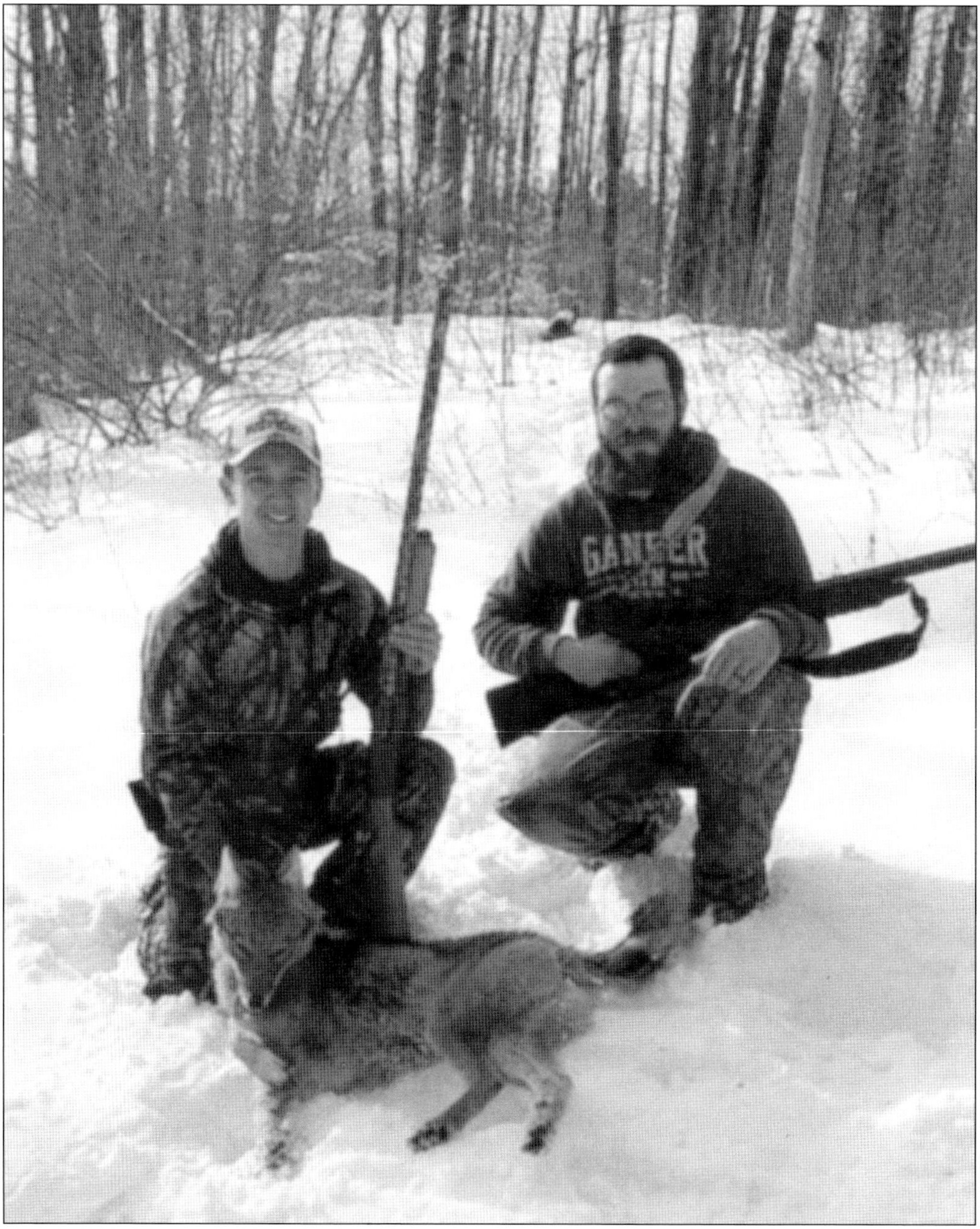

Coyote numbers in the state have been increasing over the last few years. For the past couple of decades, the population remained steady at about 20,000 to 30,000 coyotes in New York. The latest numbers from researchers at SUNY College of Environmental Science and Forestry estimate that the state's coyote population has grown to around 38,000. In this photograph, Gabe Appleton is on the left and Tom McDonald is on the right, with a coyote they hunted in the Remsen/Steuben area. (Courtesy of Tom McDonald.)

Coyotes are abundant in New York State. In recent years, they have been increasingly encroaching on communities. The summer of 2017 saw the city of Rome being terrorized by coyotes eating family pets and trespassing into peoples' lawns. Hunting and trapping coyotes is one way to help manage the population. In this photograph, posed behind the coyote from left to right, are Ryan Lawson, with hound Al; Gabe Appleton, with hound Luke; and Nate Graves, with hound Frank. (Courtesy of Tom McDonald.)

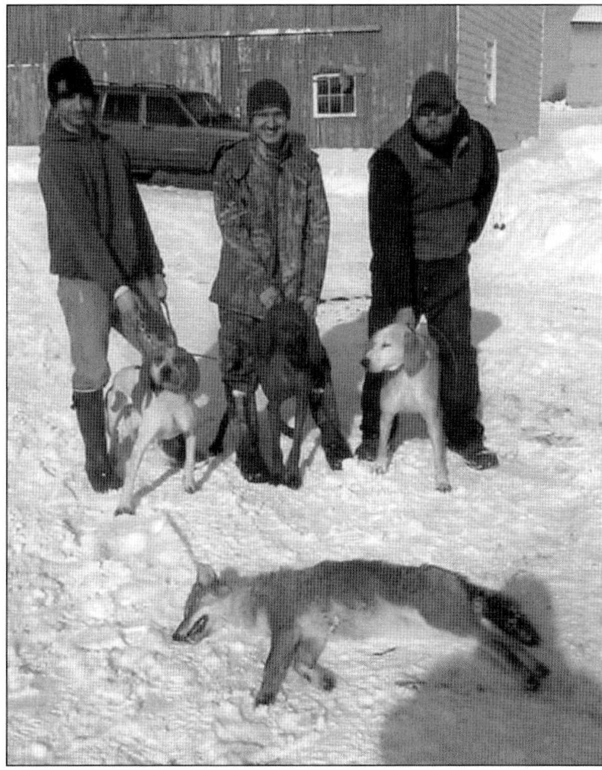

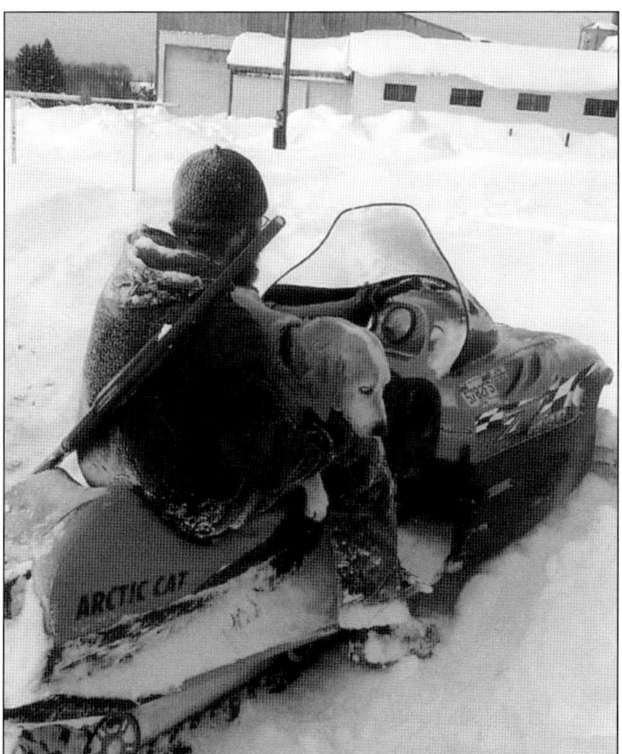

After a 12-mile run, Tom McDonald's 13-year-old hound Frank was very tired. Tom loaded old Frank onto the snowmobile and gave the veteran hound a well-deserved ride home. (Courtesy of Tom McDonald.)

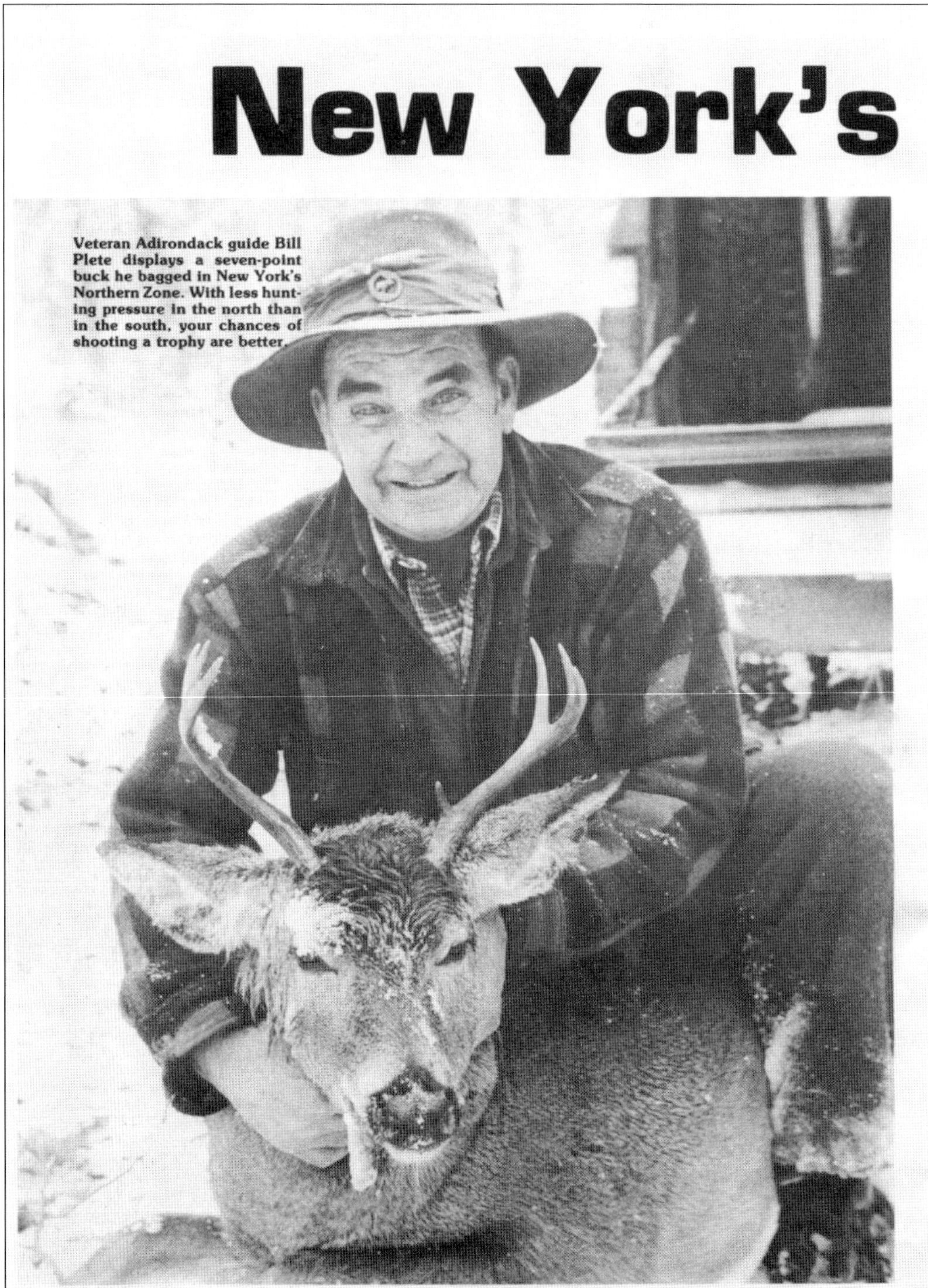

New York's

Veteran Adirondack guide Bill Plete displays a seven-point buck he bagged in New York's Northern Zone. With less hunting pressure in the north than in the south, your chances of shooting a trophy are better.

66 Fins and Feathers

Philip "Bill" Plete is seen on page 66 of the October 1982 issue of *Fins and Feathers* magazine. The article, written by Bob Peel, was titled "New York's North Country Deer." It encouraged readers to explore the Adirondack region and the Northern Tier hunting zone. (Author's collection.)

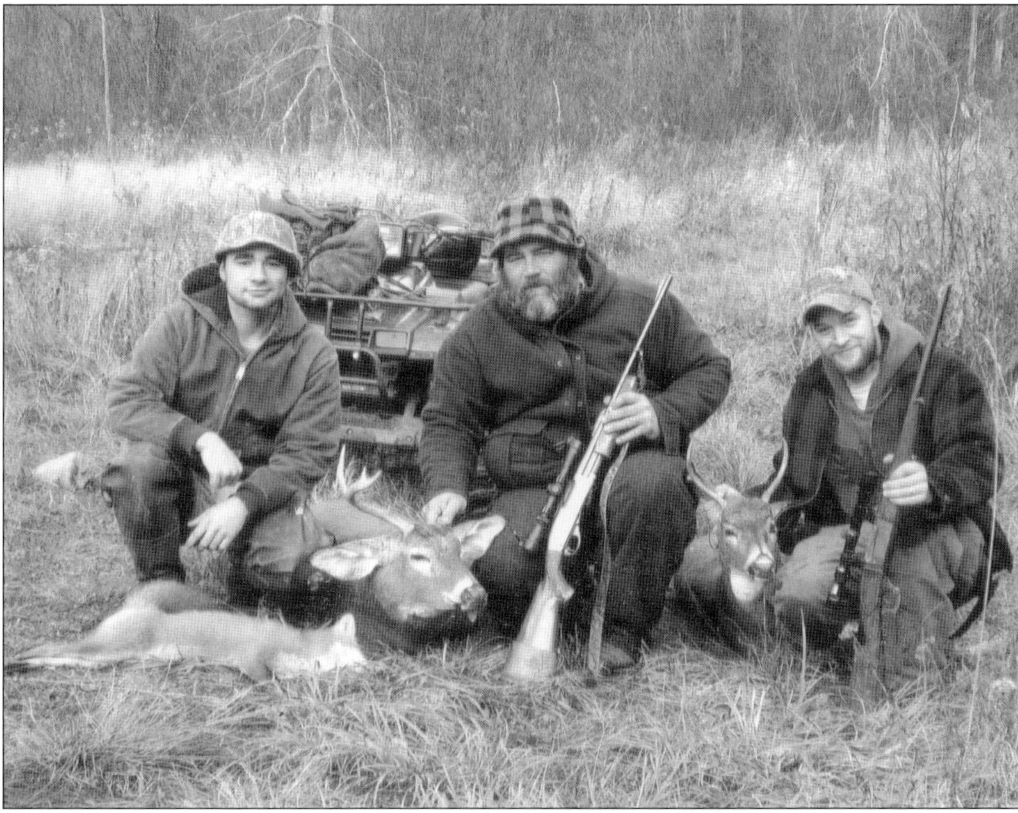

On a lucky November morning, these three men got two bucks and a red fox between them. From left to right are Bill Plete, with the red fox he trapped; Ron Plete, with his buck; and Dale Postol, with his buck. (Author's collection.)

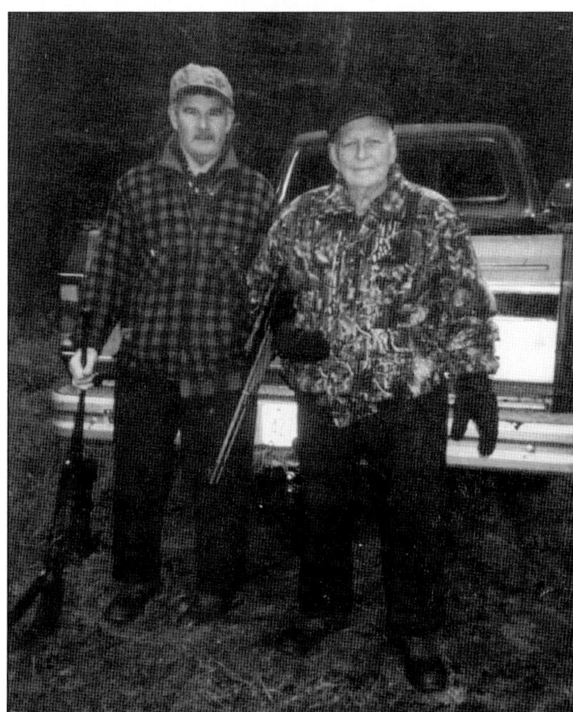

Bernard "Bill" Plete (left) and Art Johnson (right) get ready to head out into the woods to do some deer hunting. Judging by the fact that there is no snow on the ground, it was probably early in the season when this photograph was taken. (Courtesy of Ron Plete.)

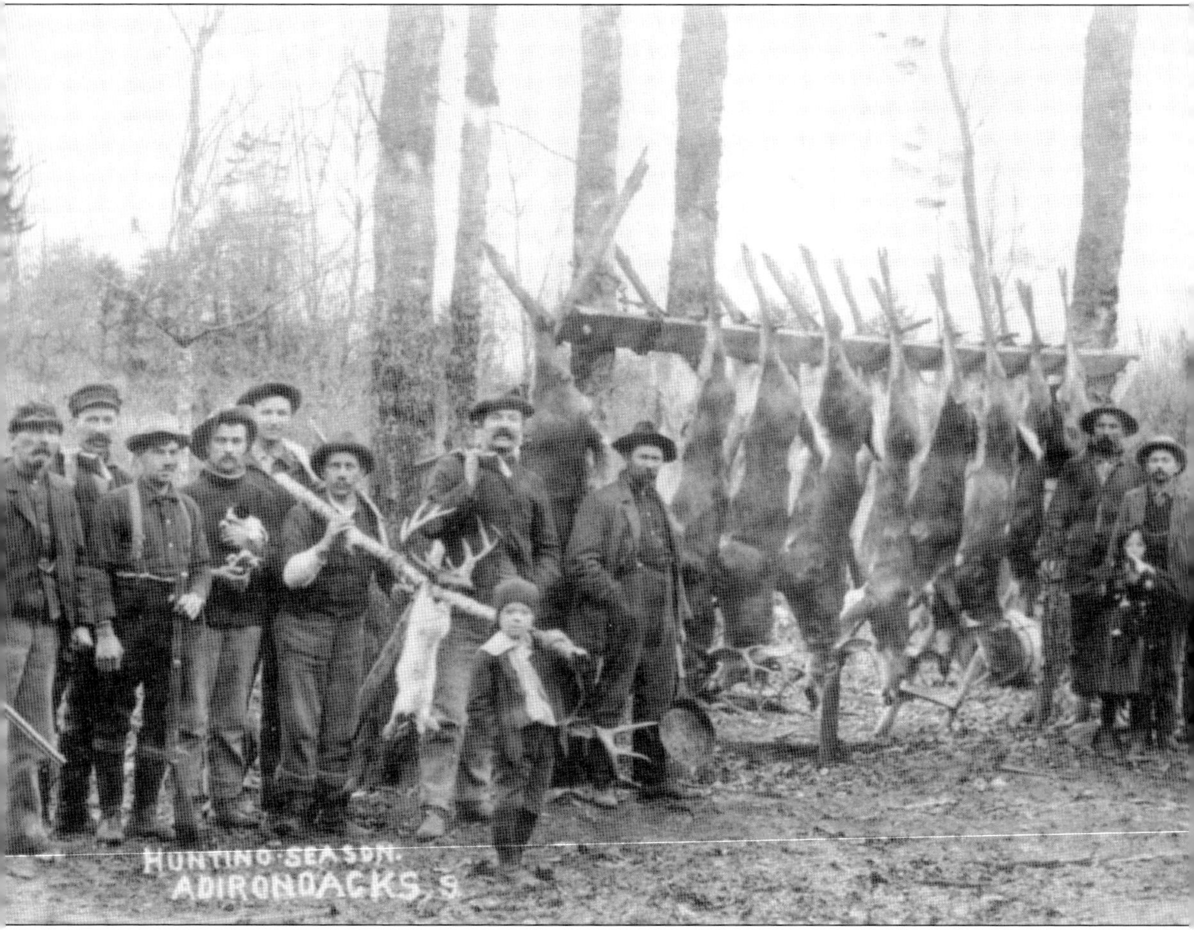

This postcard image, titled "Hunting Season Adirondacks," was taken by photographer Henry Beach. He lived in Watson and Remsen, both communities on the edge of the Adirondack Park. Beach began his photography career near Lowville, eventually expanding beyond into the Western Adirondacks. He made his career as an Adirondack photographer, traveling extensively within the park and taking photographs of tourists and locals to market for bulk sale. His work documented a time of extraordinary change in the Adirondack Mountains. Railroads were on the decline, and automobiles were taking their place. This made the park more accessible to common folk. The mountains were welcoming new generations of tourists beyond the rich families of the "Great Camps" era. Henry Beach's work overwhelmingly celebrated those plain people. A fun fact is that Beach had a son named Harry who was also a photographer, and the two men sometimes get confused as the same person. Henry Beach lived from 1863 until 1943. (Author's collection.)

Pack baskets and snowshoes like the ones in this photograph were made in the north woods by Chet Clark. His reputation for superb craftsmanship was known far and wide. Clark made his products in his Wheelertown Road home workshop. (Author's collection.)

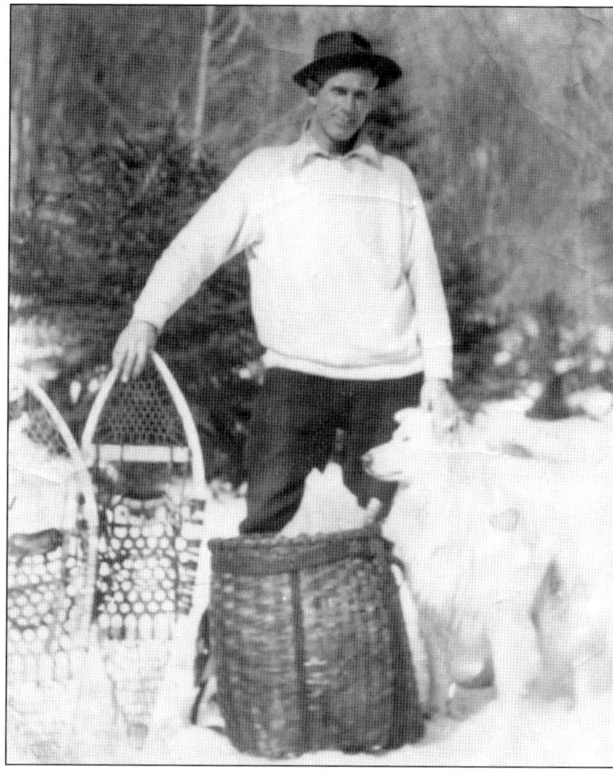

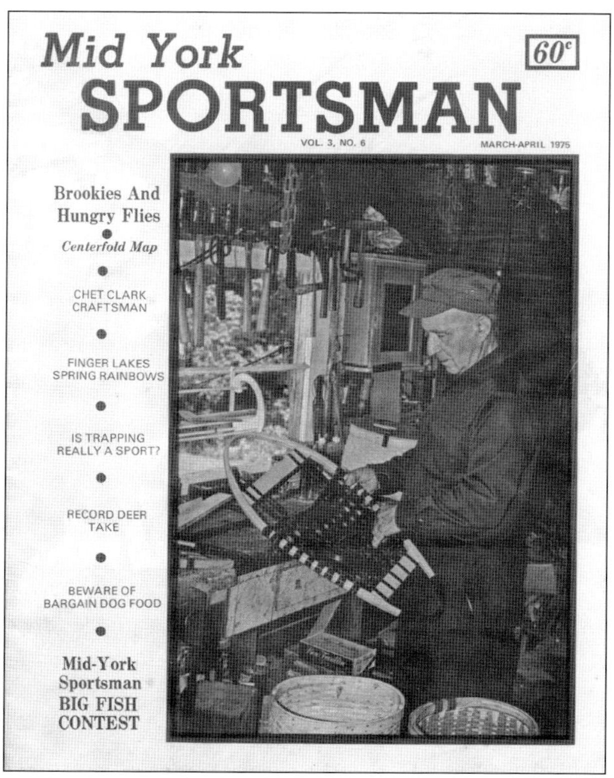

Chester "Chet" Clark was featured on the cover of *Mid York Sportsman* magazine, the predecessor to the *New York Sportsman* magazine, in the March–April 1975 issue. The magazine was founded by Paul Keesler in 1972. For several years, Keesler wrote the outdoors column for the *Utica Observer Dispatch*. In 1992, he retired as editor of the magazine. (Author's collection.)

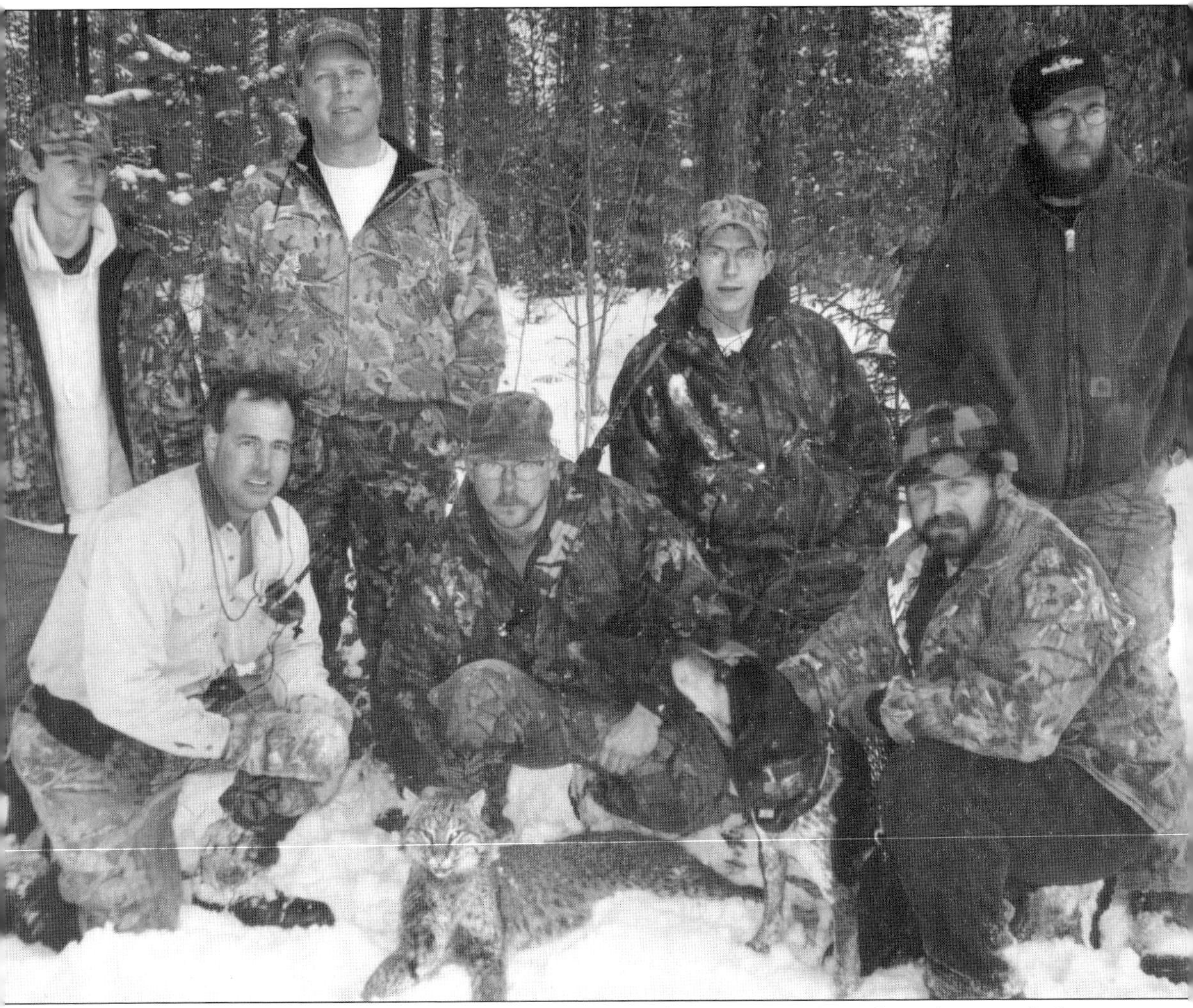

The bobcat hunting party gathered around the prize, "the Big Spring Cat," for a photograph. It was called that because it was shot in an area they referred to as "Big Spring," due to an ever-flowing spring in the swamp they were hunting. The hunt took about four hours, and everyone—dogs and people—were tired out when it was completed. Tom Murphy shot the bobcat from about six yards away. Pictured from left to right are (first row, kneeling) Perry Piacentino, Tom Murphy, and Brian Hill, with his dog Gus; (second row) unidentified, Jeff Nadeau, unidentified, and Jim Murphy. (Courtesy of Tom Murphy.)

Hunting coyotes is very popular in the Adirondack Foothills. A lot of people say one of the thrills of the sport is listening to the hound dogs as they run. From left to right are Brian Hill, Blake Yutzler, and Chris Graves. (Courtesy of Chris Graves.)

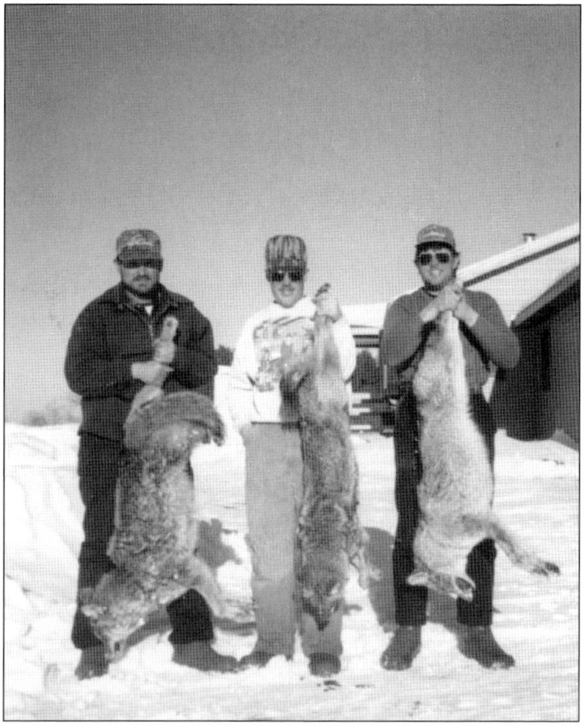

Tom Murphy shot this buck, his first, at 16 years old on the last day of the season. The buck weighed more than 200 pounds. Shooting one's first deer is a rite of passage for many. It is a moment sportsmen never forget. (Courtesy of Tom Murphy.)

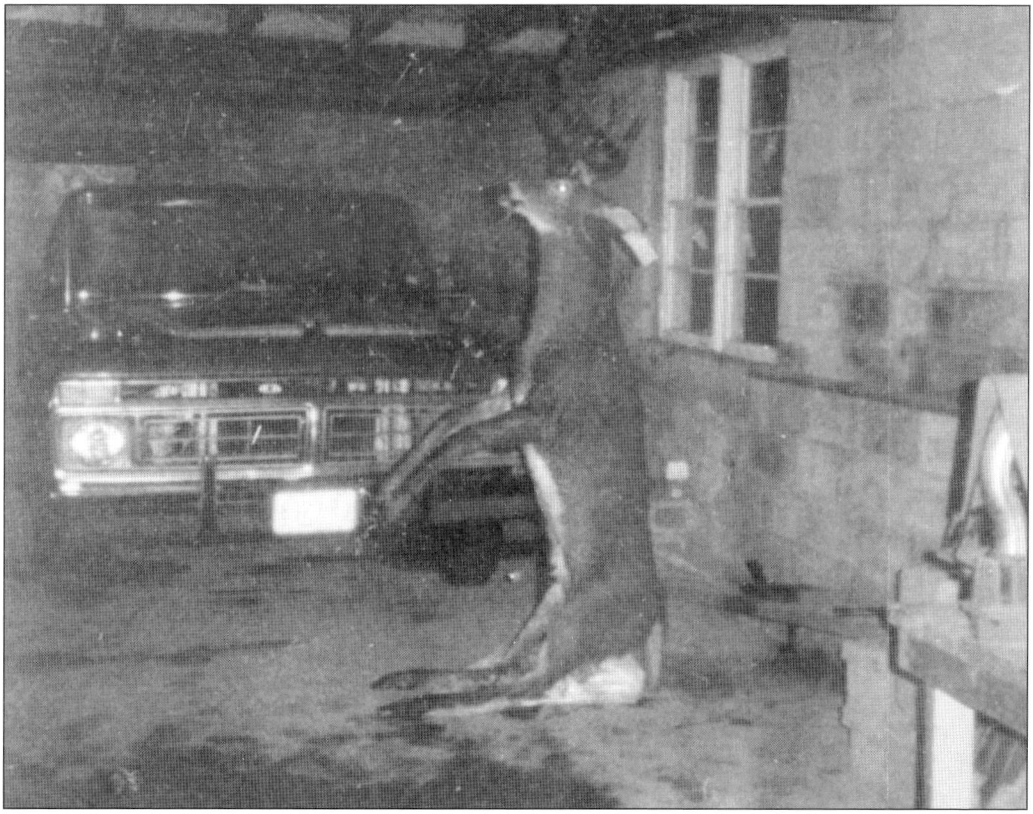

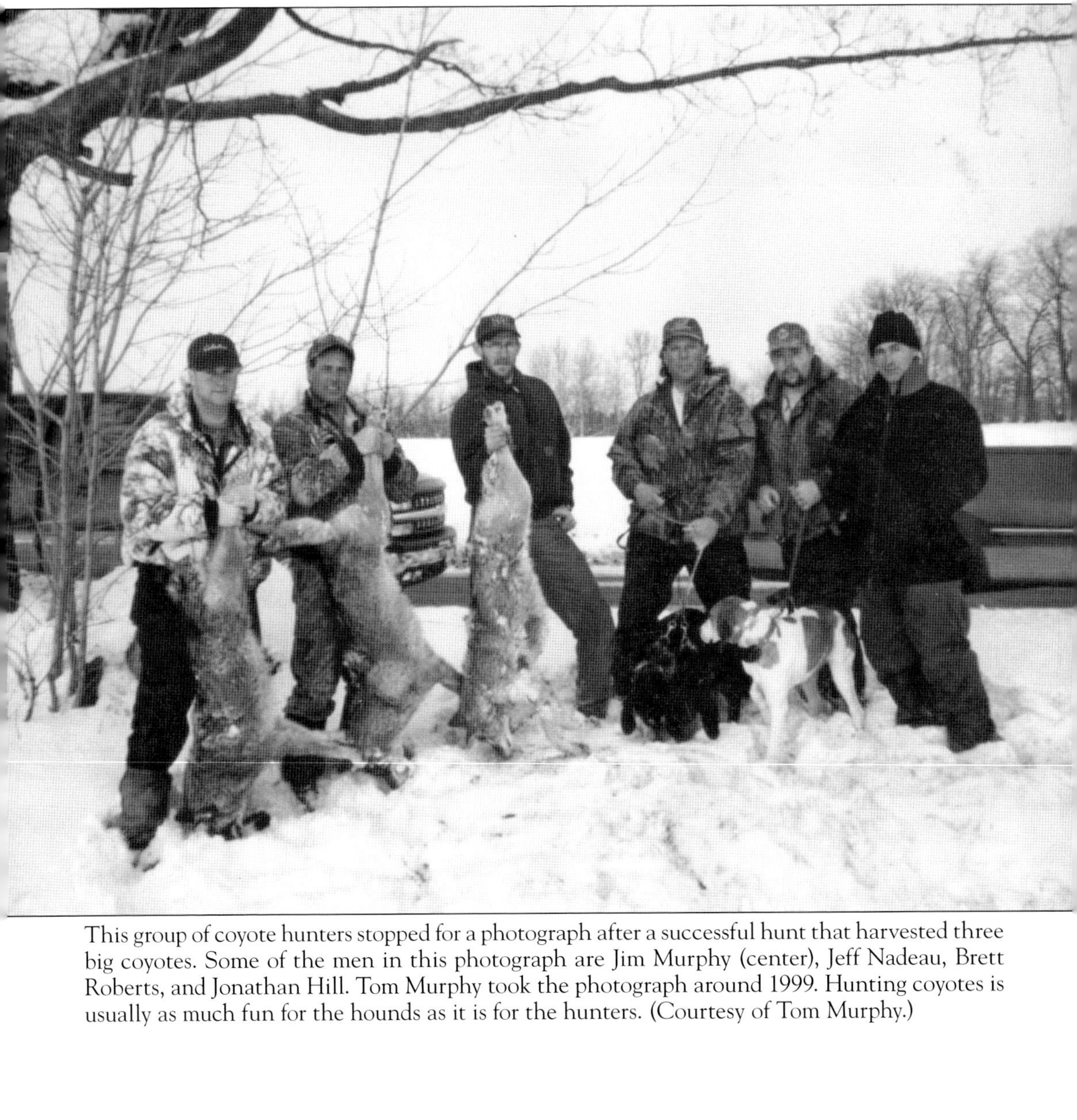

This group of coyote hunters stopped for a photograph after a successful hunt that harvested three big coyotes. Some of the men in this photograph are Jim Murphy (center), Jeff Nadeau, Brett Roberts, and Jonathan Hill. Tom Murphy took the photograph around 1999. Hunting coyotes is usually as much fun for the hounds as it is for the hunters. (Courtesy of Tom Murphy.)

Two

Fishing the Foothills

The lakes of the Adirondacks were cut into the landscape by ice glaciers moving over the earth's surface. This region's timeless beauty is made even richer by the vast amounts of freshwater fish inhabiting the numerous waterways.

Many of the lakes remain cold and clear all year long, thus providing a perfect habitat for trout. Other areas are more shallow and lush with weeds and create living space for bass and other game fish.

The Adirondacks have been a prime fishing destination for hundreds of years. Early settlers marveled at the amount of fish pulled from the lakes and rivers. Guides quickly figured out how to make money by bringing clients to the best fishing locations. Beyond the borders of the mountains and foothills, glorious stories were told and retold of the abundance of fishing opportunities within the region.

Fishing remains a popular recreation. It provides a break from the domesticated routine of daily life and offers an opportunity to engage with the real world beyond our cell phones and various electronic gadgets. It is also a great way to spend quality time with family or friends. Memories made on the water or near the water can last a lifetime.

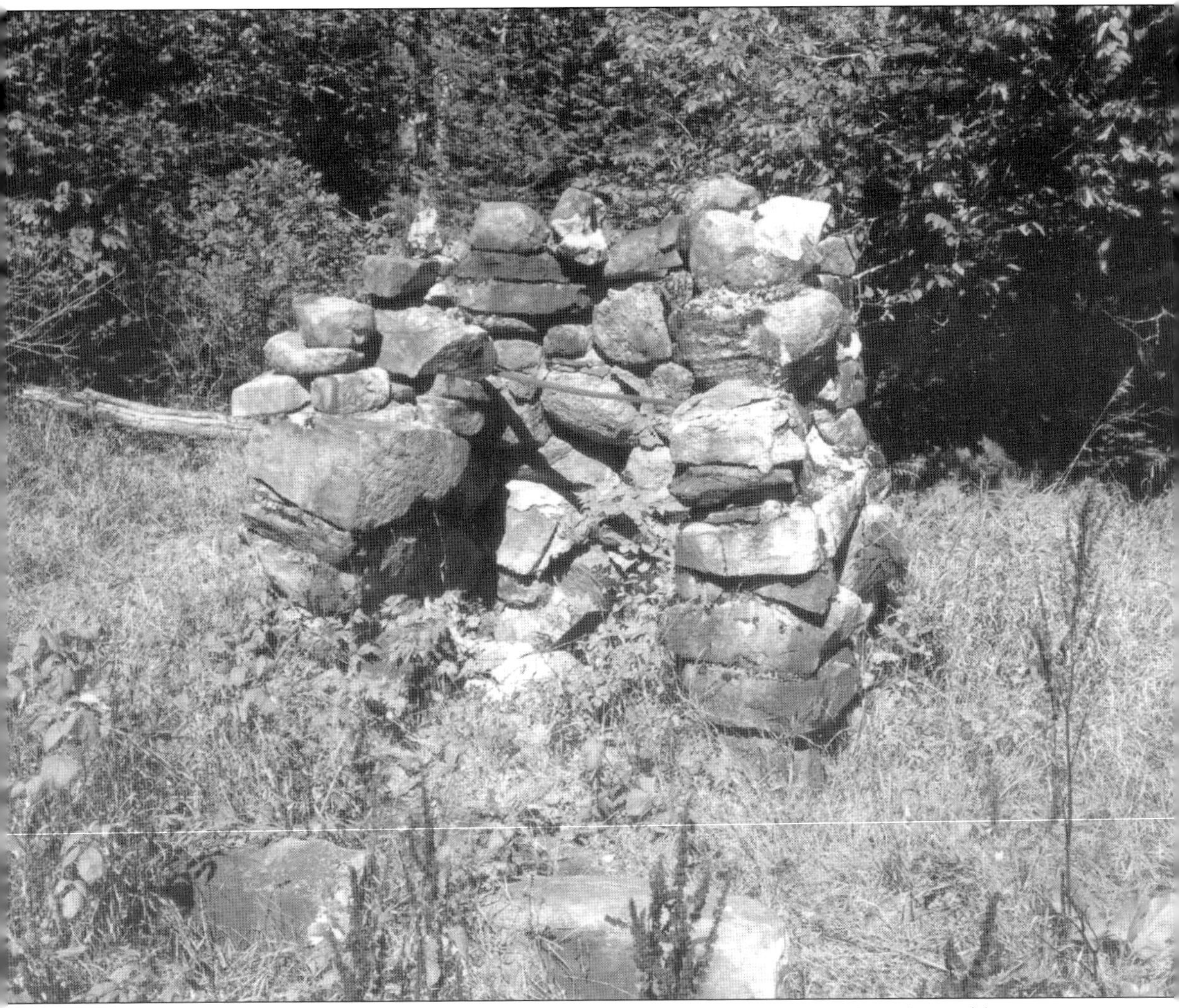

French Louie's fireplace sits undisturbed in a clearing in the West Canada Lakes wilderness area. French Louie's main cabin was at Big West. He had numerous other smaller cabins along his trap line, but Big West was his home base. He collected snakes on his travels and transported them back home in his pockets, pack, or shirt. He called them "potato bug hunters," and they were a cherished addition to his yard. Whether credit goes to the snakes or to the homemade fertilizer, French Louie had a lush vegetable garden. He was known to use the bones and fins of old lake trout as fertilizer. French Louie knew how to make the most of his resources. His iconic self-sufficiency has been inspiring generations of outdoor enthusiasts for more than a century. (Author's collection.)

Jim Arute, pleased and holding two trout in this photograph, frequently trekked to the Adirondack foothills to visit, fish, and hunt with his friend and guide, Philip "Bill" Plete. Notice the handwoven pack baskets in the background of the image. (Author's collection.)

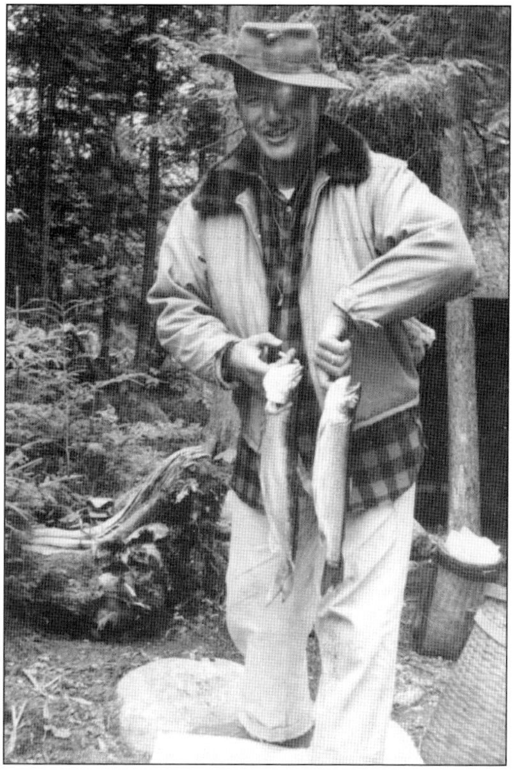

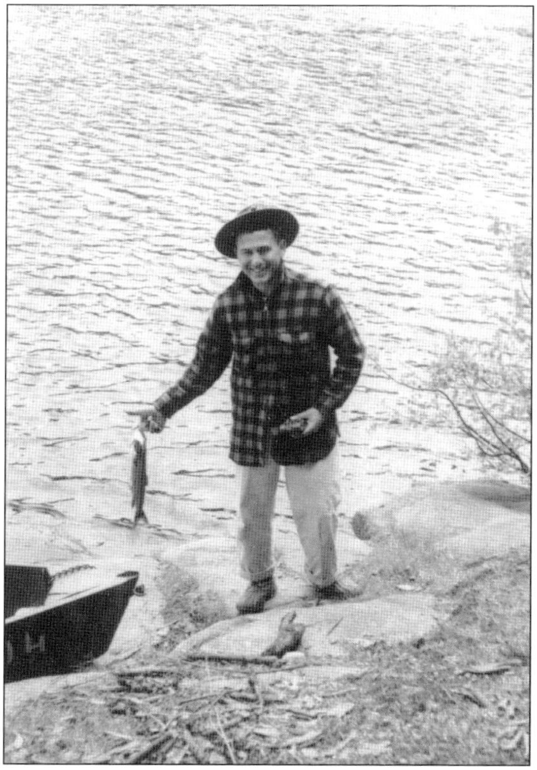

Jim Arute displays a trout he caught in Fawn Lake. Arute owned a successful construction company based in Connecticut. He was related to Jack Arute Jr., a well-known sports announcer for ESPN. Arute Field, a football stadium in New Britain, is named for the family. (Author's collection.)

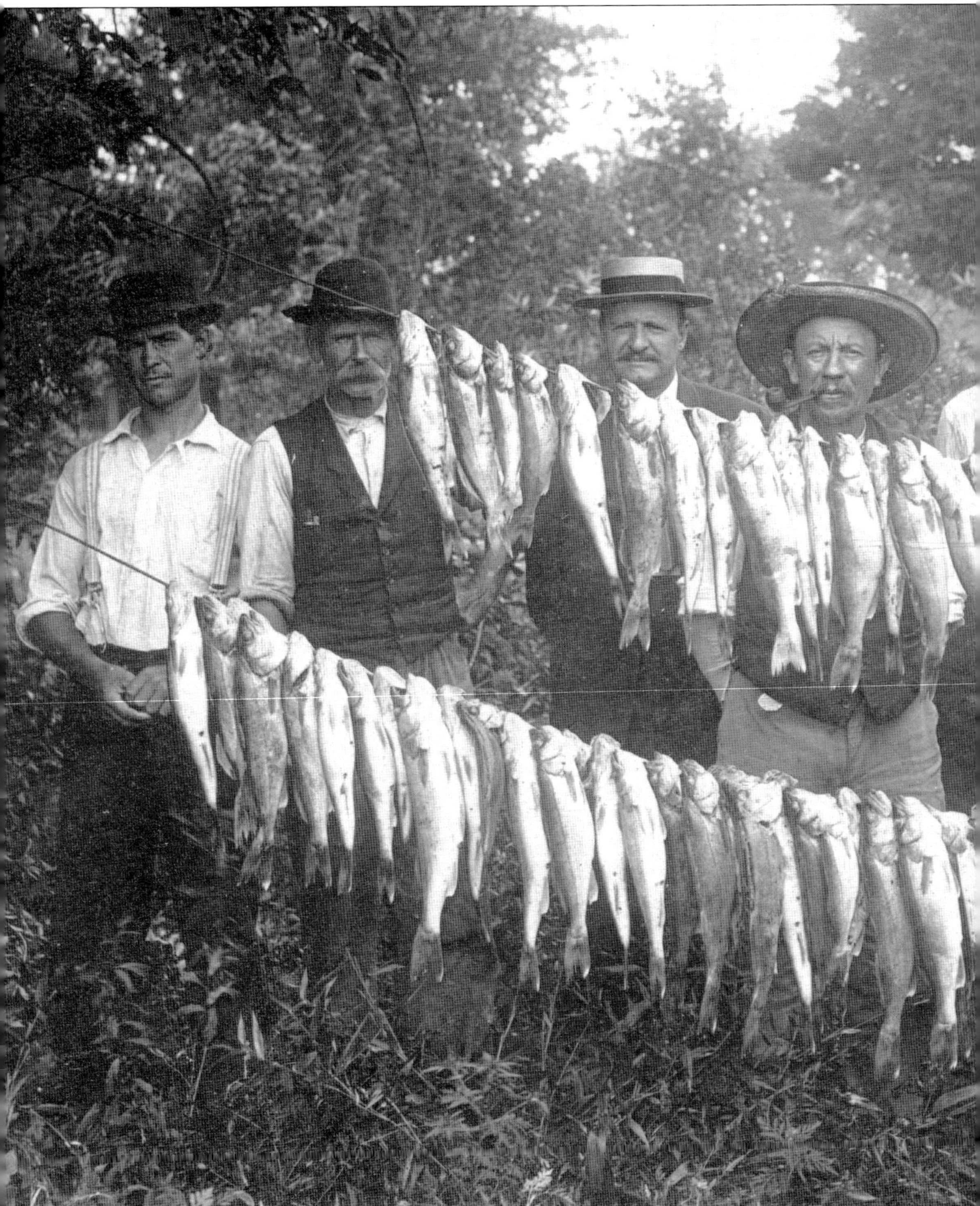

This group of fishermen in Cleveland, New York, took a picture in front of the home of Silas Potter after a very productive day of angling in the early 1900s. The party of nine men stands

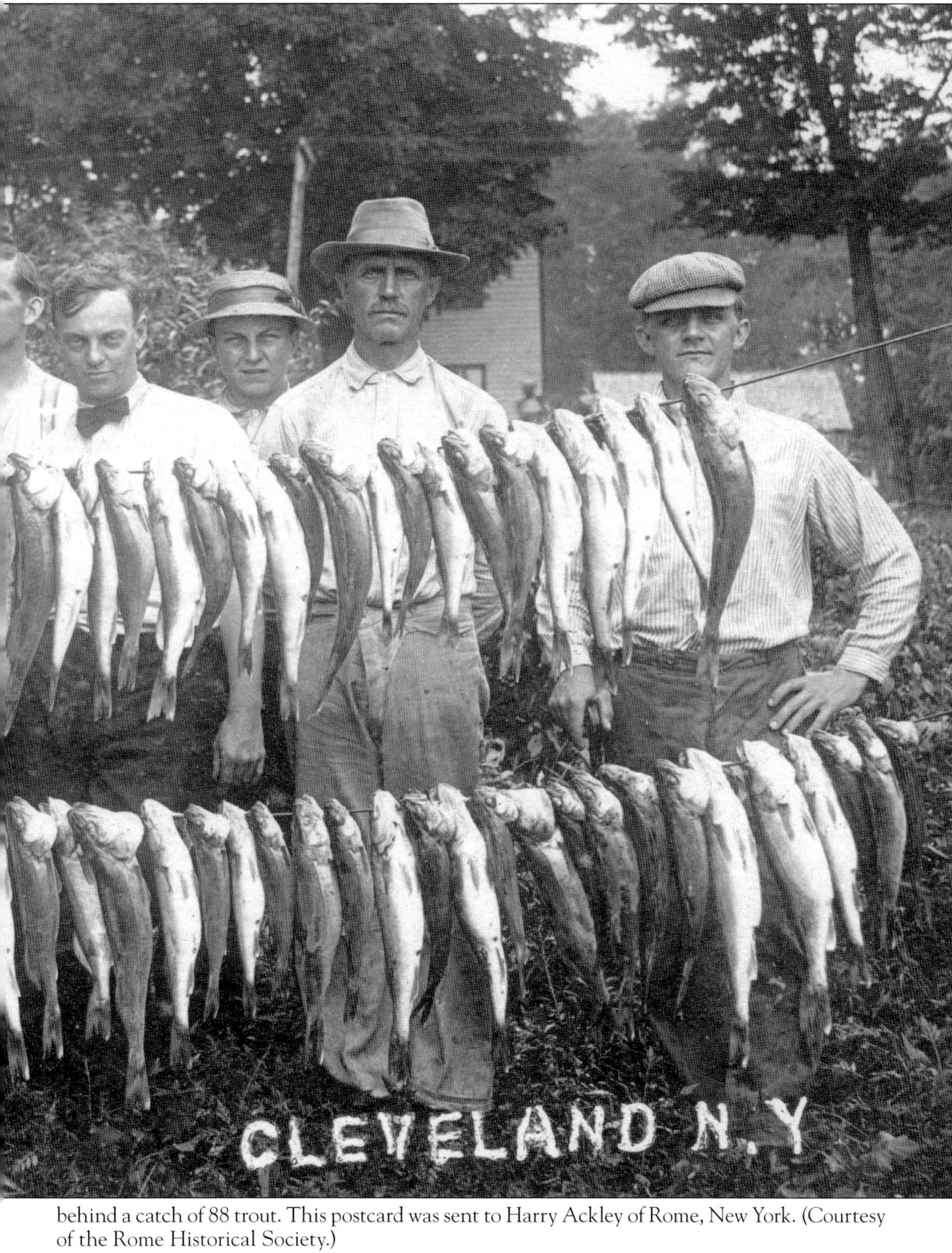

behind a catch of 88 trout. This postcard was sent to Harry Ackley of Rome, New York. (Courtesy of the Rome Historical Society.)

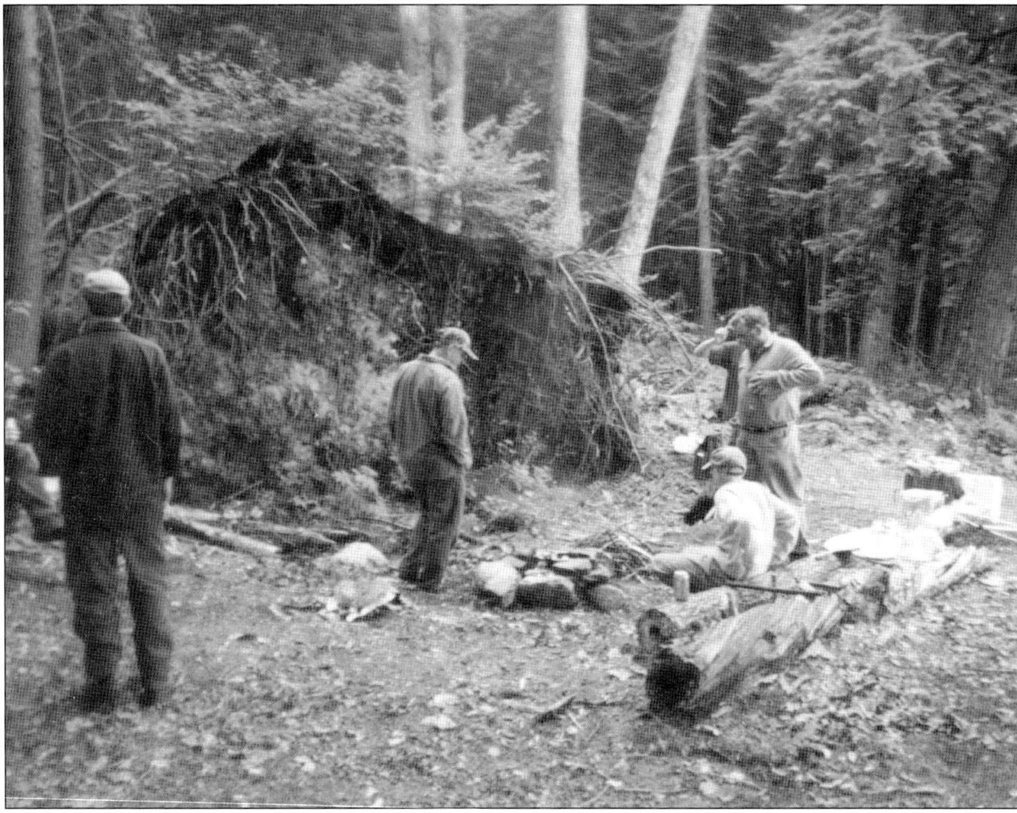

These photographs were taken on the same day during an outing at Fawn Lake. Above, the folks gathered around the campfire during a shore picnic. The same scene plays out in the image below. Carl Merritt is at the center of the photograph, looking toward the camera. Times like these, gathered together with friends and family, make for great memories. (Both, courtesy of Tom Murphy.)

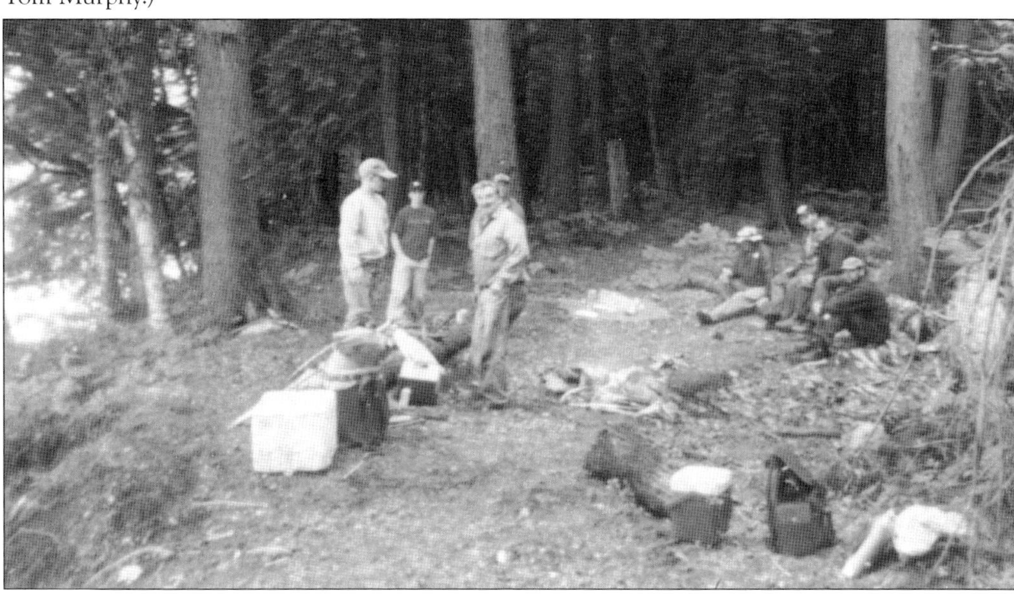

There are many spots in the Adirondacks where families can camp for free, as long as they do not mind roughing it. This scene is camping at Fawn Lake, east of Route 8 in Hamilton County. To access Fawn Lake, there is a walking path that splits and goes in two directions. The left side goes to the crude boat launch, and the right goes to the beach on the upper end of the lake. (Author's collection.)

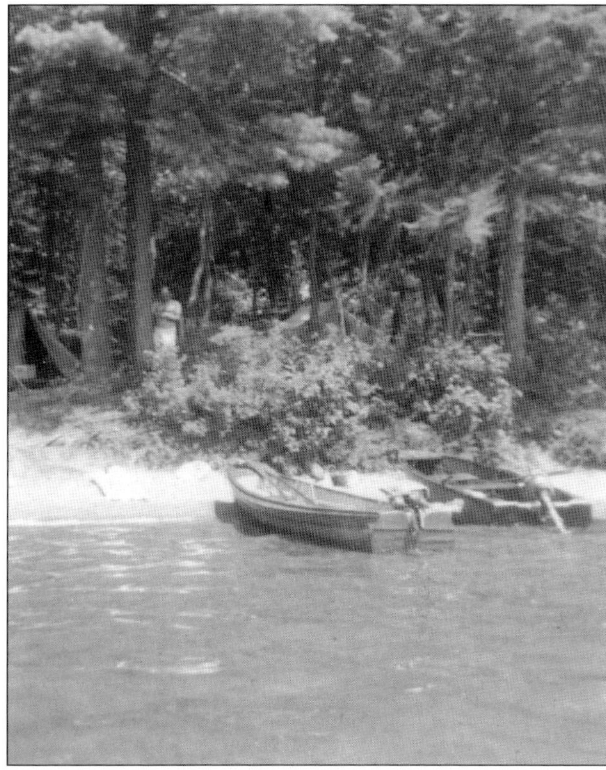

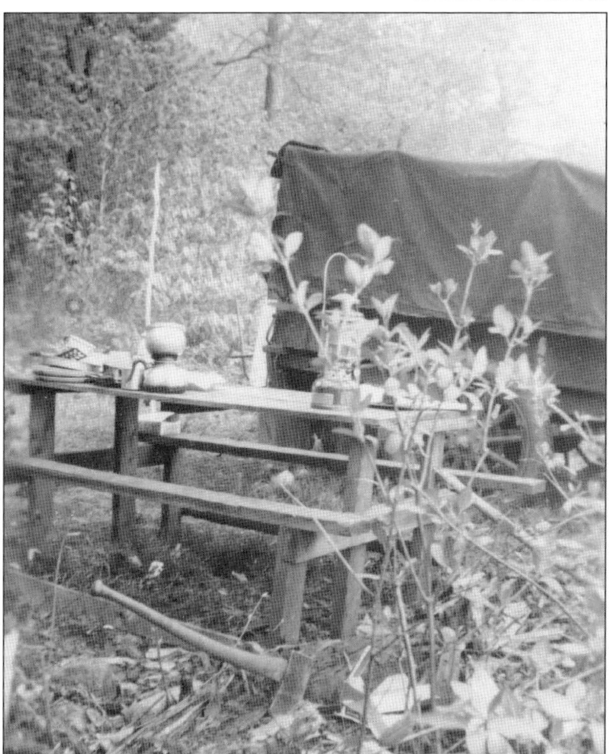

Spending time in nature is good for a person's mental and physical health. "The sights and sounds of life are not by human dwellings, not in crowded cities alone," Solomon Northup said. "The wildest places of the earth are full of them." This a typical setup that a family might use when camping in the Adirondacks. (Author's collection.)

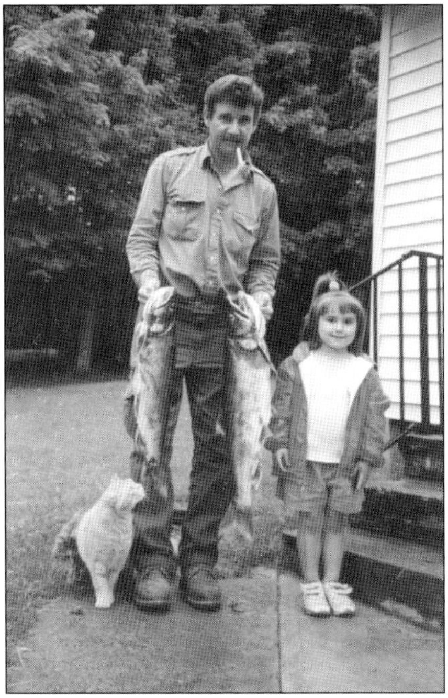

This image features four-year-old Megan Plete (the author) with her grandfather Bernard "Bill" Plete, posing in front of his home in Remsen with lake trout he caught in Hamilton County around 1993. Bill retired from working with the New York State Department of Transportation in Alder Creek at age 55 to spend more time doing what he loved: hunting and fishing. (Author's collection.)

A young Ron Plete and his father, Bill Plete, show off a mess of native brook trout they caught in a southern Adirondack waterway. Ron grew up at the family home on Fairchild Road in Remsen. The Pletes spent countless hours fishing for trout in the southern and central Adirondack waters. (Author's collection.)

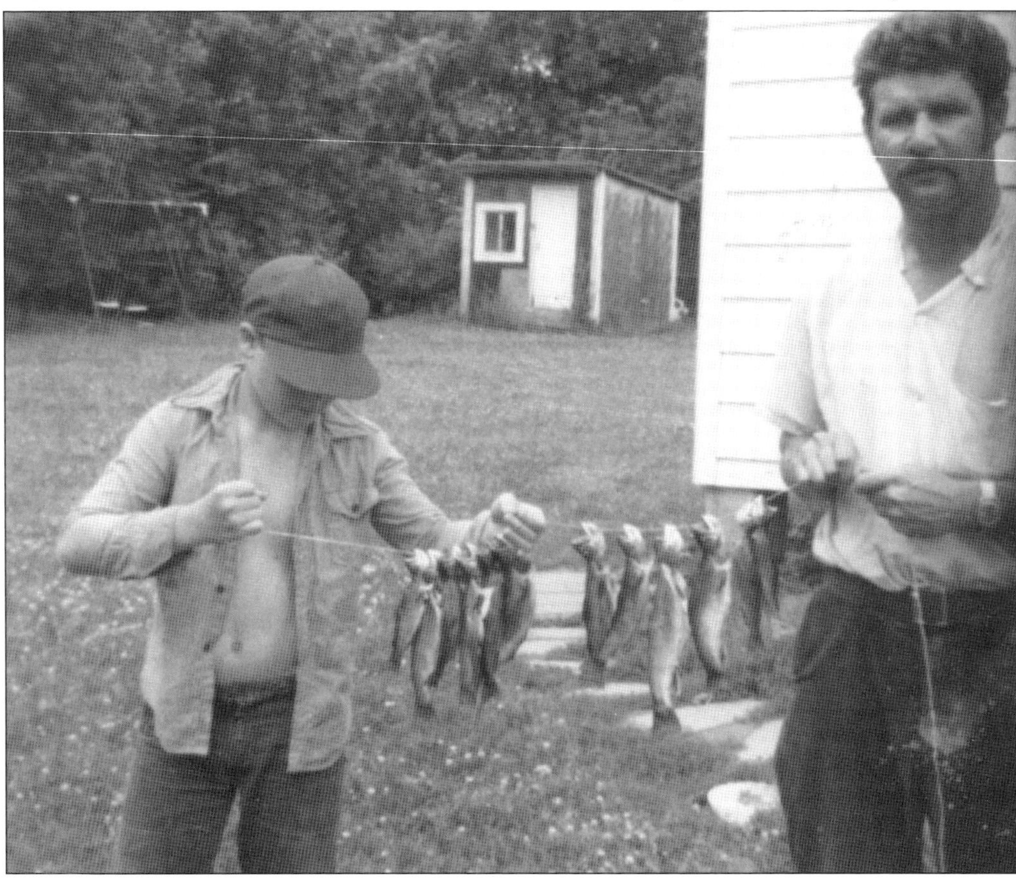

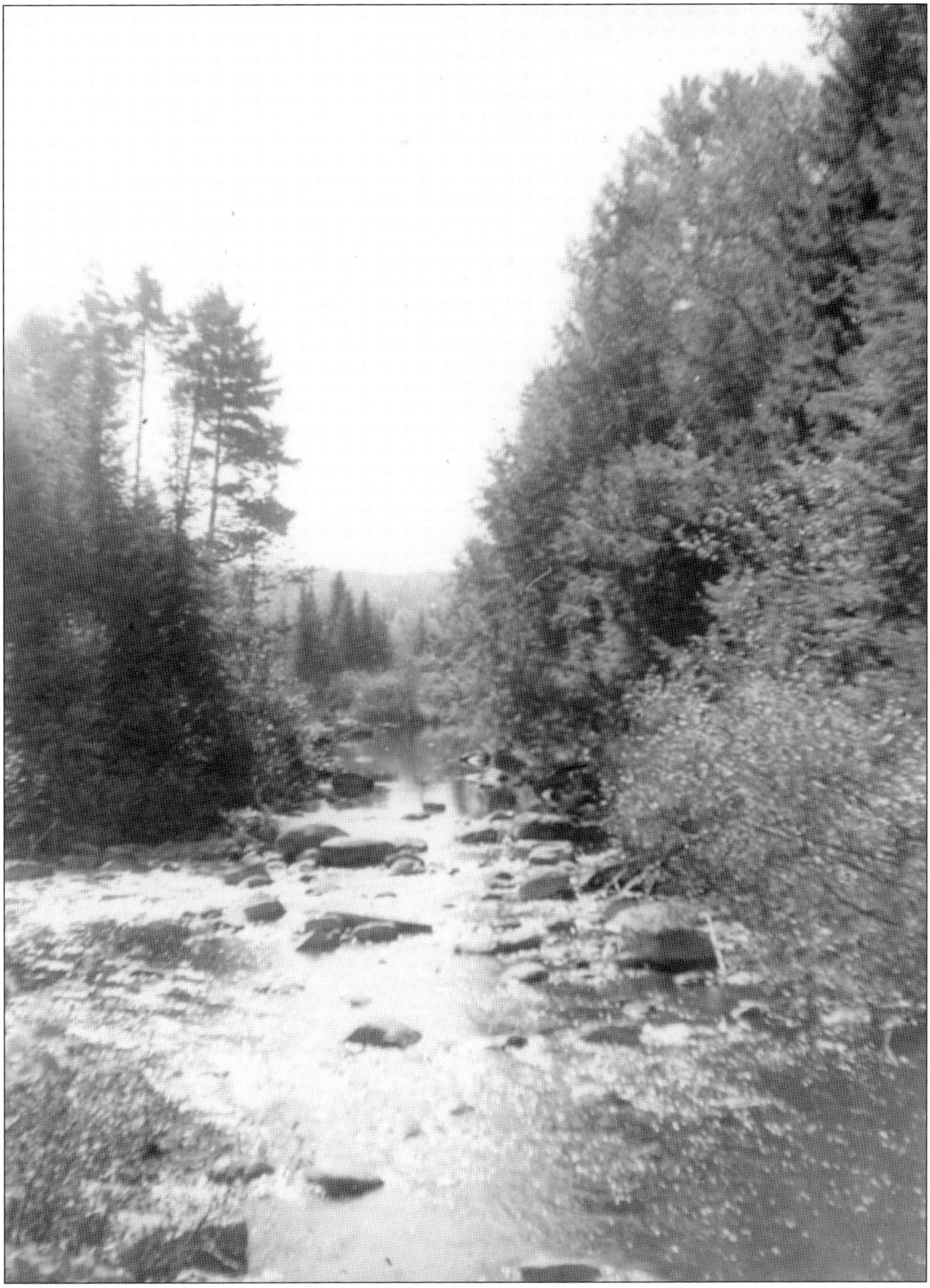

This photograph of a creek evokes a fun day of walking its bank and looking for a good hole to fish for brook trout. Brook trout can be found in many of the creeks that meander through the southern foothills of the Adirondack Mountains. The brook trout is New York State's official fish. (Author's collection.)

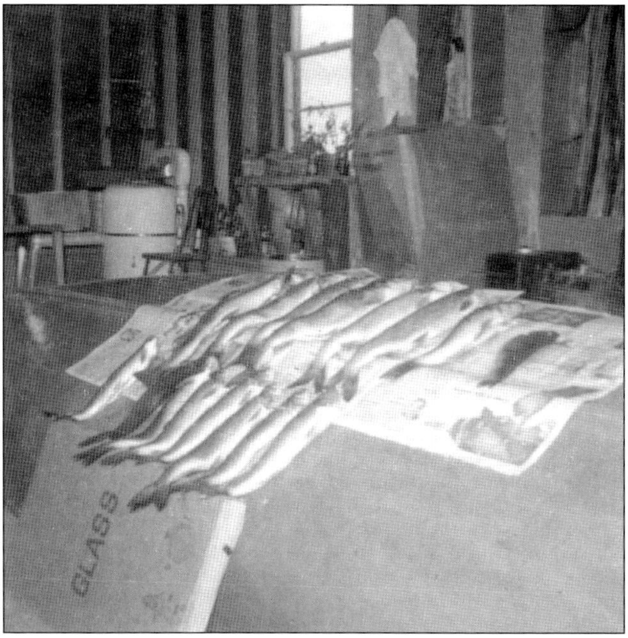

This big pile of mostly trout and a large perch were photographed after a good day's worth of fishing before they hit the frying pan. Many fishermen spent the day out on the water fishing and the night around the table socializing and telling wild tales of their outdoor adventures. (Author's collection.)

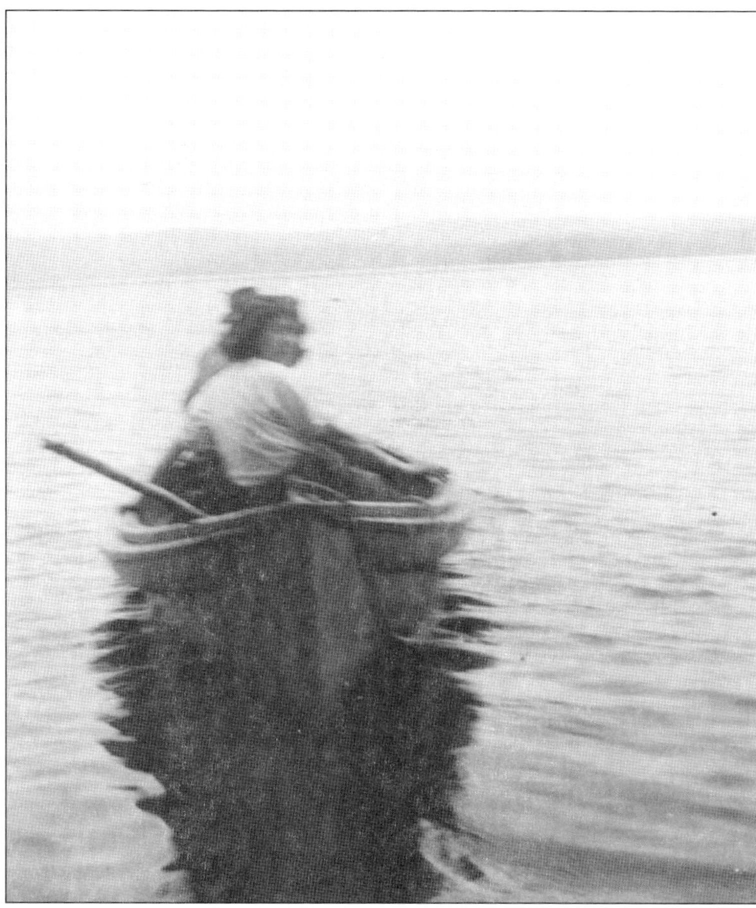

Anna Plete looked over her shoulder at the camera just as this photo was taken in the 1950s. She was spending the day fishing with her husband and a few friends in the Adirondacks. She grew up in the town of Wilmurt and raised her family in Hinckley near the lower reservoir, also known as Prospect Pond. (Author's collection.)

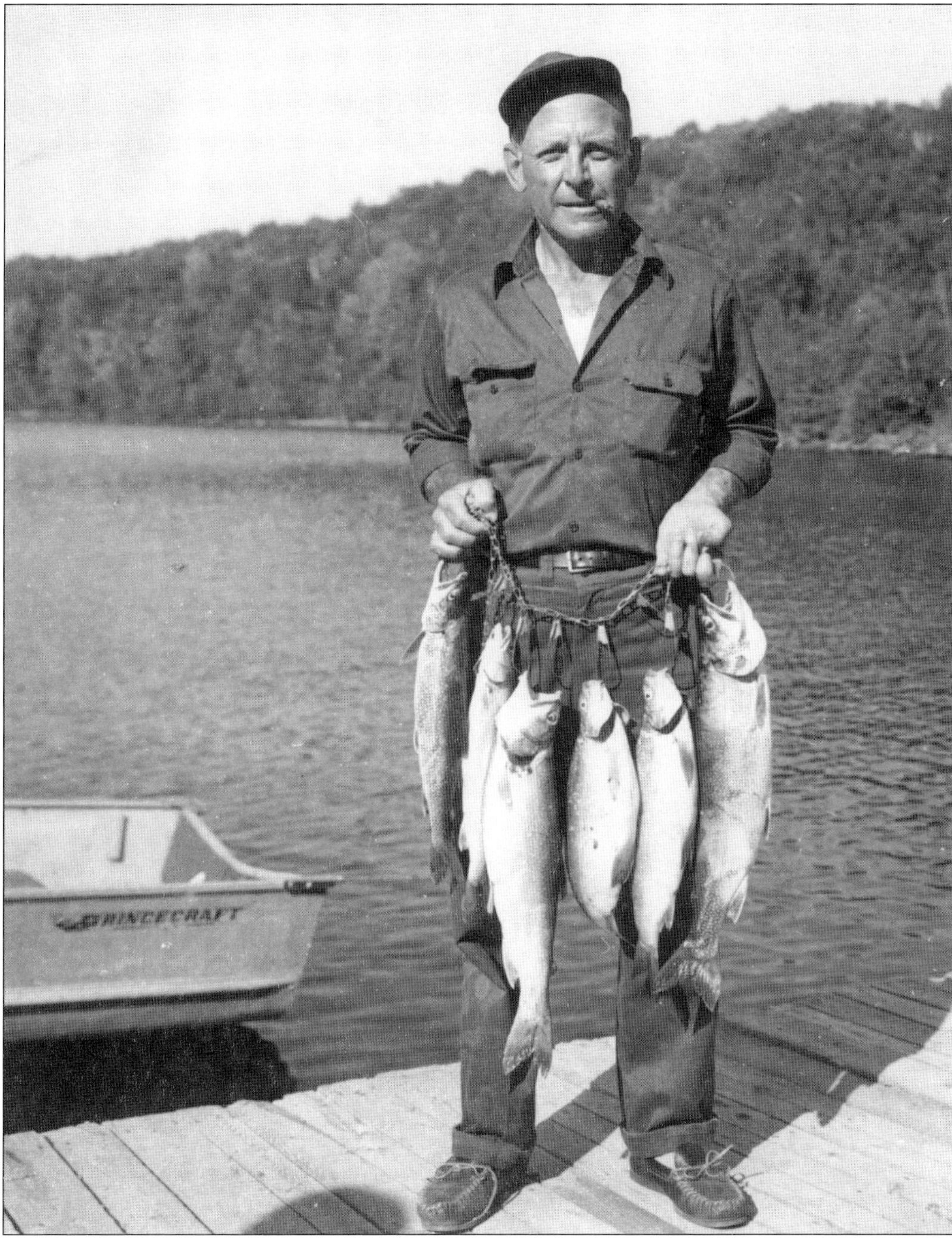

Art Johnson hunted and fished all his life. A grandson of the famous guide George Wandover, it was always in his blood. He has spent countless hours on the water and in the woods. In this photograph, he holds up a stringer of that day's catch. Johnson grew up in the Wheelertown area before leaving home to serve his country. He later settled on Briggs Road in Remsen. (Courtesy of Art Johnson.)

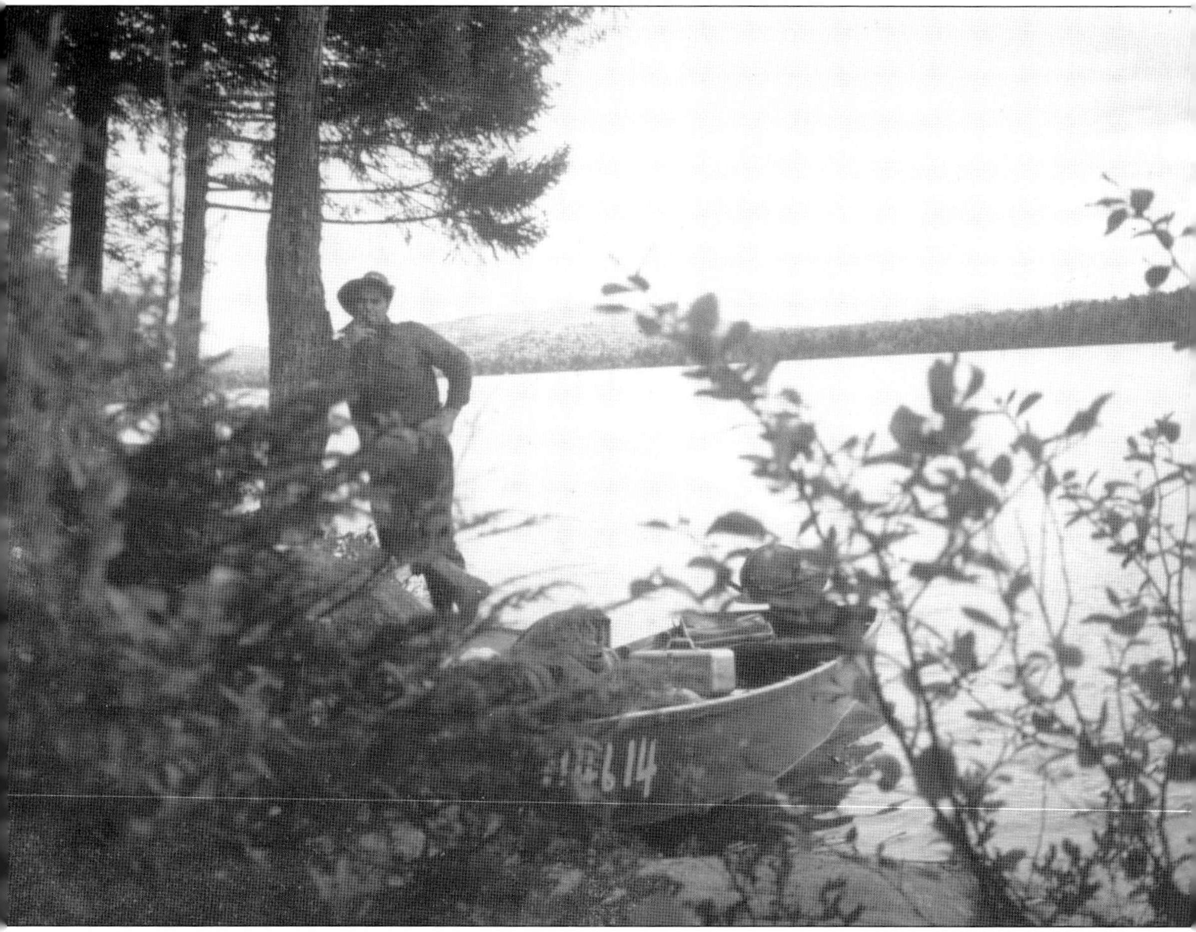

Philip William "Bill" Plete is photographed relaxing with a smoke at Fawn Lake in Hamilton County in the 1970s. He guided in the Southern Adirondacks for the Adirondack League Club. He also worked for the New York State Department of Transportation for 25 years. He lived to be in his 80s. (Author's collection.)

Bryan Postol shows off a nice brook trout while a cat named Boots looks on. Postol grew up on the family homestead on Wheelertown Road and later moved to Hawkinsville. He and wife, Wendy, have five children: Bryan, Connie, Andrea, Steve, and Dale. (Courtesy of Bryan and Wendy Postol.)

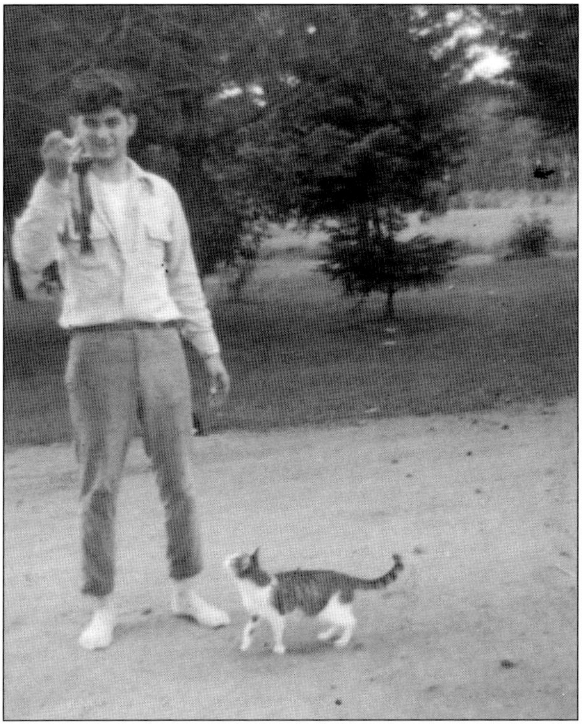

"All good things—trout as well as eternal salvation—come by grace and grace comes by art," said Norman McClean in *A River Runs through It*, published in 1976. In this photograph, Bill Simmons is on the shore of Seventh Lake with a nice stringer of trout. (Courtesy of Bryan and Wendy Postol.)

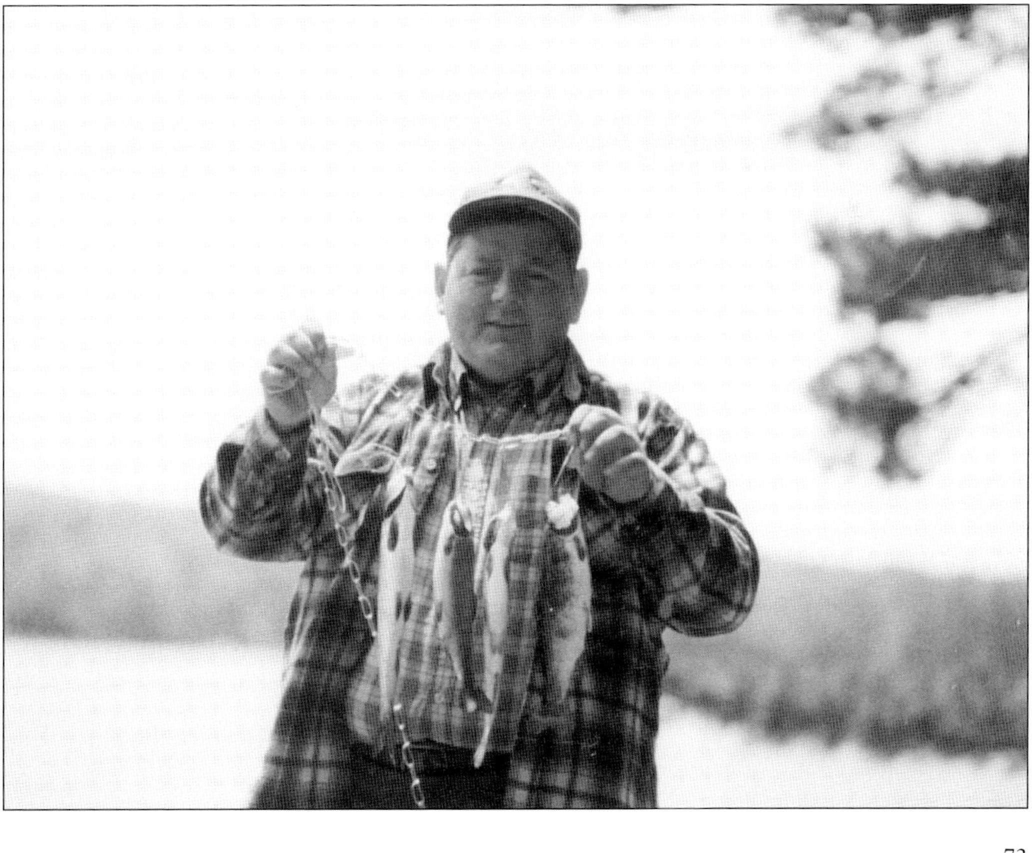

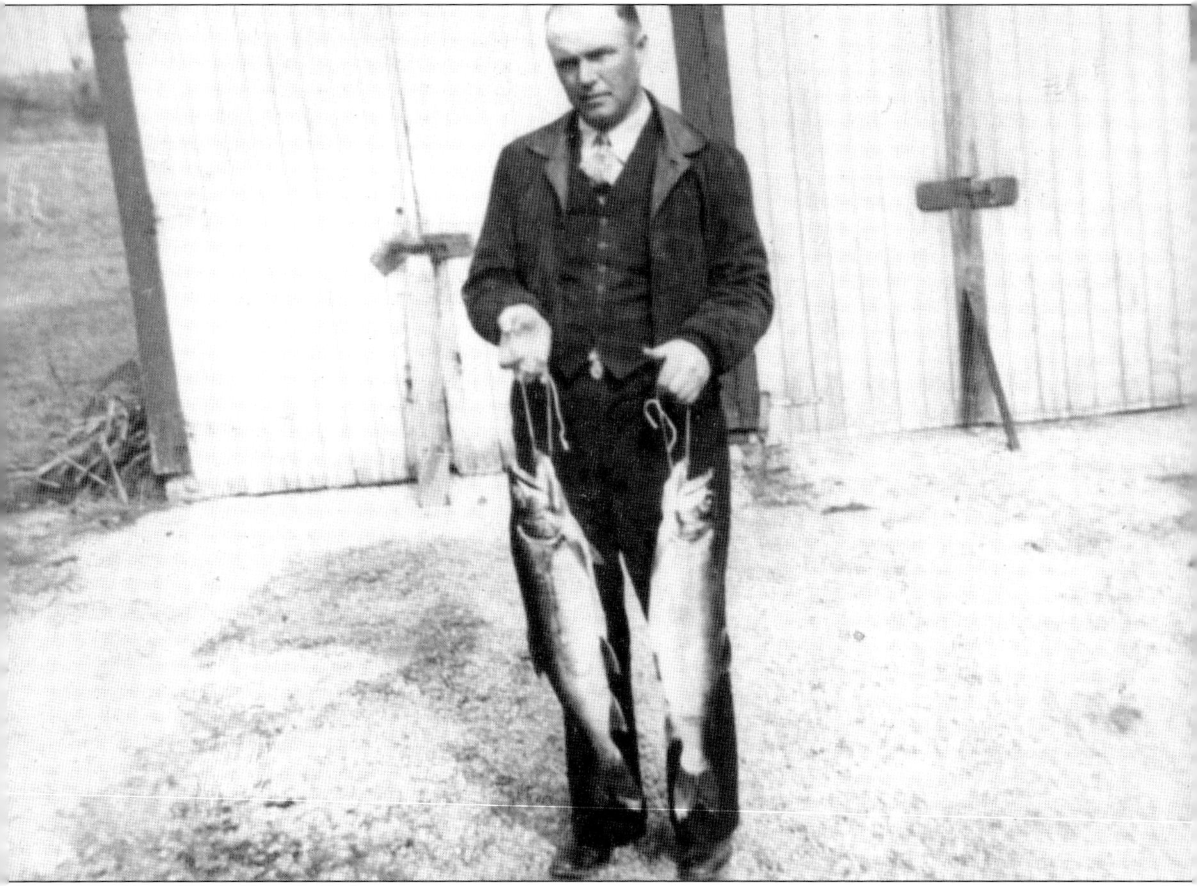

An unidentified sport lifts two heavy lake trout for the camera. As far back as the first decade of the 1800s, Adirondack guides had led visitors to the area on wilderness adventures that included fishing, hunting, trapping, and hiking. The vast forests of the area intimidated travelers, but the guides were trusted experts. (Author's collection.)

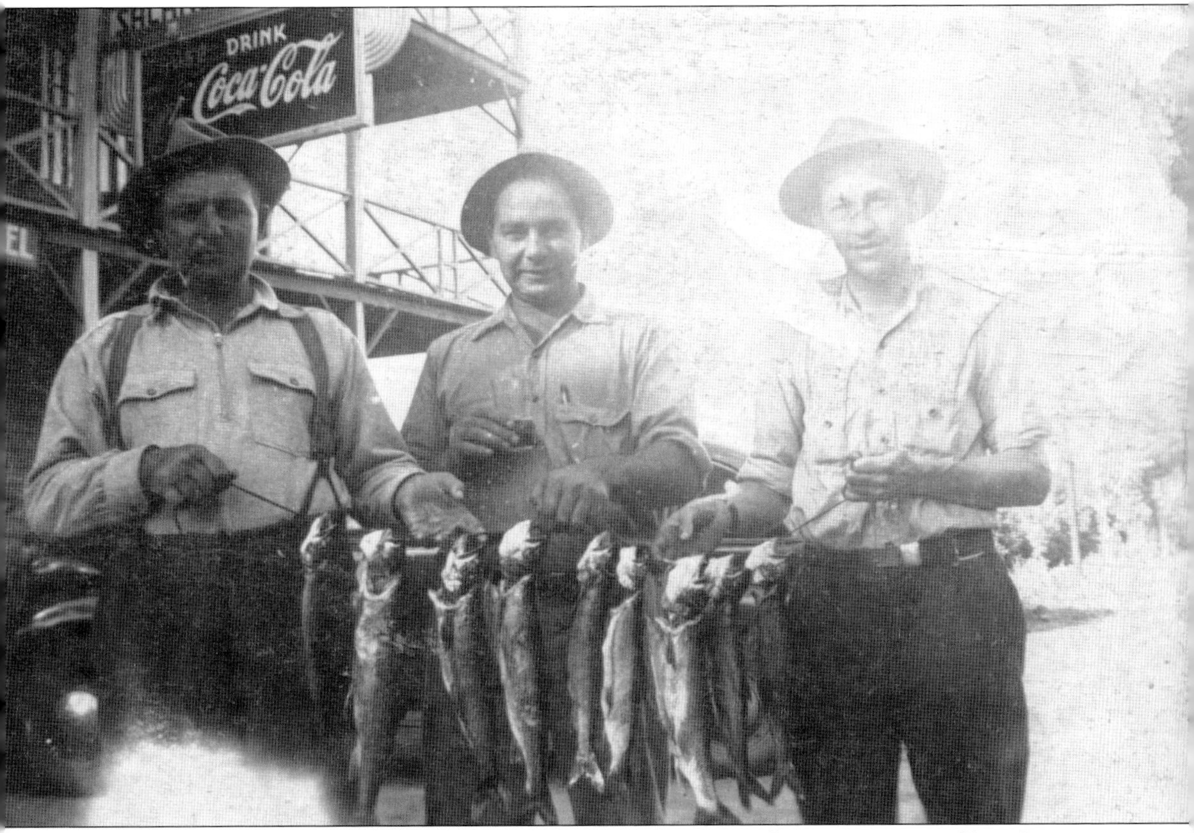

These fishermen were stopped at a hotel for a drink after catching a stringer of brook trout when they posed for this photograph. Native brook trout inhabit the lakes and streams of the Adirondacks; plus, the state stocks them, so the fishing is typically pretty good if one knows where to find them. The native "heritage" strains live longer and grow larger than domesticated strains. (Author's collection.)

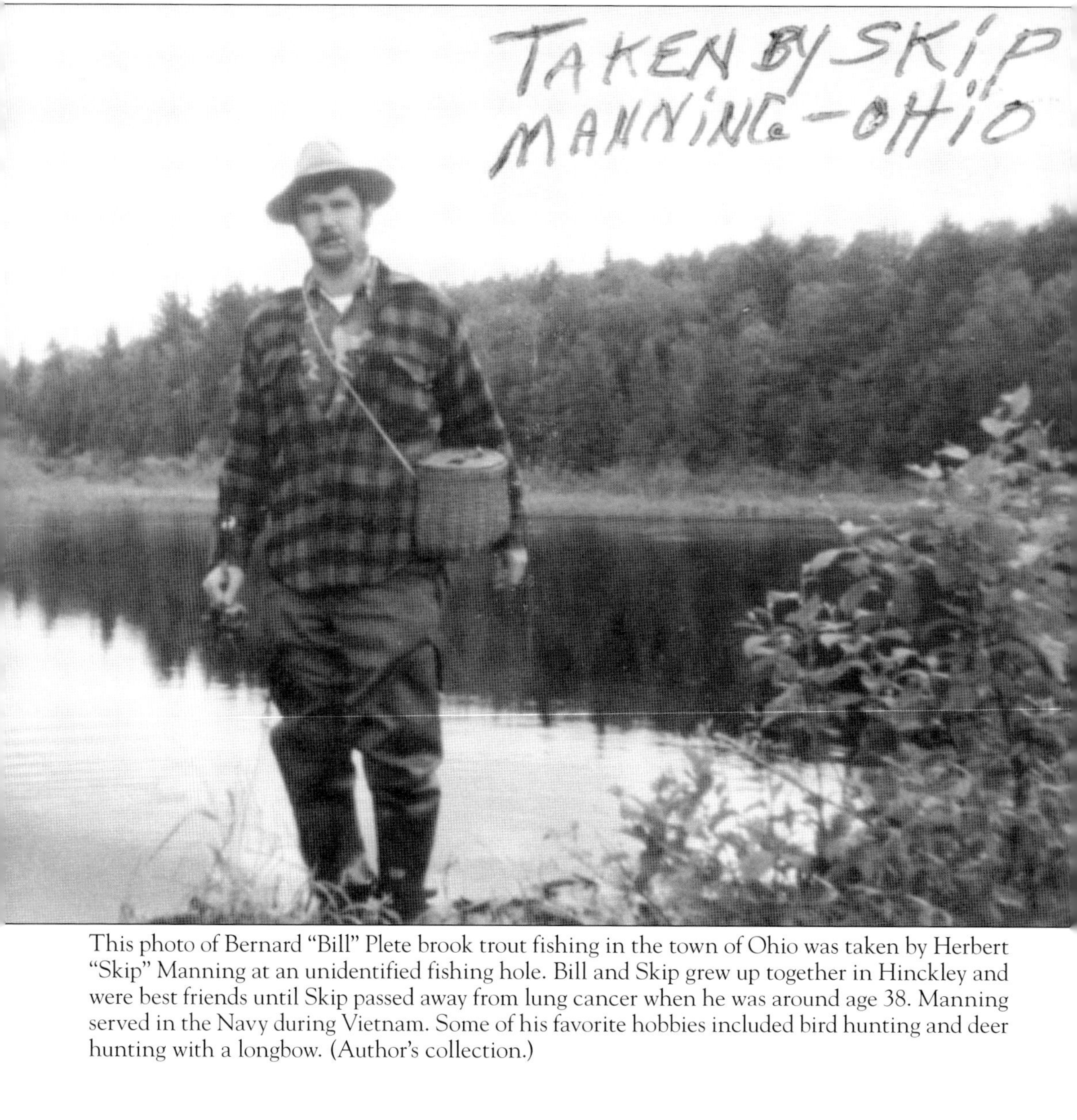

This photo of Bernard "Bill" Plete brook trout fishing in the town of Ohio was taken by Herbert "Skip" Manning at an unidentified fishing hole. Bill and Skip grew up together in Hinckley and were best friends until Skip passed away from lung cancer when he was around age 38. Manning served in the Navy during Vietnam. Some of his favorite hobbies included bird hunting and deer hunting with a longbow. (Author's collection.)

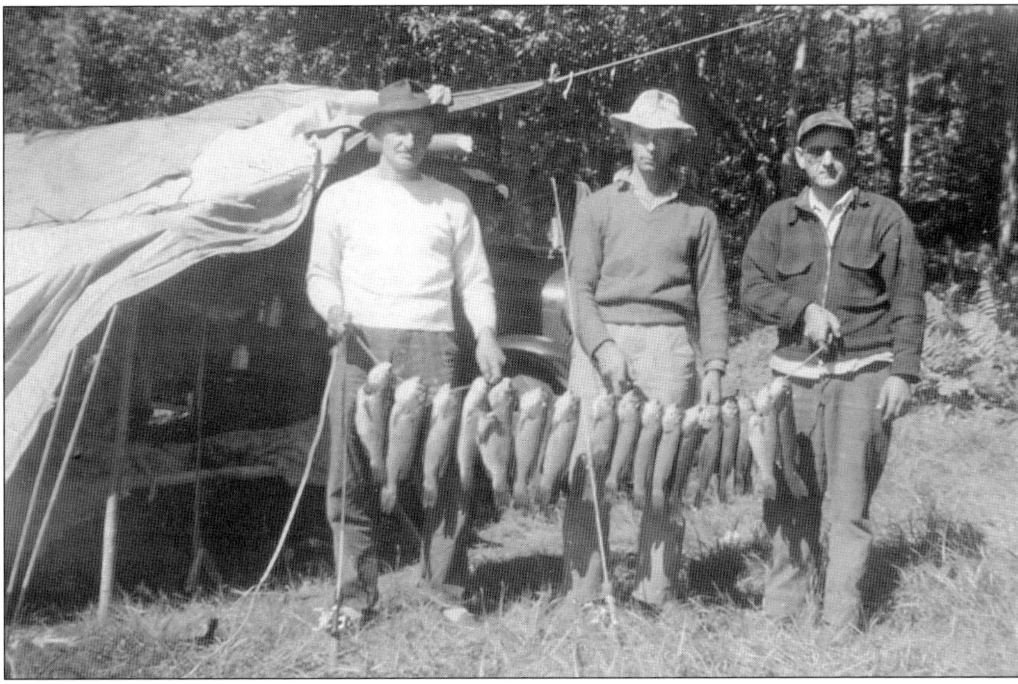

This trio of Adirondack fishermen had a productive day. The men are unidentified. (Author's collection.)

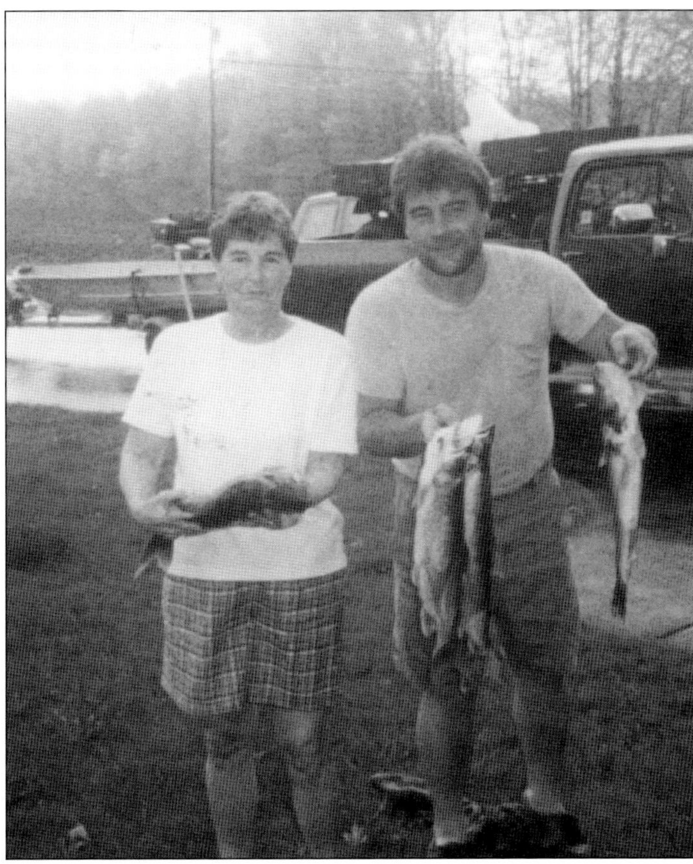

In the photograph, on the left is Helen (Plete) Woods, and on the right is her nephew Ronald Plete. Helen was the sister of Ronald's father, Bill Plete. The two pose with some Adirondack Lake trout, which, no doubt, made it to the frying pan later that evening. (Author's collection.)

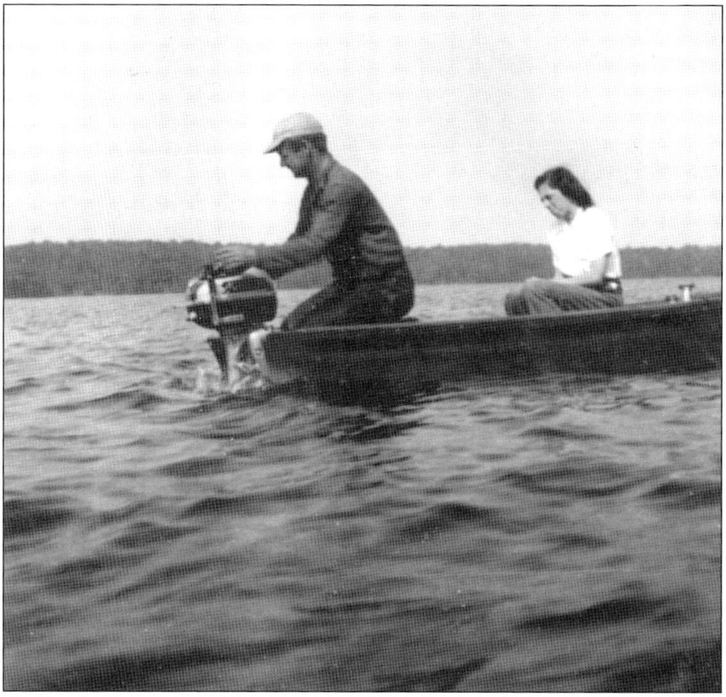

This photograph is of Nat Harvey and his wife, Curly, on their fishing boat on Fourth Lake. Nat is reversing their fishing boat to untangle a snag in the fishing line. Snags happen while fishing for trout because the fish hug the cold bottoms of the lake and the lures get caught up on branches or debris that have settled on the floor of the lake. (Author's collection.)

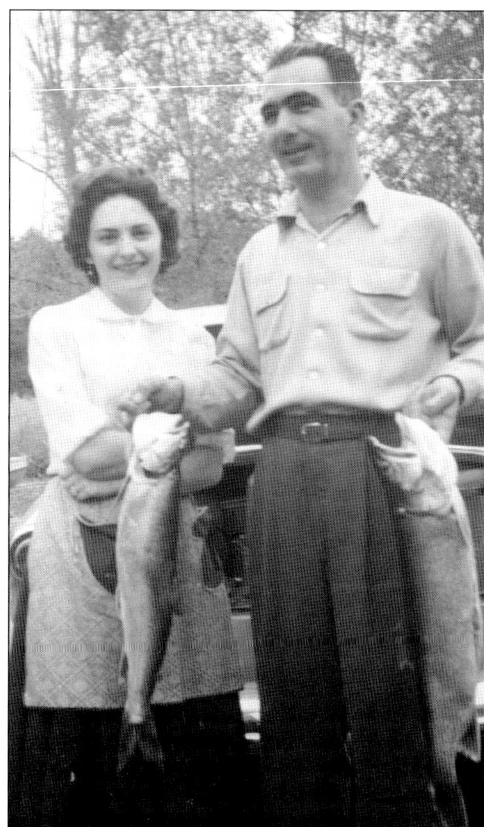

Fishing (and hunting and trapping) was just a way of life for many country folks. They lived their lives in close harmony with nature. The cycle of the seasons determined what they would pursue. It was a simple and wholesome way to live. This couple is unidentified. (Author's collection.)

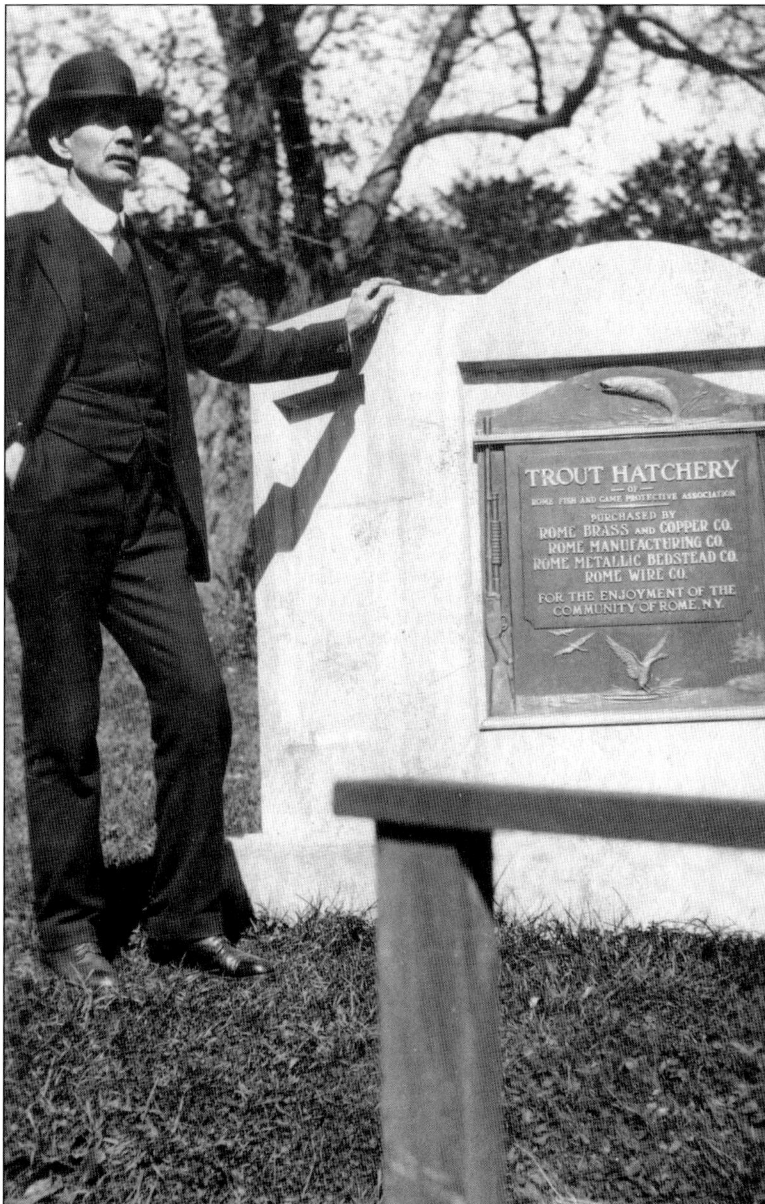

The Rome Fish Hatchery, New York State's largest hatchery, started out as a privately owned organization. In 1915, the first fish hatchery was established on the property by Harry Ackley. A pioneer in trout production, Ackley raised trout to large sizes for stocking in public waters in and near the Adirondacks. Around 1920, one small fish farm was built nearby on the property of Dr. George Reid, and one was built by the Rome Fish and Game Club. In 1930, the Fish and Game Club sold its parcel of land for the sum of $1 to the State of New York to develop a fish hatchery. In 1932, the state purchased the Reid farm, giving them exclusive rights to all springs on the property. This was the beginning of today's Rome Fish Hatchery. Annual production at the facility now totals nearly 160,000 pounds of brook, rainbow, and brown trout. Hatchery staff plays a major role in producing trout for airplane and helicopter stocking of remote Adirondack waters. (Courtesy of the Rome Historical Society.)

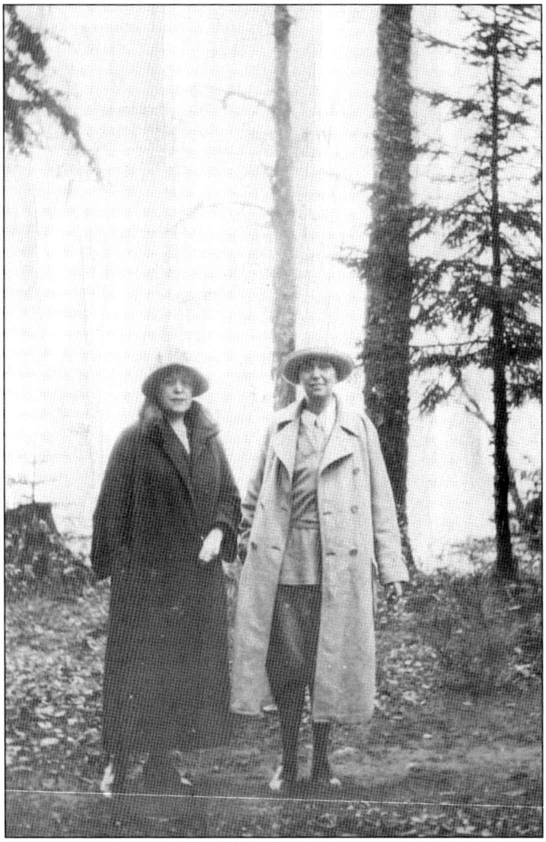

Two of the wives of wealthy businessmen who were involved in the Rome Fish Hatchery pose for a photograph while attending a trout conference in Cranberry Lake. The women are Mrs. Ackley and Mrs. Rabenald. (Courtesy of the Rome Historical Society.)

The original trout reservoirs at the Rome Fish Hatchery were built into the old frame of the defunct Black River Canal, which closed in 1925. The Black River Canal began in Carthage; it flowed to Rome and served as a feeder for the larger Erie Canal. (Courtesy of the Rome Historical Society.)

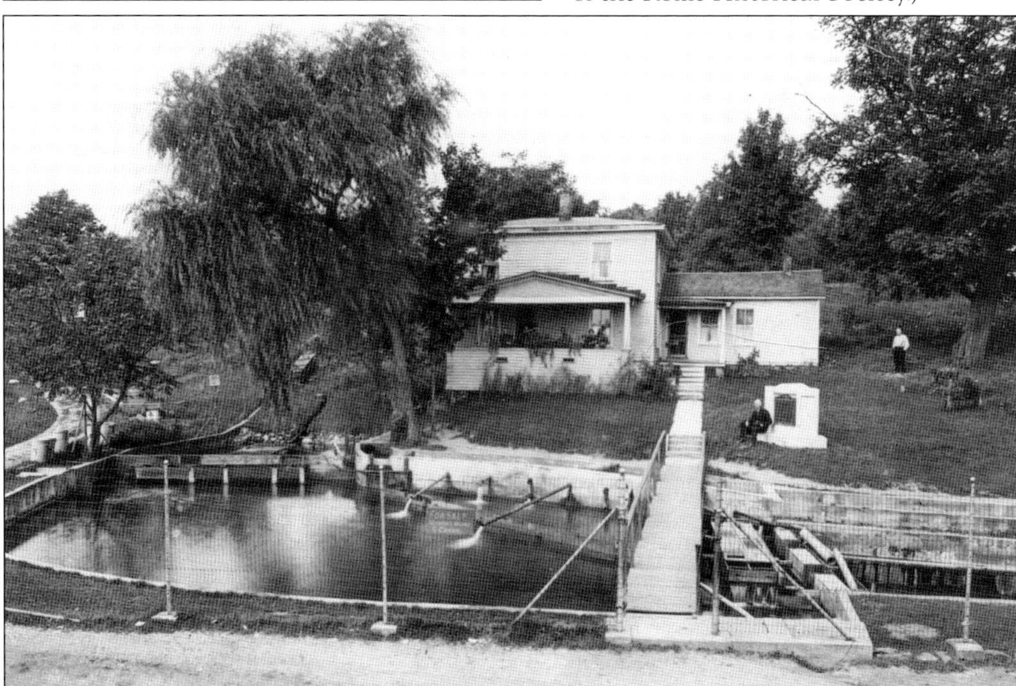

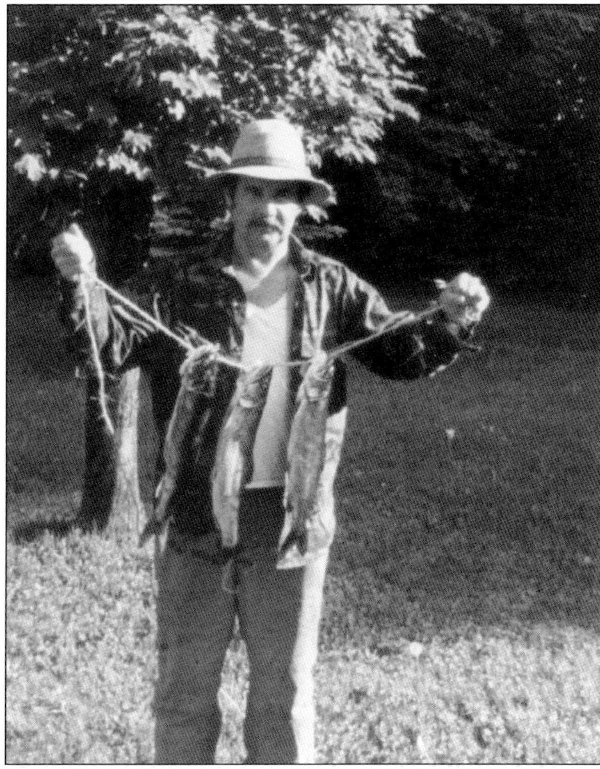

Bernard "Bill" Plete (right) and Neil Smith (below) were lifetime friends. Both spent their boyhood on the banks of the Hinckley Reservoir. (Both, author's collection.)

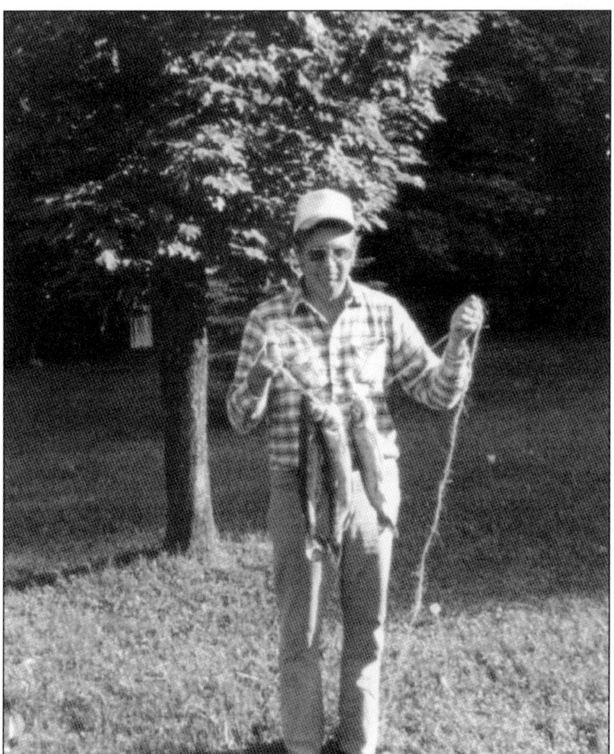

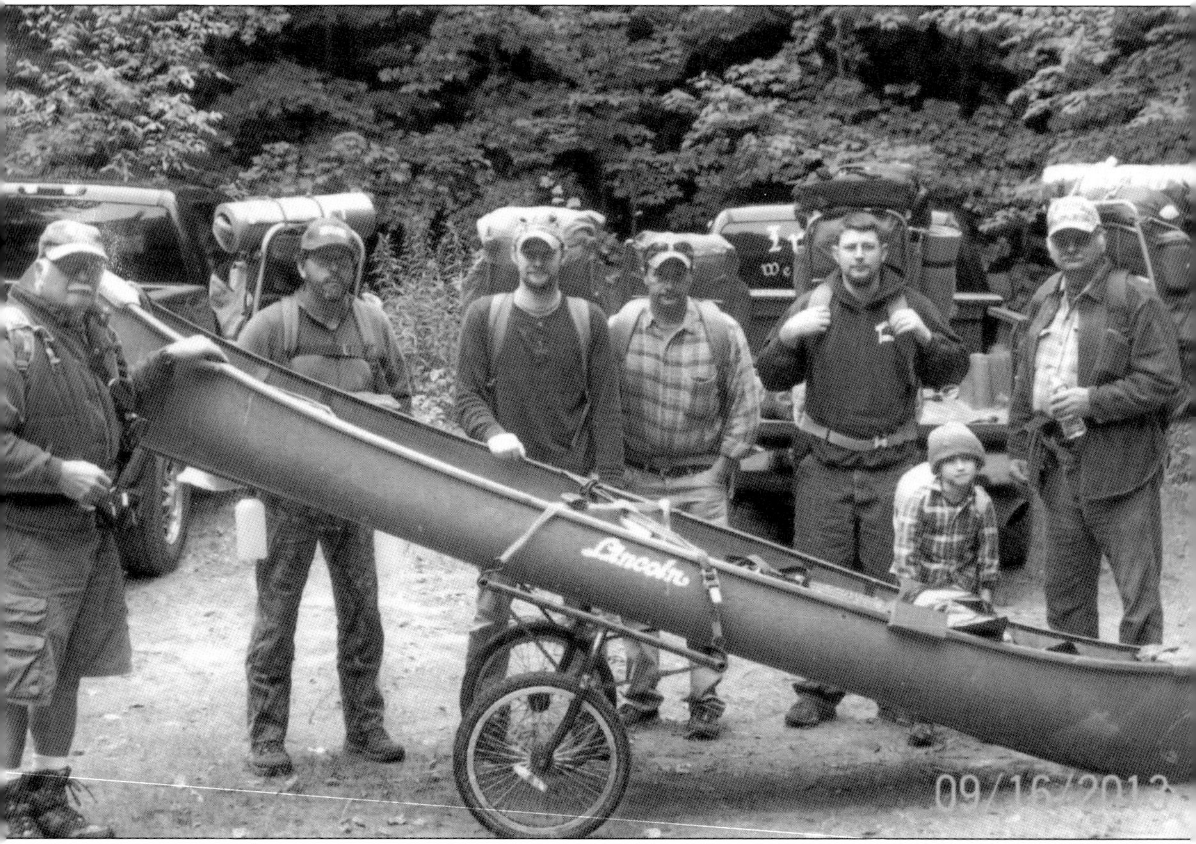

The men who took part in the 2013 Annual West Canada Lake Wilderness Hike pose together for a photograph before they headed out on their trip. The trip has become somewhat of a family tradition. They carried all their supplies in on their backs. The September weather was perfect for hiking and bug season had already passed, so it made for a pleasant trip. Dale and Bryan Jr. lugged the canoe the whole way in so that they could do some fishing. This became quite a difficult task as the trail became narrow and uneven. Some of the crew had traveled from Tennessee. From left to right are Jack Postol, Mark Postol, Dale Postol, Bryan Postol Jr., Steve Postol, Darryl Musser, and Bryan Postol. Missing from the photograph are Tony Postol and his dog Coe. (Author's collection.)

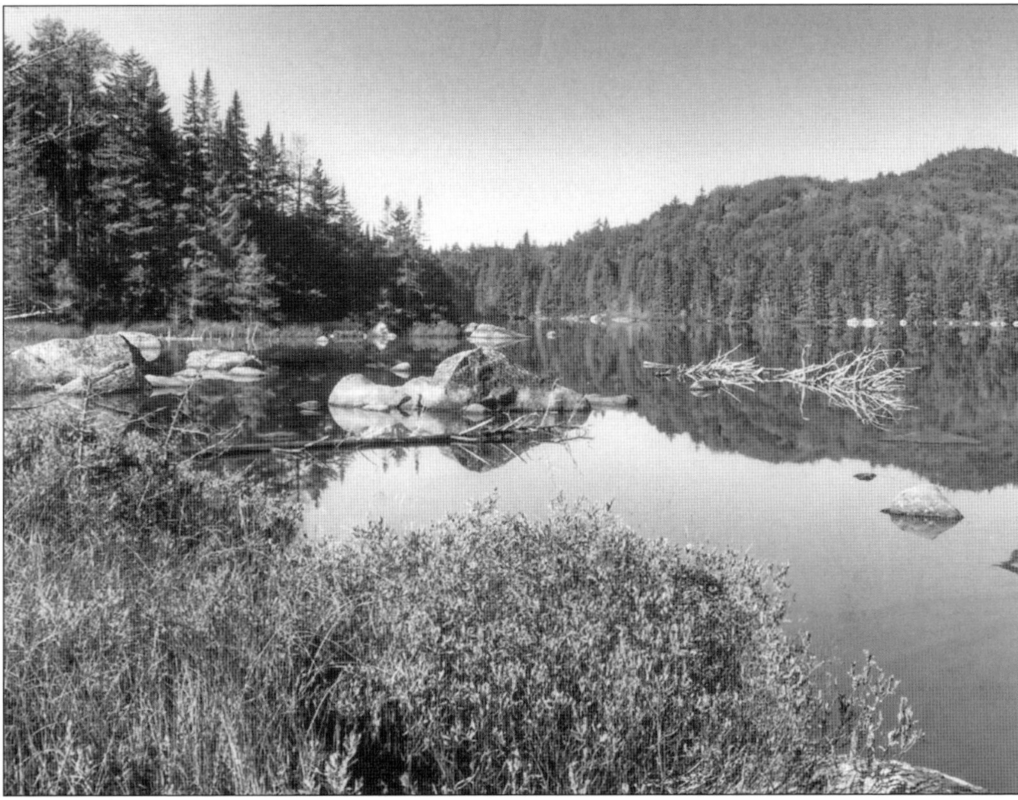

In the year 1906, brothers Eldridge and John Spears were hiking in the West Canada Lake Wilderness near Brook Trout Lake. The two were from a little town called Northwood, which was mostly flooded by the construction of the Hinckley Reservoir. On the trail in, they came upon the hermit French Louie, who made his home in this wilderness area. The brothers recounted their impression of Louie: "A rather short man, a bit stooped, grizzled and gray, with arms and hands that seemed to reach gorilla-like almost to his knees. Rather old, yet plainly a man of great strength." The book *Adirondack Characters and Campfire Yarns* by William J. O'Hern describes the brothers' experience staying at French Louie's camp. Both of these photographs are of Brook Trout Lake, nearby which the brothers met famous ol' French Louie. (Both, author's collection.)

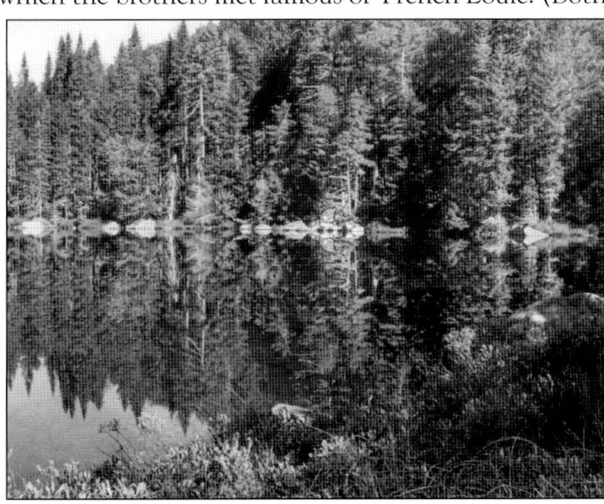

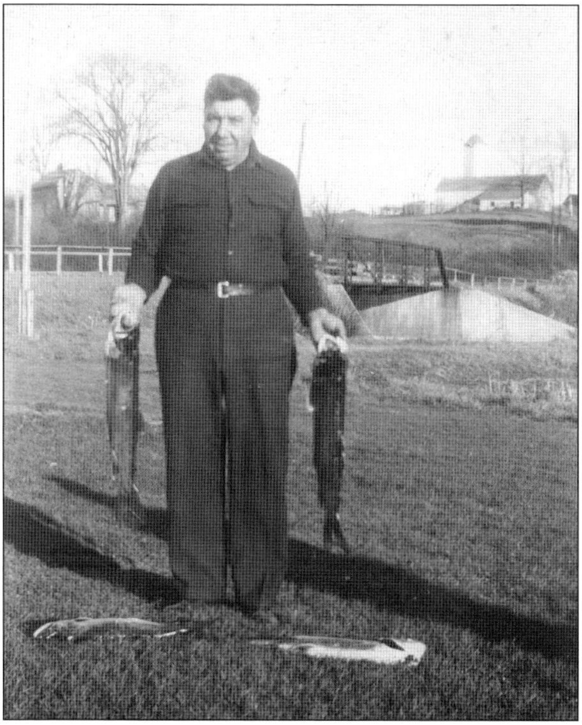

This man, probably a Barley from Grant, holds up two lake trout and has two in the grass near his feet. The Adirondacks are full of lots of different kinds of fish, including small and largemouth bass, pike, musky, pickerel, panfish, perch, rock bass, shiners, brown trout, rainbow trout, lake trout, and more. (Author's collection.)

Jeff Evans shows off a pike he caught through the ice on Delta Lake. Delta Lake, which is actually a reservoir that was created by damming up the Mohawk River, is a popular spot for winter ice anglers. Construction of the dam flooded the community of Delta, which was located on the river's west bank. Most of the structures in the village were torn down and moved to new locations. (Courtesy of Jeff Evans.)

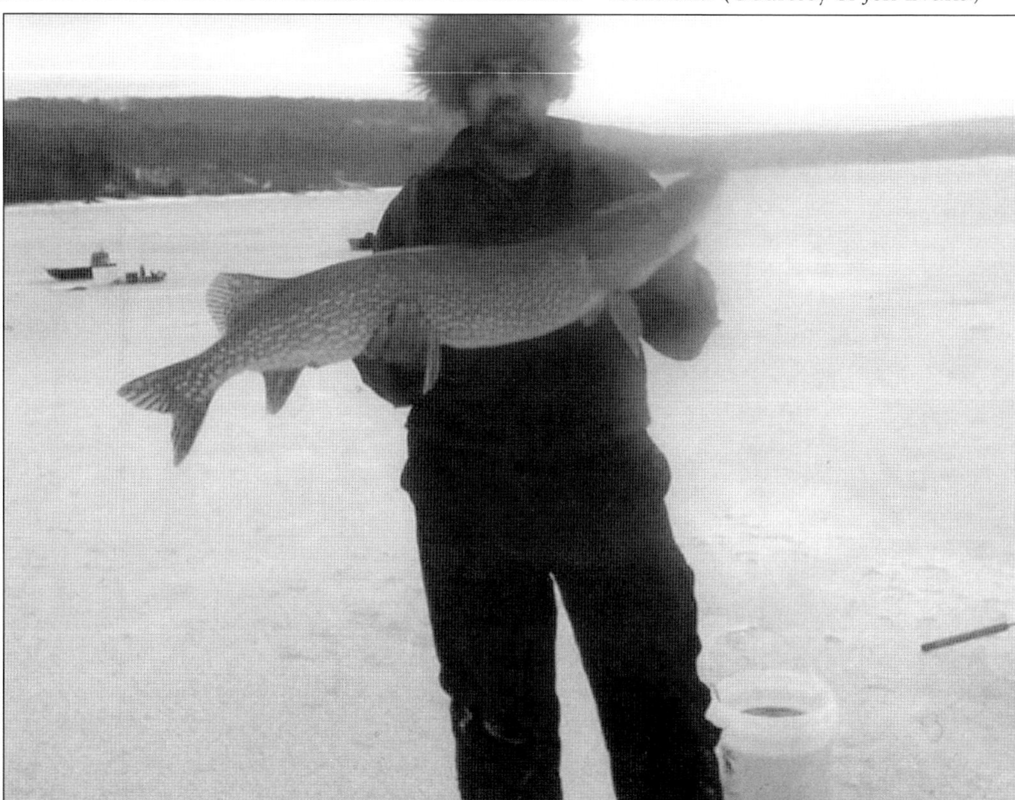

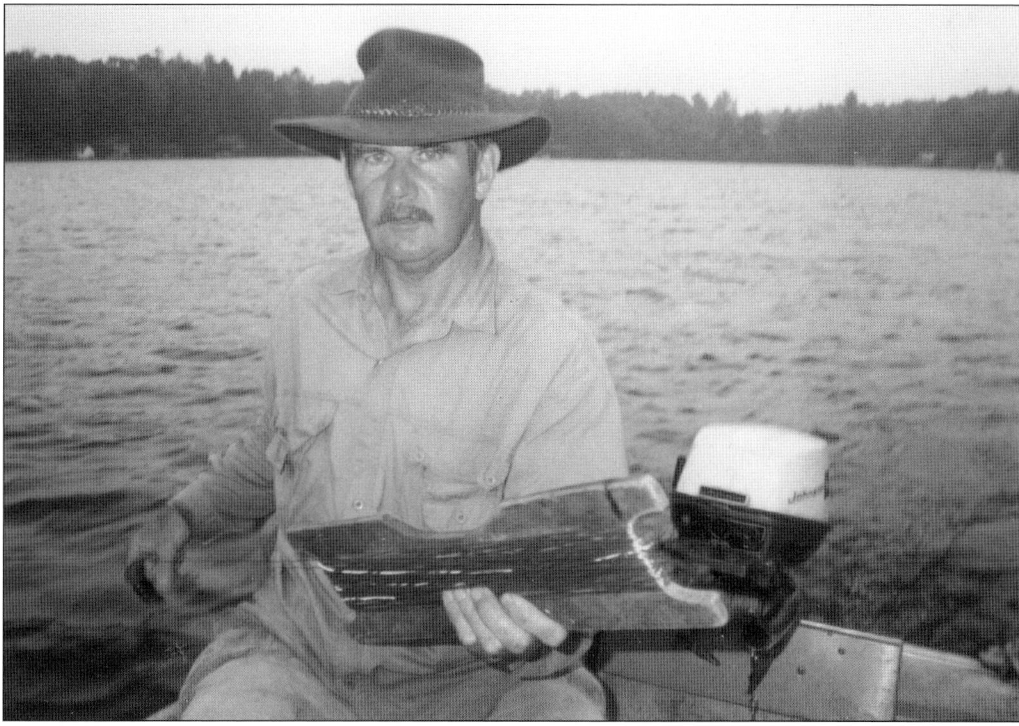

Bernard "Bill" Plete hand lines for lake trout with a copper line. This method for catching lake trout is not very common anymore. (Author's collection.)

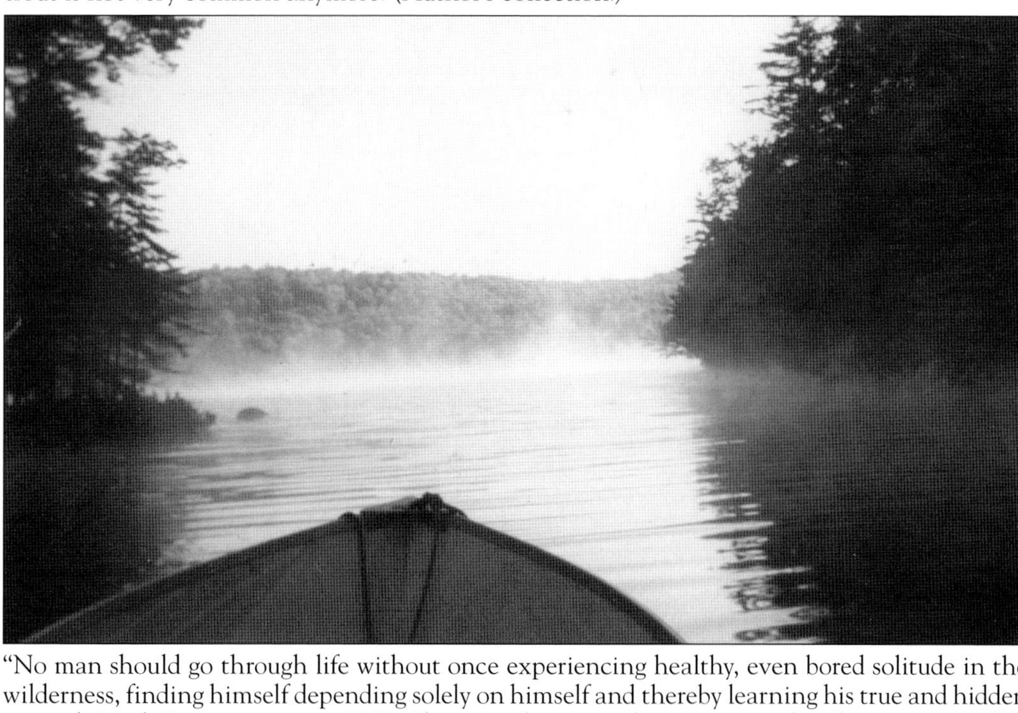

"No man should go through life without once experiencing healthy, even bored solitude in the wilderness, finding himself depending solely on himself and thereby learning his true and hidden strength," Jack Kerouac wrote in 1960. This quote has masculine pronouns, but the concept applies to everyone. (Author's collection.)

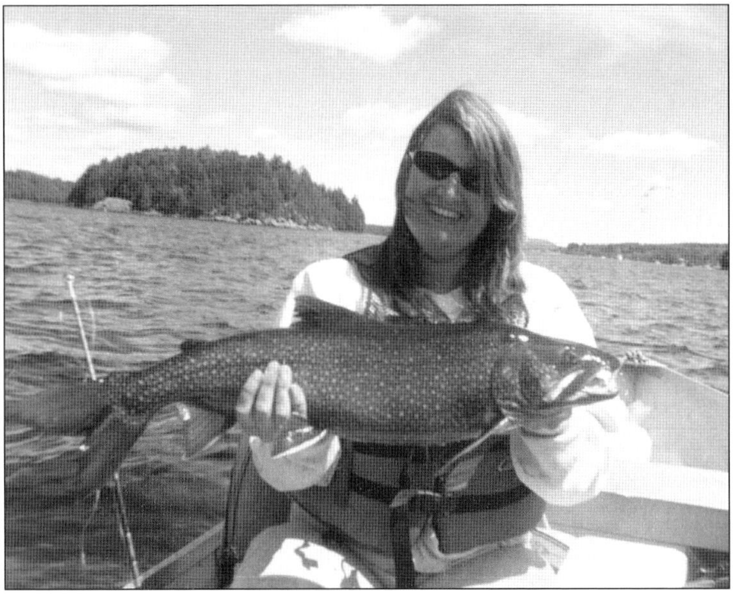

Kathleen "Leenie" Plete shows off an eight-pound lake trout she caught while fishing Tupper Lake with her brother. Later that same day, she caught a large whitefish on the same lake. She is the second daughter and youngest child of Bernard "Bill" Plete and Karen Weaver Engell. She grew up in Remsen and now lives in Parish with her family. (Author's collection.)

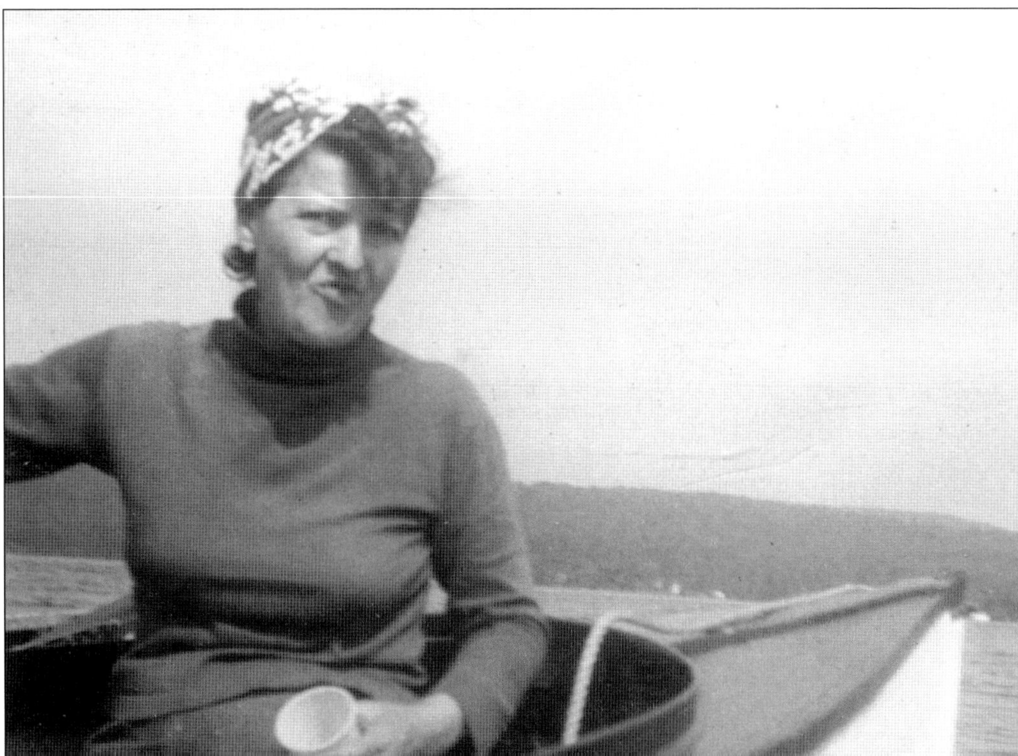

Although the percentage of women participating in outdoor sports has increased over the past decade (according to the US Fish and Wildlife Service survey), women fishing, hunting, and trapping is not a new phenomenon. Above, Francis Tallman was photographed fishing lake trout on Piseco Lake, her favorite place to fish. Her first husband and both of her children succumbed to tuberculosis when she was a young woman. She later married her second husband, Earl Tallman. (Author's collection.)

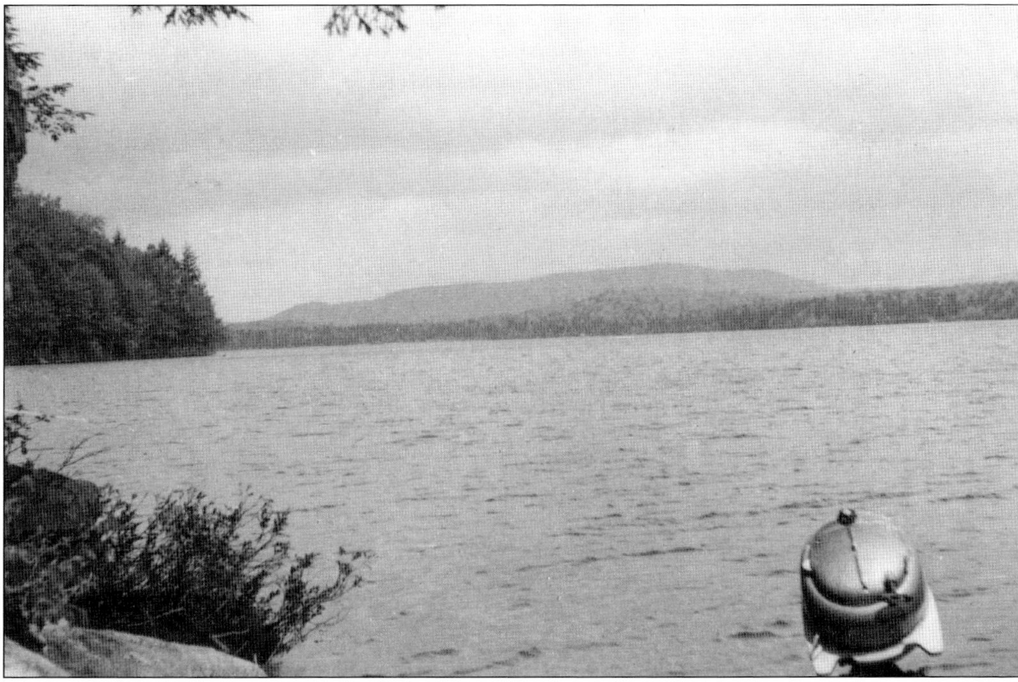

Fawn Lake is as popular for its clear water, sandy beach, and nice backcountry campsites as it is for its fishing. The water is full of trout, smallmouth bass, yellow perch, pickerel, and white sucker fish. Wild brook trout can be caught from shore there in the spring season near deep water. The lake is not large, but it is very beautiful. (Author's collection.)

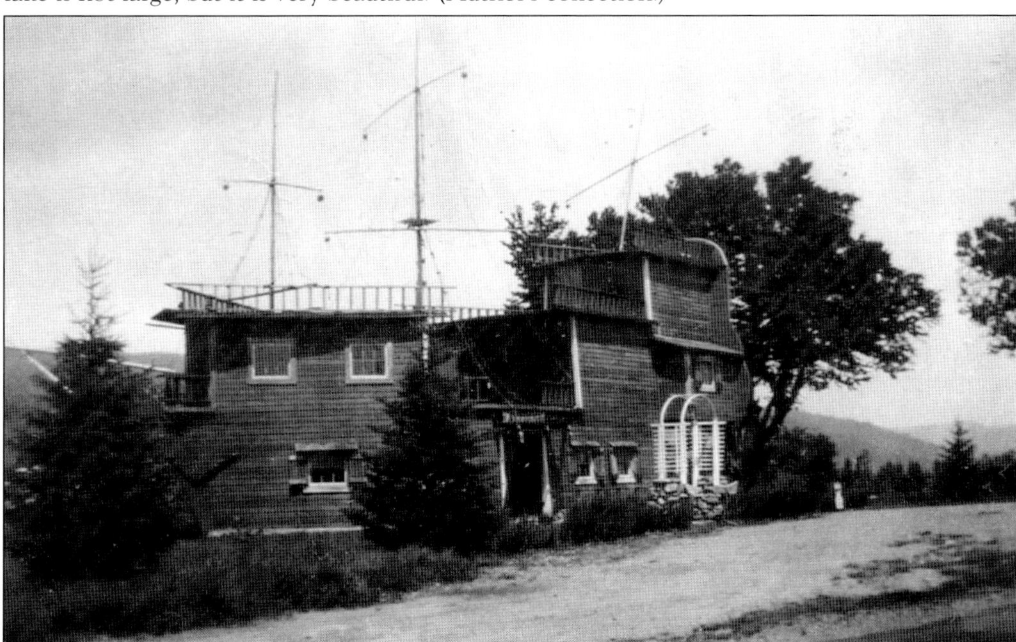

The Mayflower was a fun roadside peculiarity on the northbound side of Route 8 headed toward Speculator. The Adirondacks had many of these gimmicky things along the main highways through the park. This structure has now fallen into disrepair. (Author's collection.)

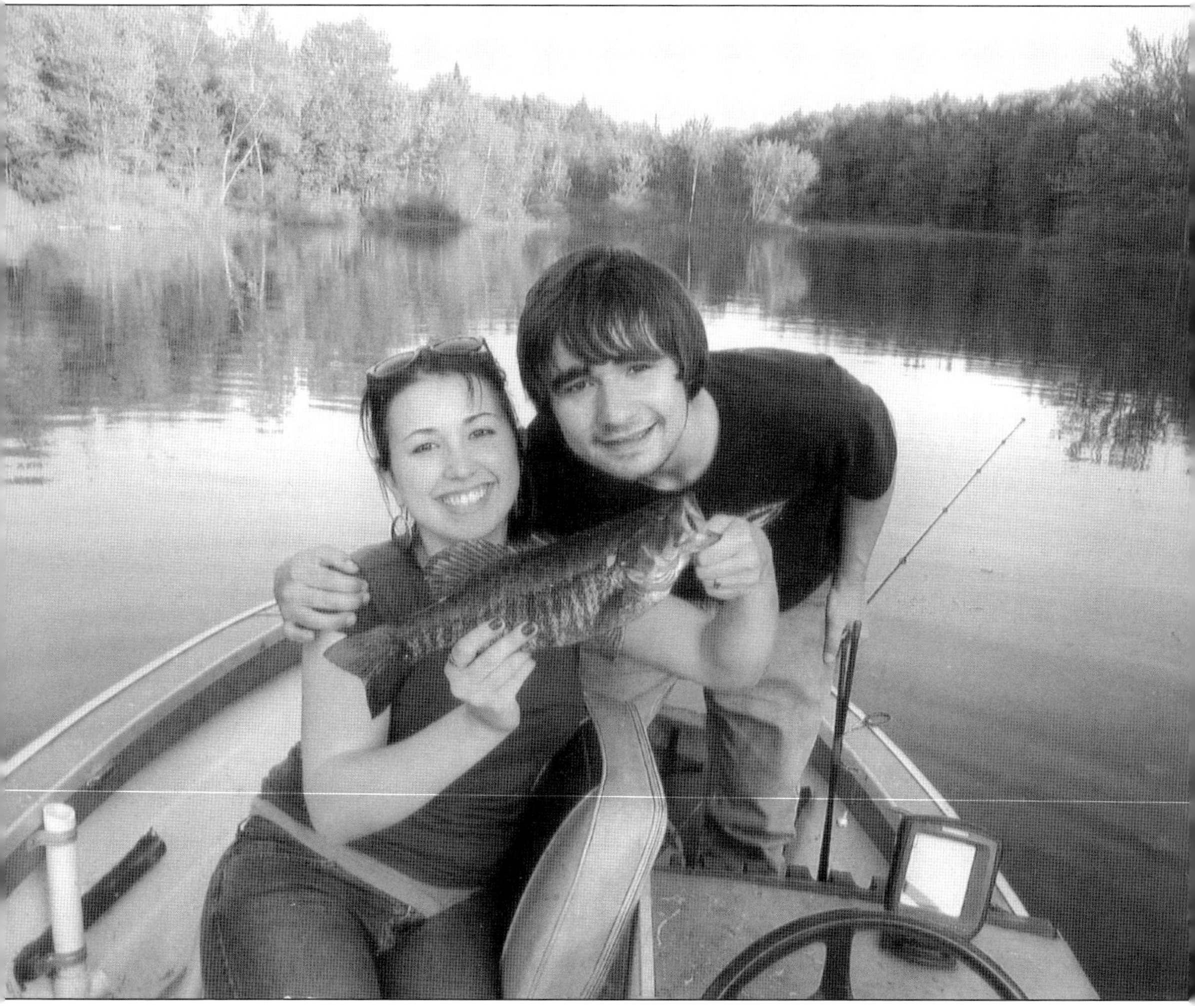

Bass are a lot of fun to catch because they give a good fight. "Let bass be given permanent status as the working class of American gamefish," Pat Smith wrote about bass in *Old Iron Jaw: Lamar Underwood's Bass Almanac*, 1979. "He's tough and he knows it. He's a factory worker, truck driver, wildcatter, lumberjack, bar room bouncer, dock-walloper, migrant farmhand, and bear 'wrassler.' Whether it's a backwater at noon, a swamp at midnight, or dockside at dawn, he'll be there waiting. He's a fierce-eyed, foul-mouthed, tobacco-chewing redneck who has traveled to every corner of the nation, paying his way and giving no quarter." In this photograph, author Megan (Plete) Postol and her brother Bill Plete stop to pose with a bass Megan caught on Hinckley Reservoir, which forms a portion of the border of Oneida County and Herkimer County. (Author's collection.)

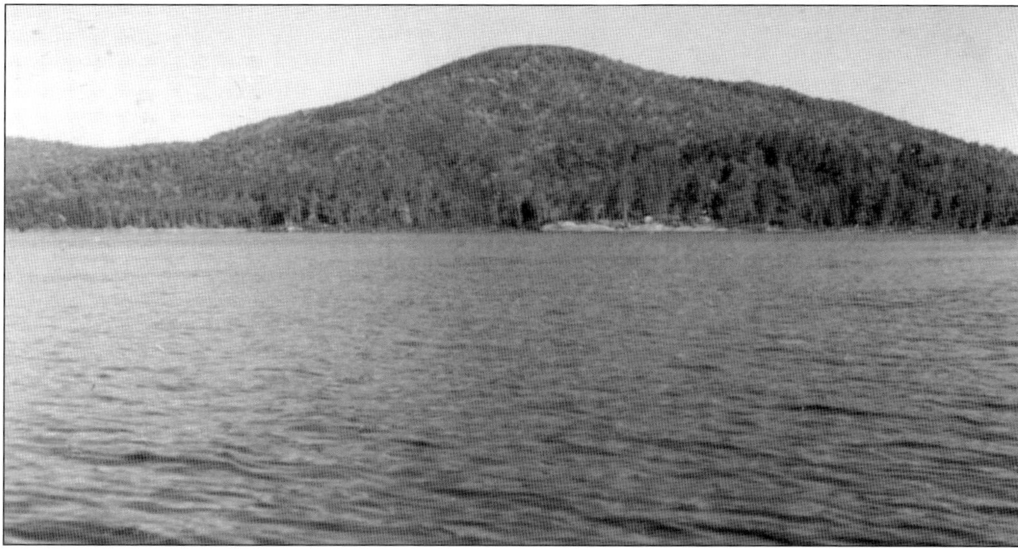

The Adirondacks has a seemingly endless array of beautiful lakes and ponds. In the 1970s, these lakes were threatened by acid rain. Some small lakes in the Adirondack Park were found to be so abnormally acidic that the fish that previously inhabited the waters were no longer able to live there. Many of the affected lakes have since recovered. (Author's collection.)

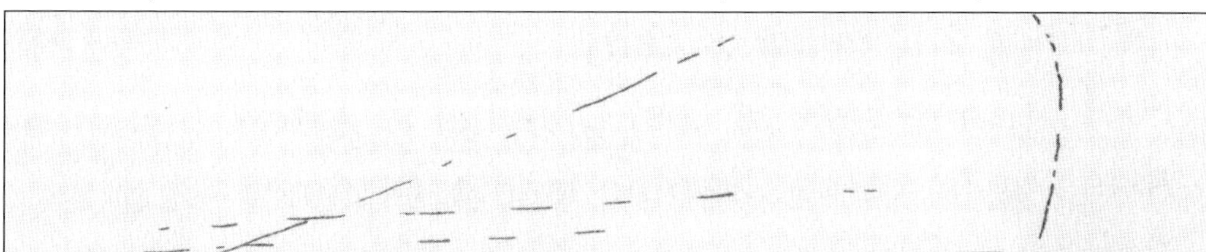

In addition to the bodies of water affected by acid rain in the 1970s, some species of trees were also being damaged. The Adirondack Park had a higher percentage of injury from acid rain than other parts of the country. This image is from a 1970s New York State Department of Conservation brochure. (Author's collection.)

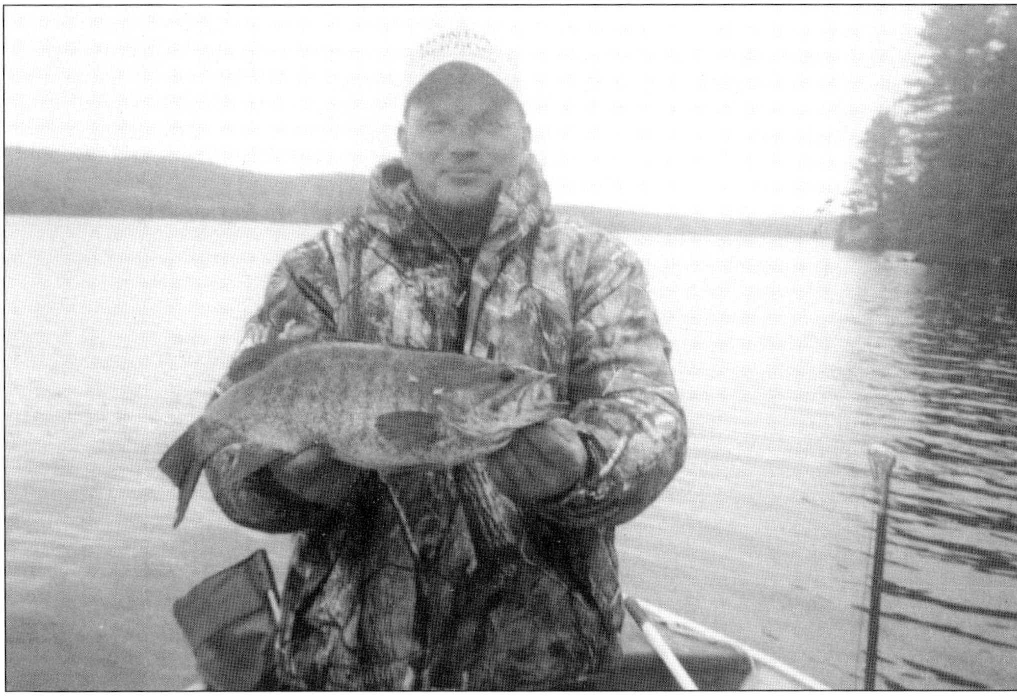

Bass can be found in many Adirondack lakes, including Long Lake, Forked Lake, Cranberry Lake, Eighth Lake, and others. Both largemouth and smallmouth bass are enjoyable to catch and are a popular fish to pursue. In this photograph, Brian Countryman is seen with a catch-and-release bass he caught in an Adirondack lake. (Courtesy of Ron Plete.)

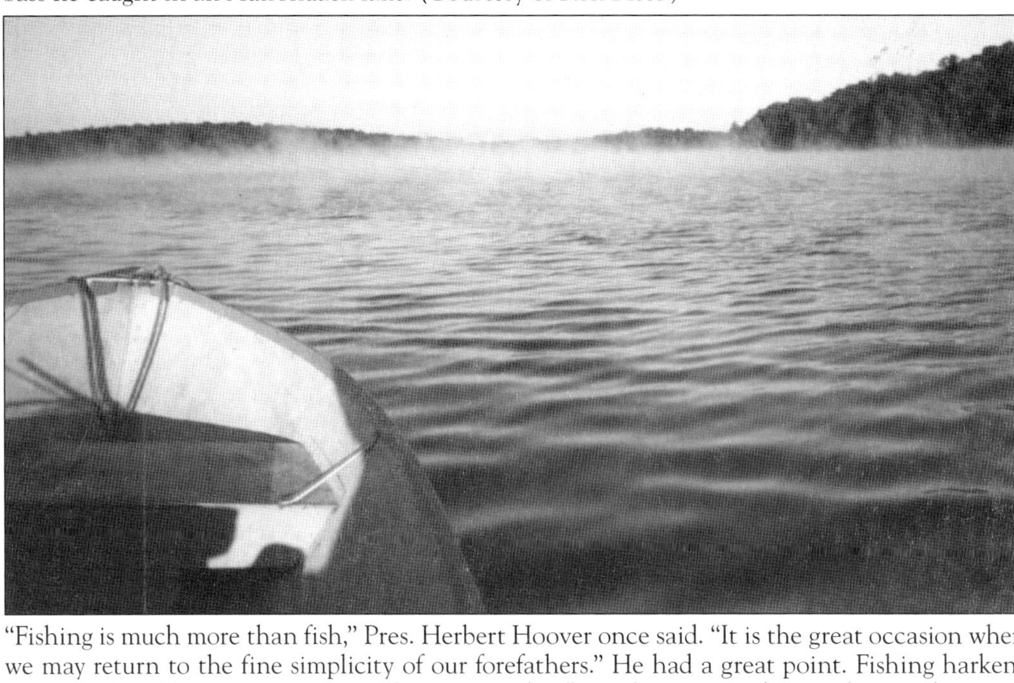

"Fishing is much more than fish," Pres. Herbert Hoover once said. "It is the great occasion when we may return to the fine simplicity of our forefathers." He had a great point. Fishing harkens back to a humbler time, reconnects humans to the flow of nature, and gives them a chance to immerse themselves in the authentic world. (Author's collection.)

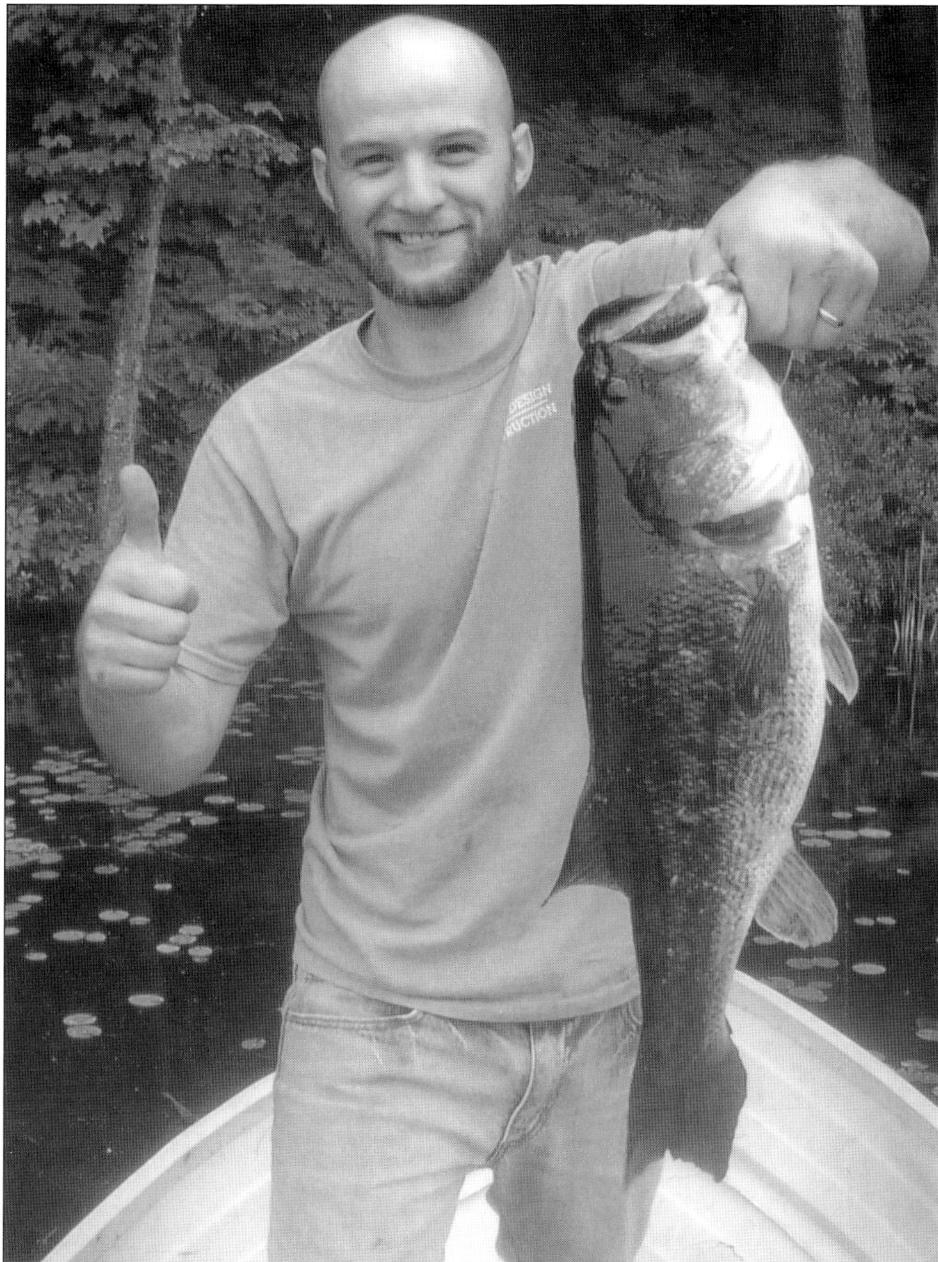

On a Fourth of July overnight fishing trip with Bill Plete, Dale Postol caught this five-and-a-half-pound largemouth bass. They were fishing for bass along the shores of the backsets of the lake. They both had Senko fishing lures on their poles. This bass took a swipe at Postol's pole but missed it. He tried to convince it to hit it again. Plete was working his line too. Finally, Postol remembered he had a spare fishing pole rigged up with a Rapala. He grabbed that pole and cast the Rapala at the bass. The bass hit it swiftly, and Postol was finally able to land it. The bass put up a good fight. Later that night, during the trip, a thunderstorm moved in. They were sleeping in a tent, and it rained heavily; they were soaked. They packed it up early the next morning and went home. (Author's collection.)

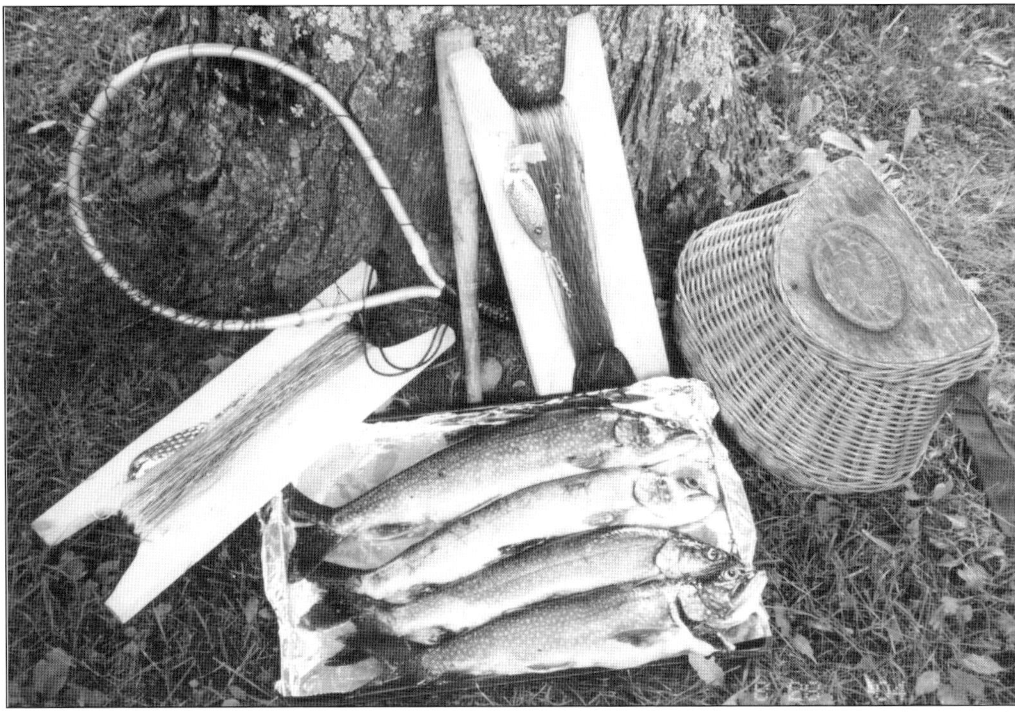

Hand-line fishing for trout is a technique that the old-timers would use when fishing in the Adirondacks. Sometimes, this technique is called "pulling copper," because of the pulling movements of the fishermen's hand and the copper line used. The fishing rig setup consists of a carved board, the copper line, and the fishermen's lure of choice. The copper line is spun upon the board and usually marked by feet or yards so that the fishermen can know the depth of the water. The line is released into the water and tugged near the bottom of the river to attract the trout. The concept is simple but surprisingly difficult. Fishermen can feel more of the action on the bottom when using this method because there is nothing between them and the line. (Courtesy of Tom Murphy.)

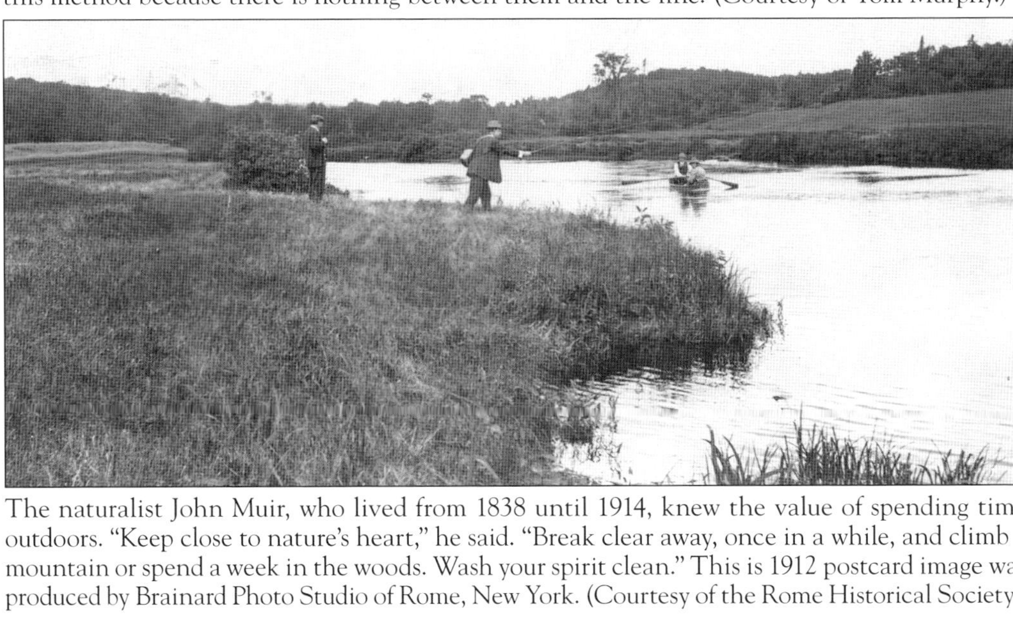

The naturalist John Muir, who lived from 1838 until 1914, knew the value of spending time outdoors. "Keep close to nature's heart," he said. "Break clear away, once in a while, and climb a mountain or spend a week in the woods. Wash your spirit clean." This is 1912 postcard image was produced by Brainard Photo Studio of Rome, New York. (Courtesy of the Rome Historical Society.)

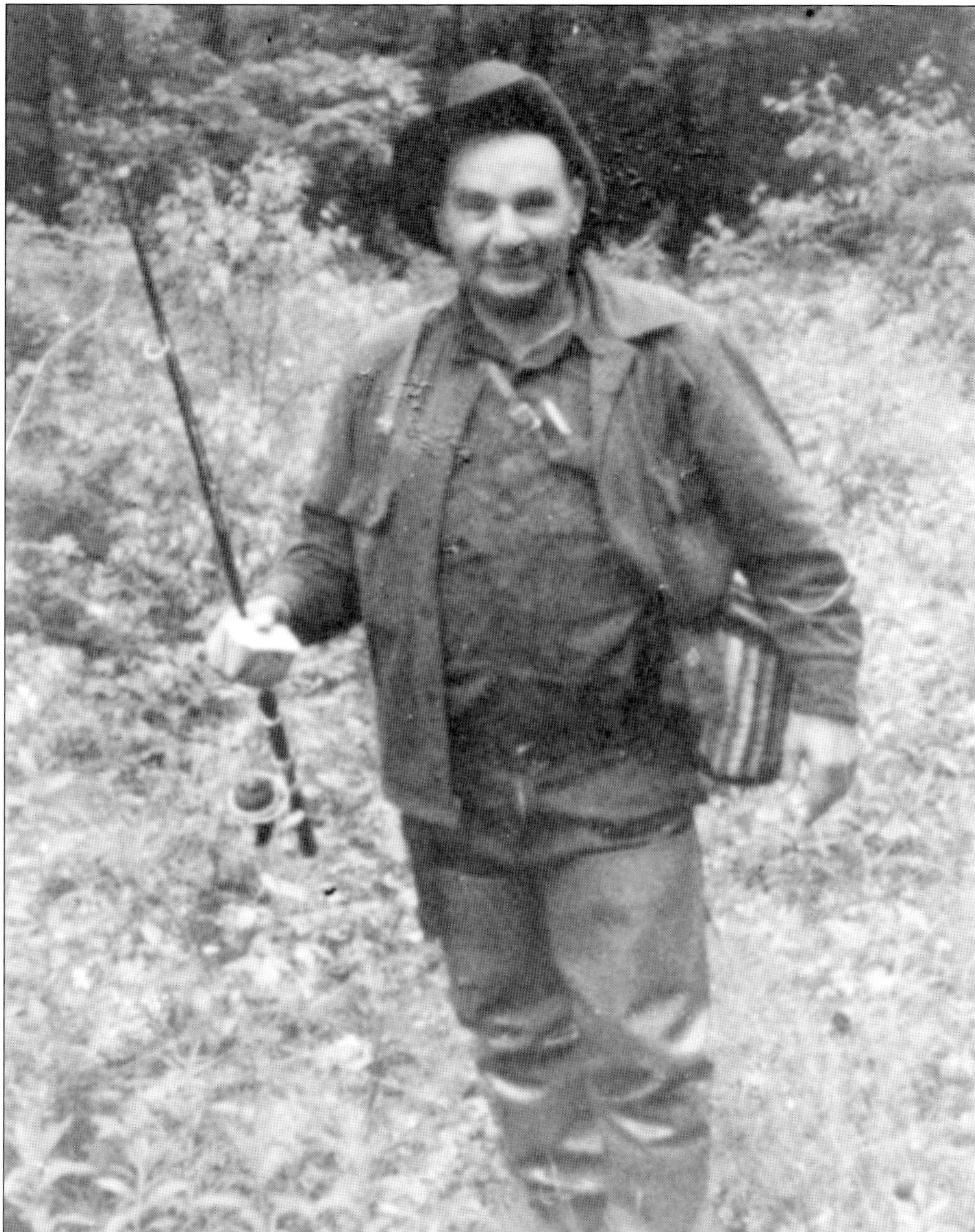

Pictured here while brook trout fishing is Adirondack guide Philip "Bill" Plete. His family emigrated from Italy in 1894 and settled in the upper Italian district of Hinckley. He was the youngest son in the large family of 10 children. His family was one of the many that had to relocate when the state decided to build the Hinckley Dam and Reservoir to supply the Erie Canal with water. They resettled on a farm on Briggs Road in Remsen. In addition to guiding, Plete worked for the New York State Department of Transportation for 25 years. After his marriage in 1936, he moved back to Hinckley with his wife, Anna, and they raised two children: Bill and Helen. (Author's collection.)

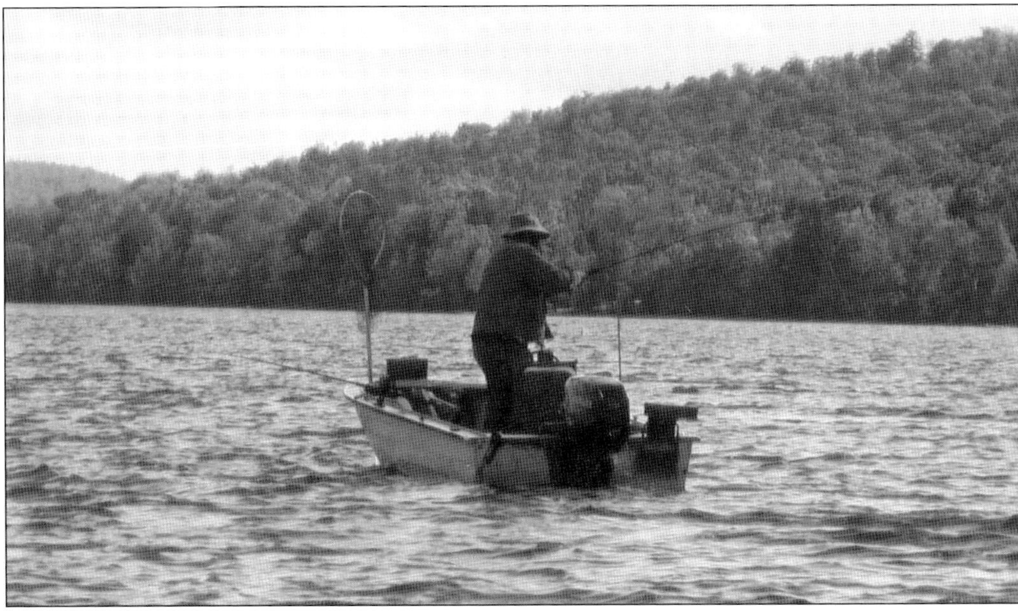

Above, Ron Plete reels in a fish while in his boat on Piseco Lake. Piseco Lake is a popular spot in the Southern Adirondacks. The three state campgrounds along its shore make it easily accessible. It has a large population of lake trout, landlocked salmon, and whitefish. The name "Piseco" is said to have come from a Native American that was known to an early surveyor. Below, Panther Mountain overlooks the lake. Hiking to Echo Cliff on Panther Mountain is a popular activity for campers and visitors. (Both, author's collection.)

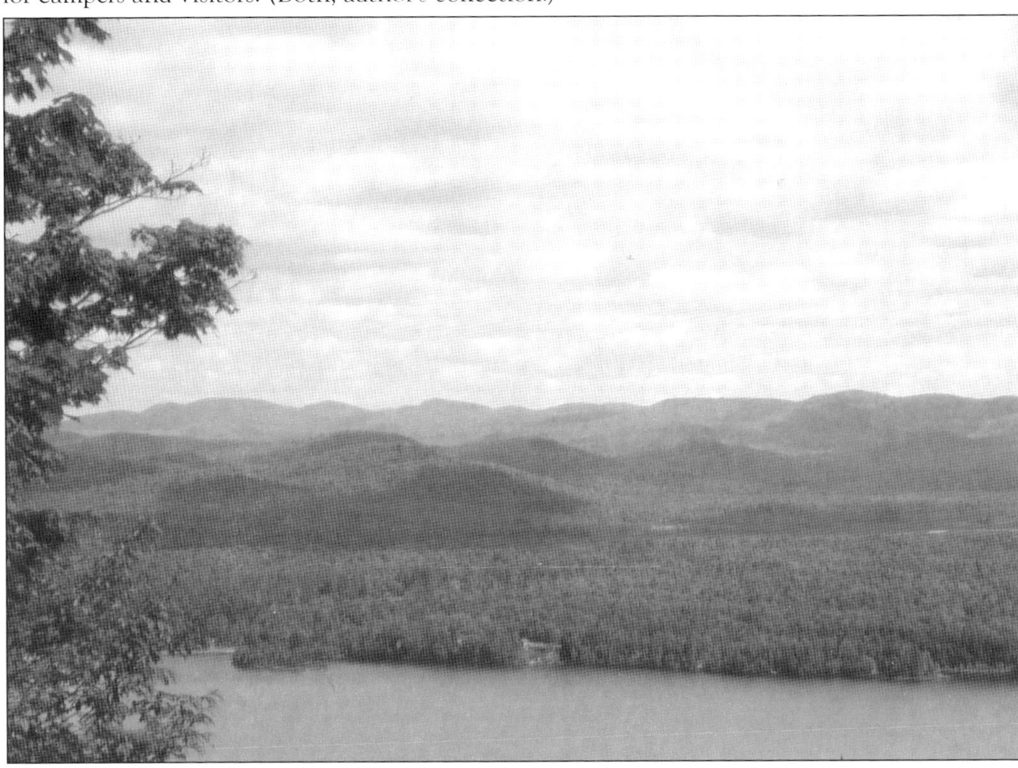

Three

North Country Trappers

Trapping animals has been a part of human history since the prehistoric ancestors. The ways of trapping have evolved, but the roots of the sport trace back to the dawn of time. In New York State, trapping was carried out by settlers who had come from Europe to make a life in this new land. The state's economy was built on the fur trade. In the Adirondacks, the sport of trapping grew in popularity in the 1800s and 1900s, partly inspired by the famous trappers, hermits, and guides who made their home there.

The fur boom of the 1970s saw trapping once again explode in popularity among the blue-collar folks of the foothills. Although not as commonplace as it once was, the tradition of trapping furbearers continues in the Adirondacks and all over the country. Instead of making a living off trapping, most trappers pursue it as a passion and hobby. The anticipation of checking the trap line and the connection to nature are the two most cited reasons that trappers continue the sport in the present. With cooperation among trappers, other sportsmen, and those beyond that community, solid ethics, and the notion of conservation, fur trapping can continue for generations to come.

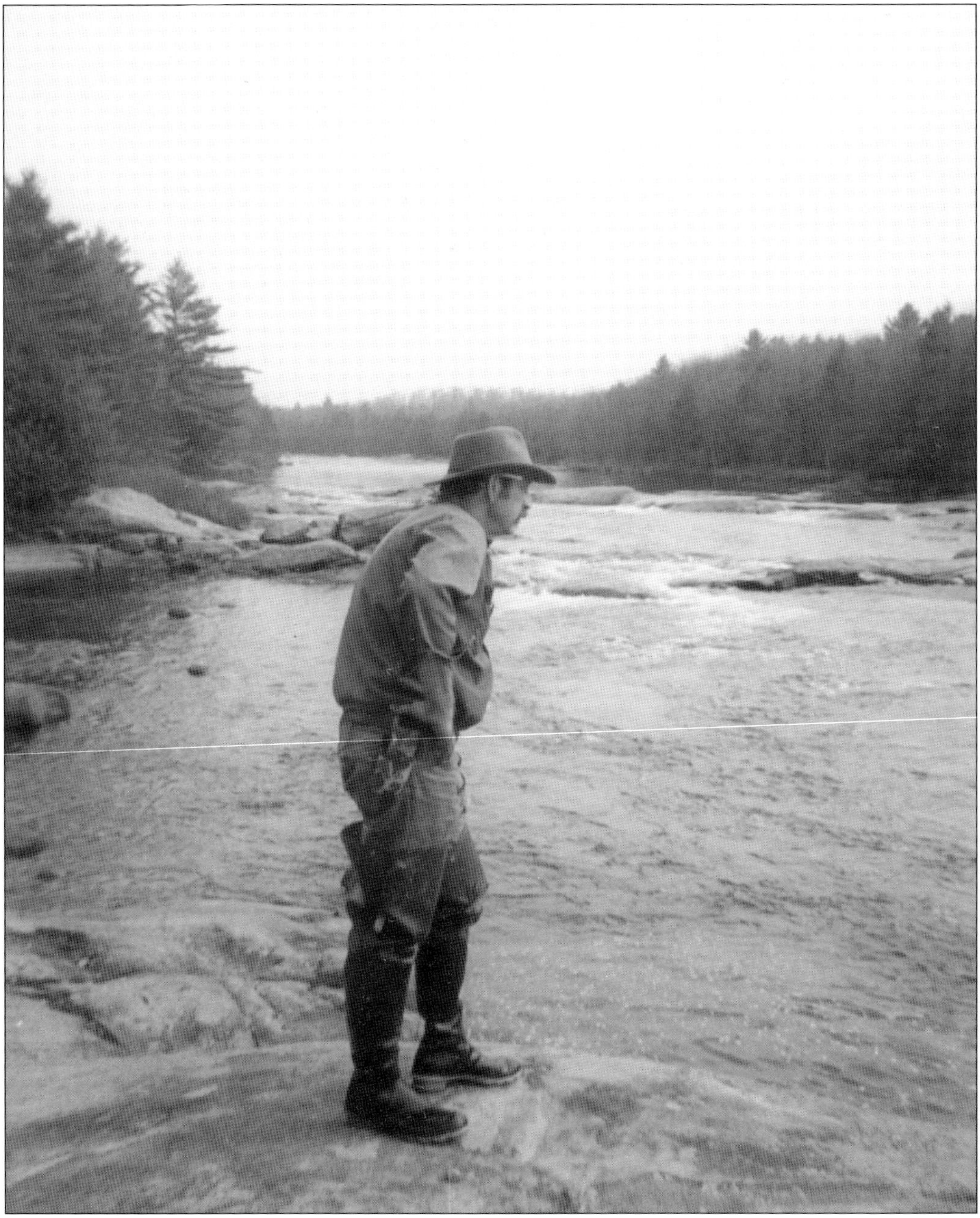

Steve Hitchcock, of Remsen, has trapped all over the Adirondacks. His years of trap line experience have earned him an expansive database of accumulated knowledge. It has not come easy. He has fallen through the ice on a bitter 12-degree day, he has confronted a bear stealing his beaver out of a trap, and he has weathered the night in a makeshift pine branch shelter after being trapped in a flash snowstorm. Hitchcock is the kind of tough old sportsman described in this quote from the film *Jeremiah Johnson*: "The story goes that he was a man of proper wit and adventurous spirit suited to the mountains." Trappers are like that—rugged by necessity, tougher than nails, and self-reliant. Trapping demands that kind of discipline and dedication. Hitchcock personifies all of what it means to be a trapper. (Courtesy of Steve Hitchcock.)

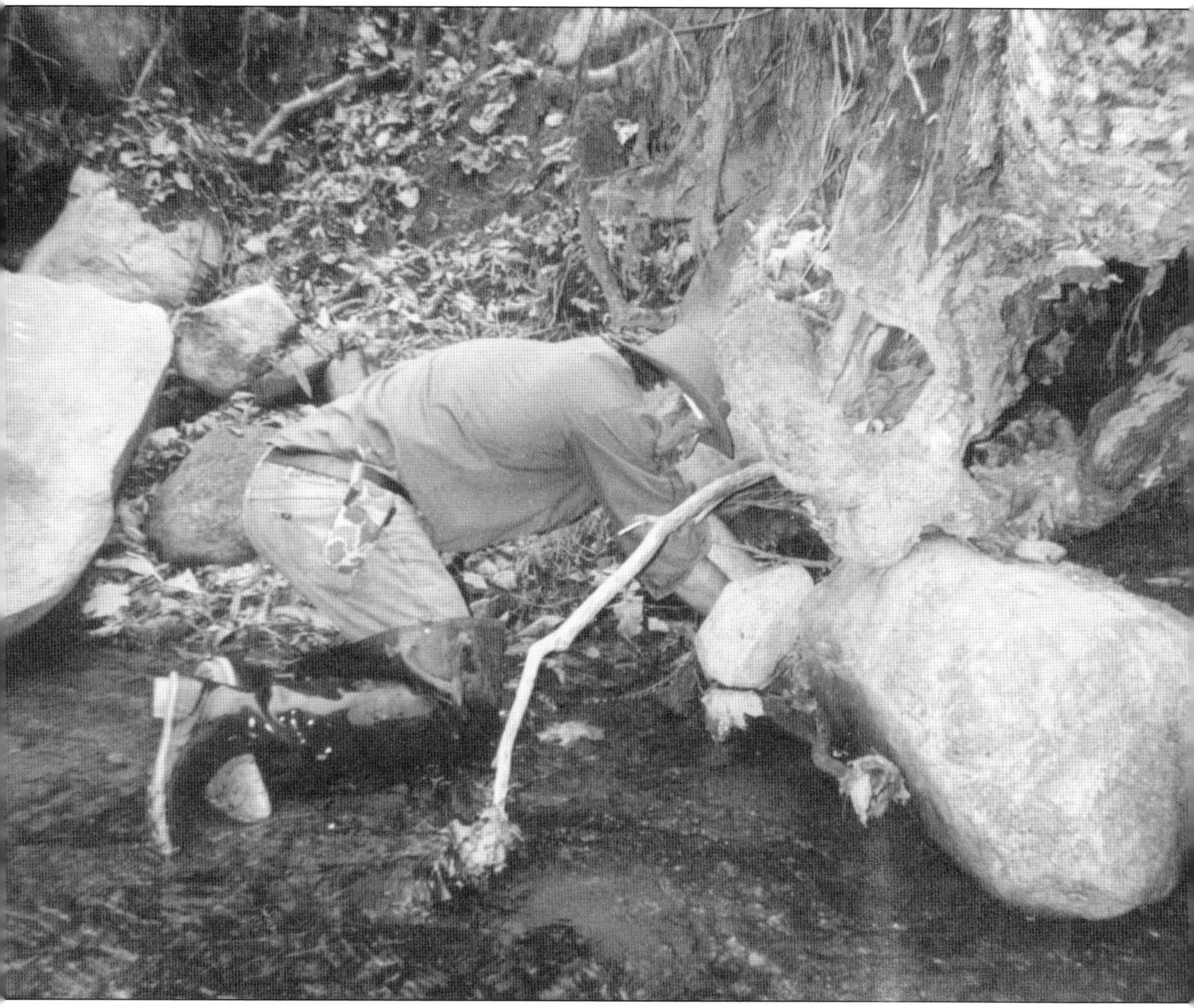

Hitchcock's favorite critters to trap are mink and fisher, but for different reasons. To trap mink, he utilizes his knowledge and experience, but to trap fisher, he listens to his instincts to choose the right location. (Courtesy of Steve Hitchcock.)

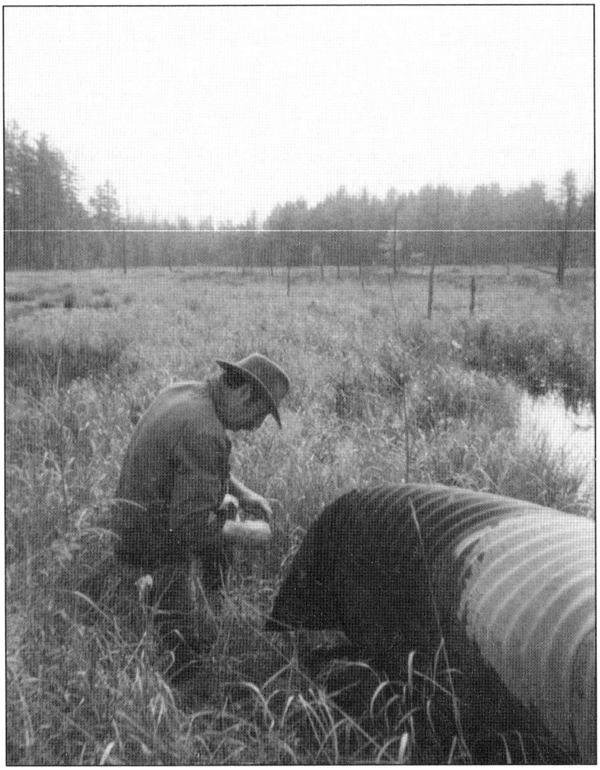

Steve Hitchcock is a self-taught trapper. He got his start around age 10, trapping muskrats for spending money. When he started, a muskrat would bring in about 75¢. Back then, there was not as much how-to literature to learn from as there is today. He read the *Fur-Fish-Game* magazine for some tips, but mostly, he had to learn by doing. After muskrats, he progressed to raccoon and fox. He trapped his first fox at age 14 with a 1.5 Victor long-spring. (Both, courtesy of Steve Hitchcock.)

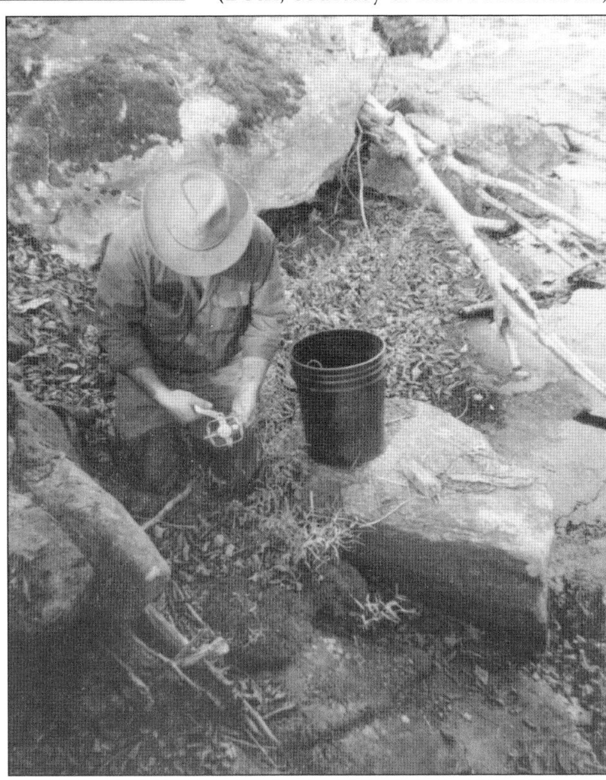

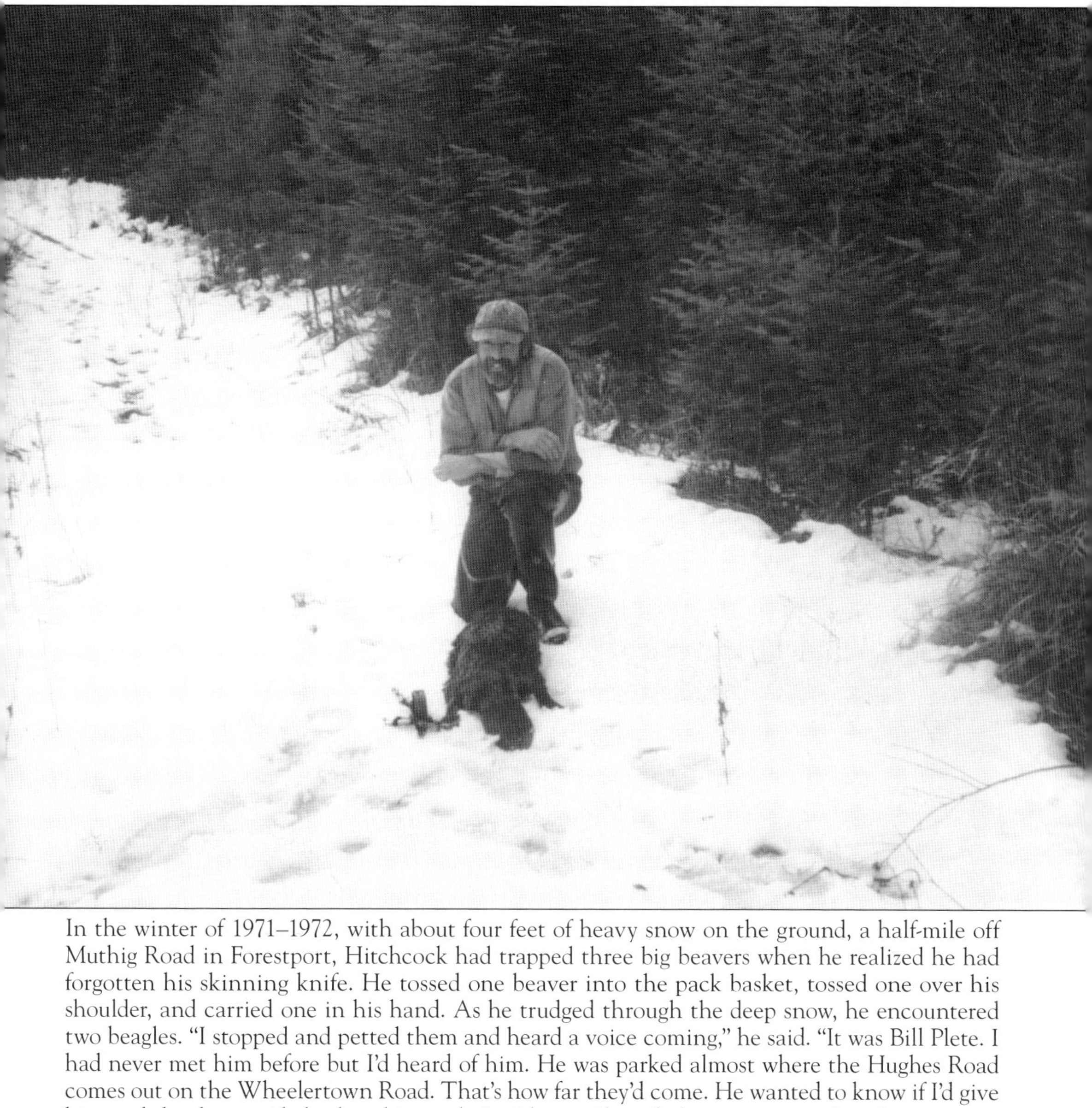

In the winter of 1971–1972, with about four feet of heavy snow on the ground, a half-mile off Muthig Road in Forestport, Hitchcock had trapped three big beavers when he realized he had forgotten his skinning knife. He tossed one beaver into the pack basket, tossed one over his shoulder, and carried one in his hand. As he trudged through the deep snow, he encountered two beagles. "I stopped and petted them and heard a voice coming," he said. "It was Bill Plete. I had never met him before but I'd heard of him. He was parked almost where the Hughes Road comes out on the Wheelertown Road. That's how far they'd come. He wanted to know if I'd give him and the dogs a ride back to his truck. I said sure, if you help me to carry these beavers out. It was cold that day too. After that, in my travels I'd find where there were quite a few snowshoe rabbit tracks, I would call him up or stop to let him know. He always appreciated the daylights out of that." (Courtesy of Steve Hitchcock.)

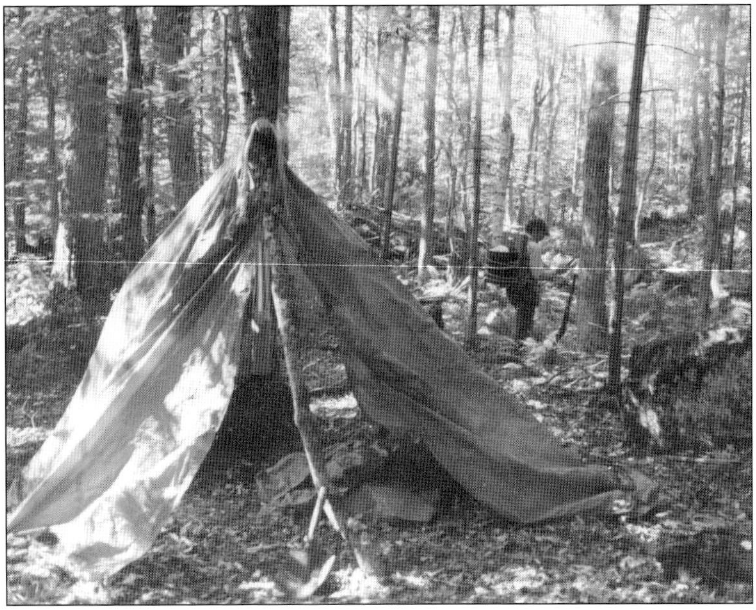

Hitchcock set up this temporary camp to scout the area in the Forestport area of the Adirondacks. The range was full of black bears. He set out a line of sets targeted for fisher, but when he returned to check, the bears had decimated the sets. (Courtesy of Steve Hitchcock.)

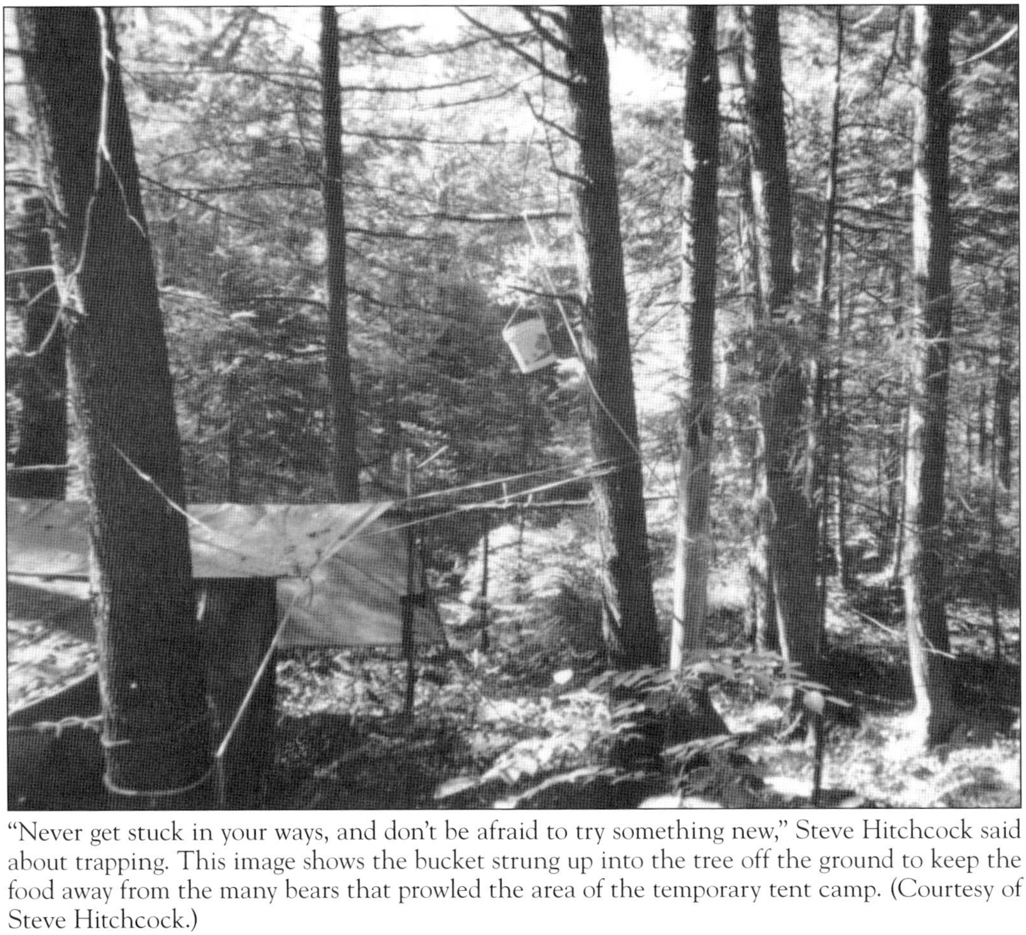

"Never get stuck in your ways, and don't be afraid to try something new," Steve Hitchcock said about trapping. This image shows the bucket strung up into the tree off the ground to keep the food away from the many bears that prowled the area of the temporary tent camp. (Courtesy of Steve Hitchcock.)

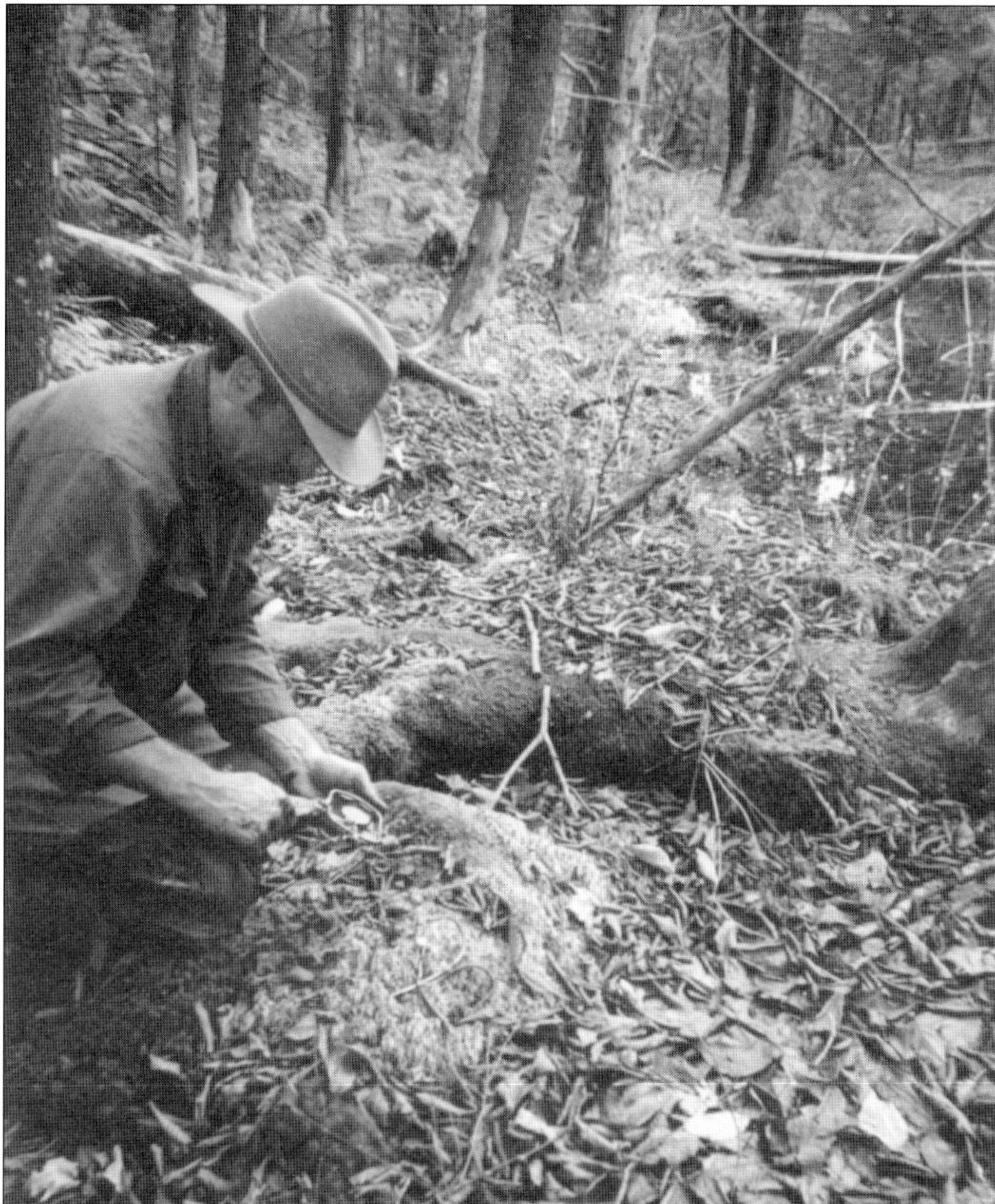

Steve Hitchcock brought his friend Dwayne with him to visit E.J. Dailey at his Trapper Supply House in the 1970s: "E.J. was mixing up lure," Hitchcock said. "It stunk to high heavens, but I didn't think anything of it because it didn't bother me. E.J. was kind of a gruff old guy. He looked up at us and said, 'What'd ya want?' I told him I wanted to buy some traps. I looked over to Dwayne, and he's turning green. Suddenly he tore out the back door. So I went out and E.J. came out behind us and stood in the door. Dwayne had puked all over the big old maple tree in the yard. I looked over to E.J., and he said, 'Geez, I love that tree,' and he went back in. Then he told me the traps were in the front room. I picked out a few. E.J. said, 'What are ya using them for?" I told him fox. He said, 'Put them back." And he showed me what I needed. He taught me a lot about which size traps to use." (Courtesy of Steve Hitchcock.)

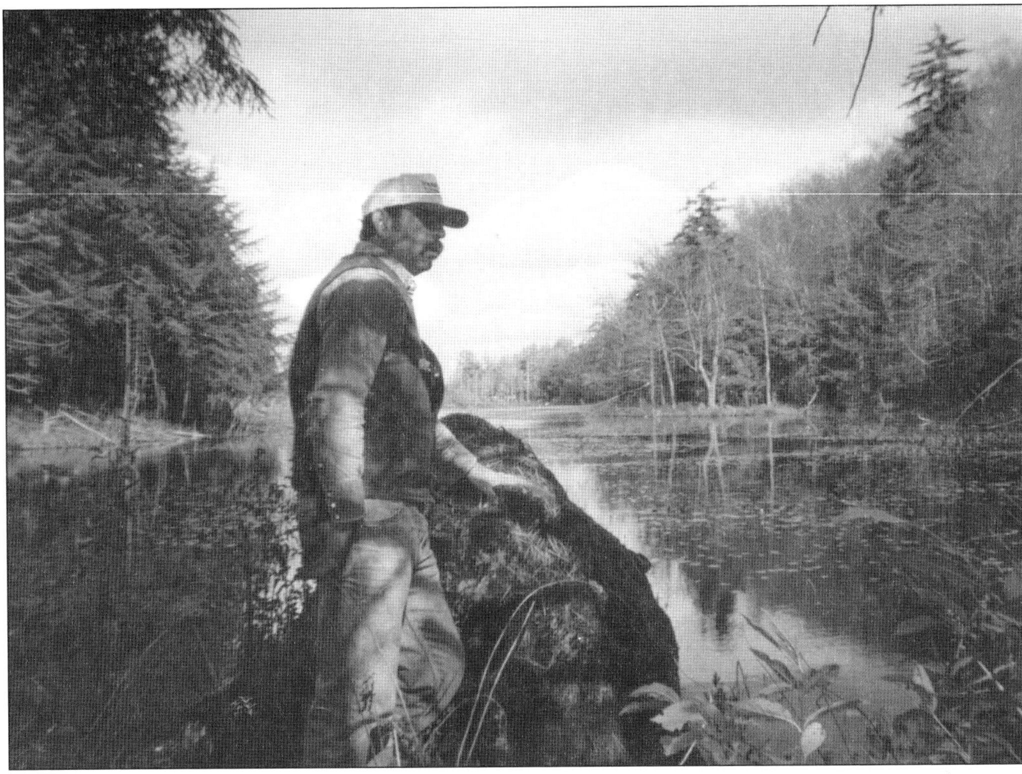

One year, Steve Hitchcock was becoming frustrated because he was not making any catches. Day after day, he found empty sets. Then finally, the action picked up. "Every day out on the line is different," Hitchcock said. "You never know. It was getting to be well into November and I had hardly caught a thing. I was beginning to wonder." At the end of the season, Hitchcock ended up with 130 raccoons, almost 700 muskrats, 18 fishers, 10 foxes, 40 mink, and about 120 beaver. Hitchcock was bringing muskrats home that year by the five-gallon bucketful. (Both, courtesy of Steve Hitchcock.)

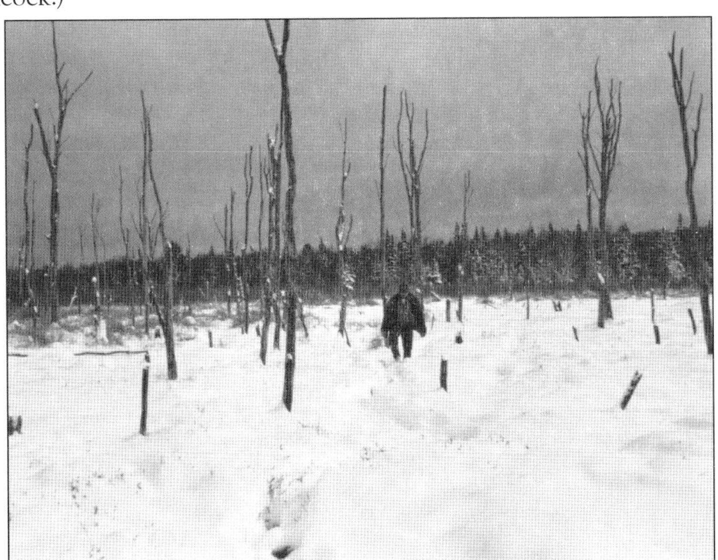

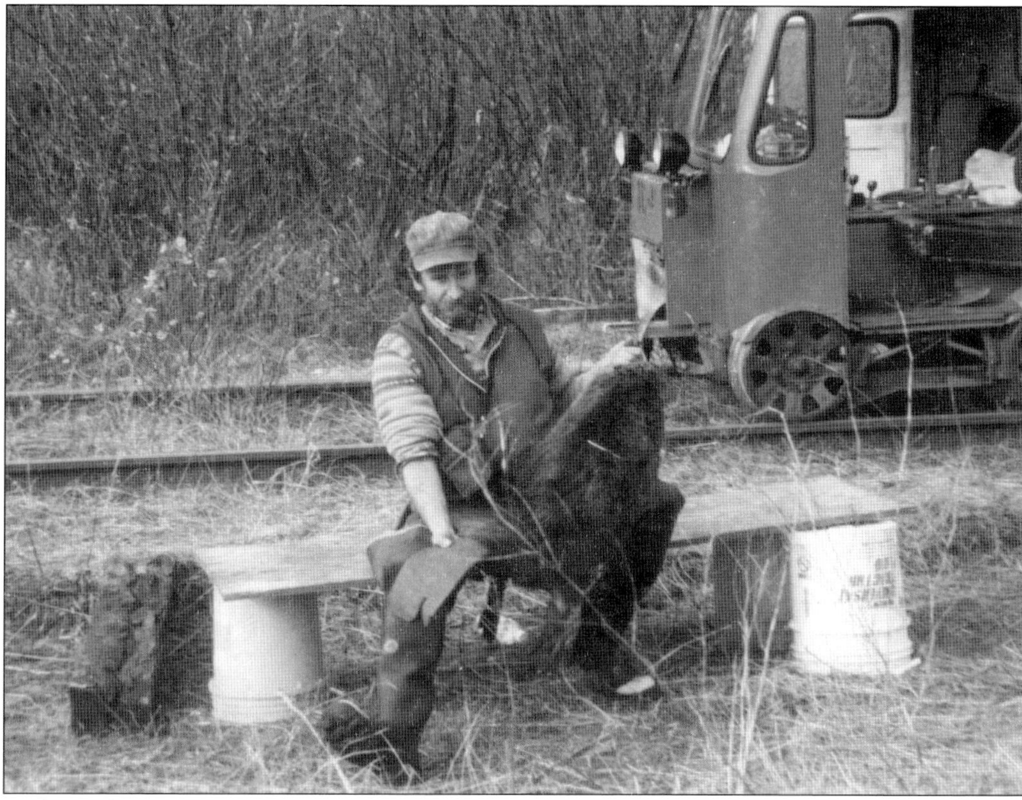

In the early 1990s, Steve Hitchcock and Kenny Lyon trapped for the railroad removing nuisance beavers. They had a base camp in Sabbattis, near Tupper Lake. Kenny Lyon's nickname was "Fur Fish and Game." He was from Forestport, New York. He camped in a tent and trapped, even after a liver transplant left him in poor health, carrying his anti-rejection medication with him into the wilderness. (Courtesy of Steve Hitchcock.)

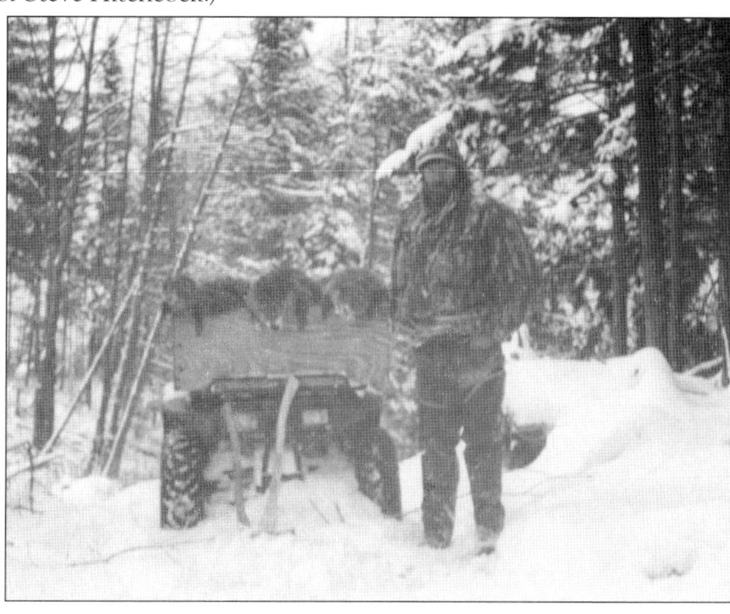

Kenny Lyon is posed next to a stack of fur during a railroad beaver line trip. He and Hitchcock would spend weeks to months in the cold Adirondack wilderness trapping beaver. (Courtesy of Steve Hitchcock.)

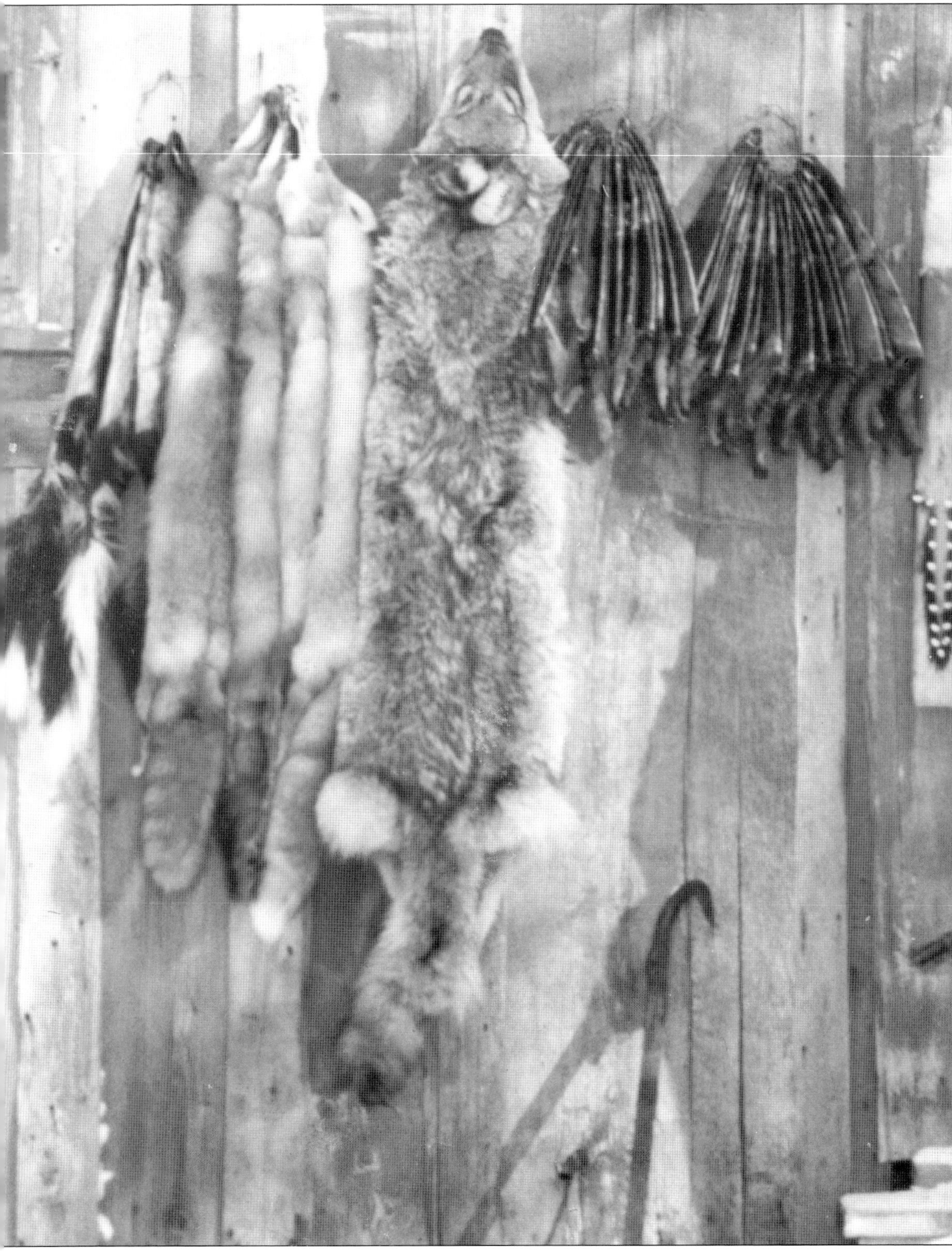

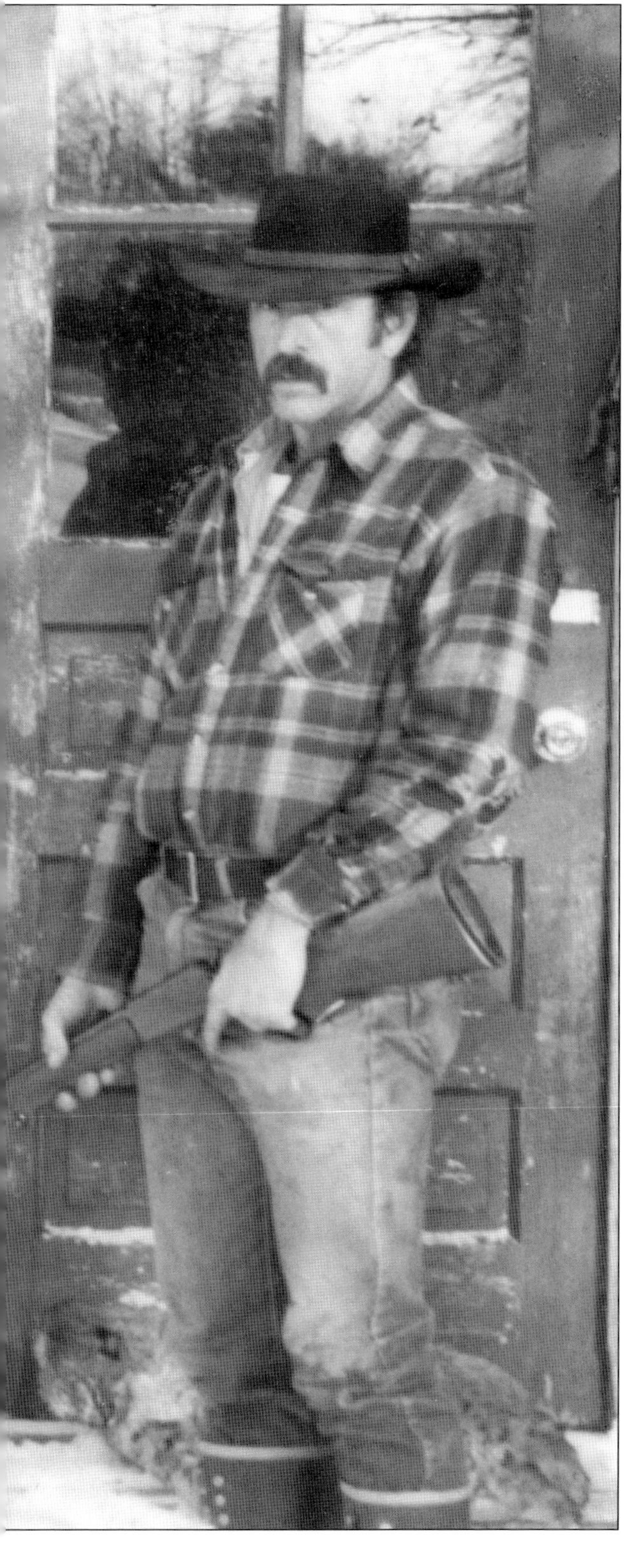

For many, a life spent outdoors is a life well lived. Many sportsmen garner great satisfaction from their outdoor pursuits. There is nothing quite like immersing oneself into the natural world, finding one's strengths and realizing one's limitations. Nature is a beast, and there can be great fulfillment for those who can rise to its challenge. Steve Hitchcock says that when it comes to trapping, it's "five percent know-how, ninety five percent hard work." (Courtesy of Steve Hitchcock.)

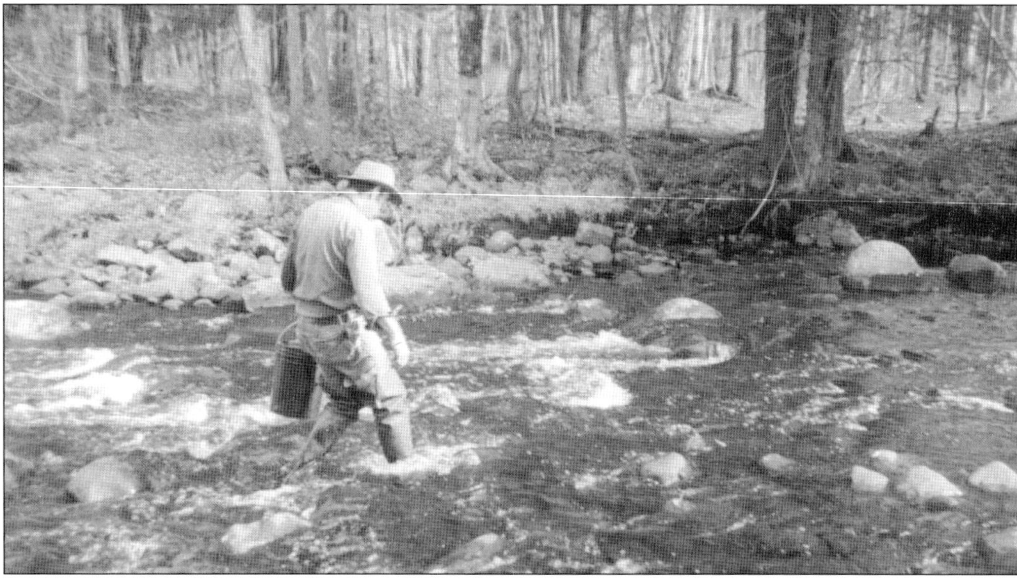

Trapping and spending time in nature helped Steve Hitchcock cope with PTSD after his military service. He said at that point, he wanted to be out in the woods rather than around people. He now serves as commander at the Remsen VFW Memorial Post 982. (Courtesy of Steve Hitchcock.)

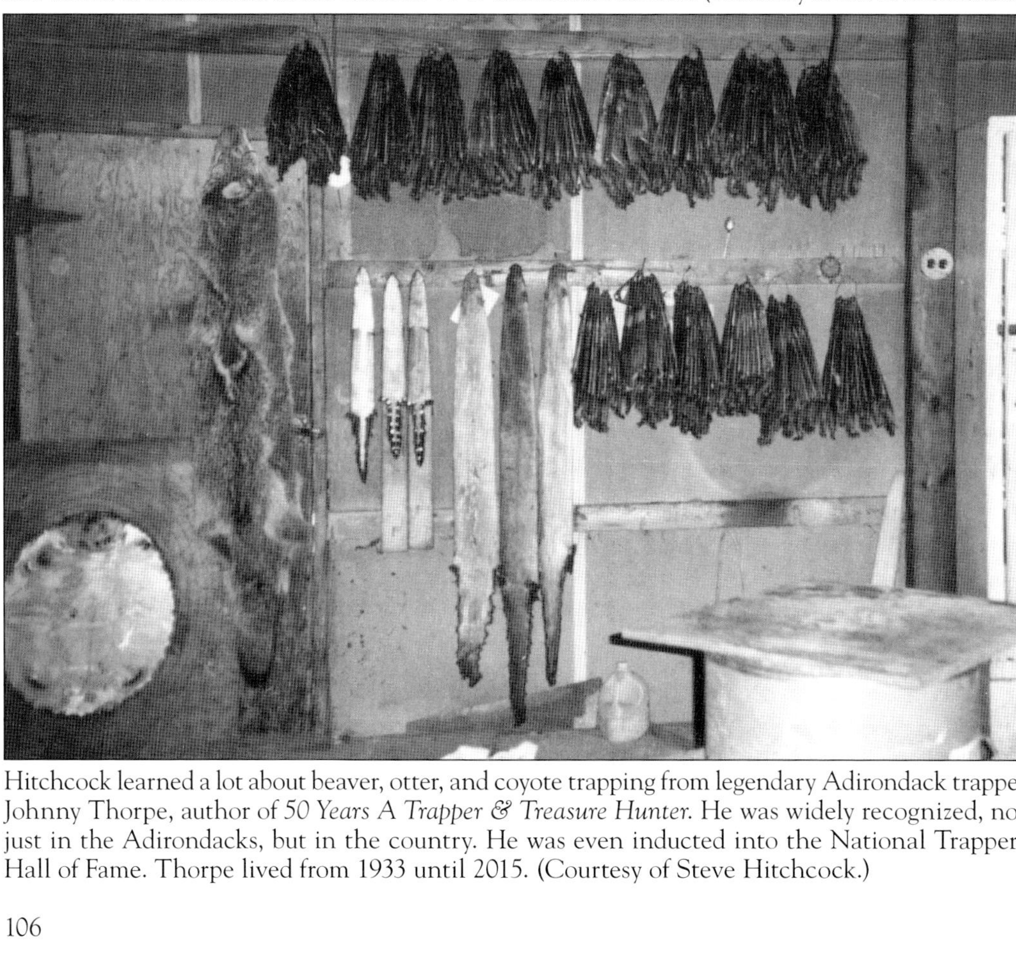

Hitchcock learned a lot about beaver, otter, and coyote trapping from legendary Adirondack trapper Johnny Thorpe, author of *50 Years A Trapper & Treasure Hunter*. He was widely recognized, not just in the Adirondacks, but in the country. He was even inducted into the National Trappers Hall of Fame. Thorpe lived from 1933 until 2015. (Courtesy of Steve Hitchcock.)

There is a rich tradition of fur trapping in the foothills of upstate New York. Here, Adirondack guide Philip "Bill" Plete poses with friends in front of a season's catch of beaver pelts. Joe Robenski is the man kneeling. The man on the left is certainly not dressed for trapping in his tailored suit. Notice the woven pack basket, a typical example of a trapper's pack. (Author's collection.)

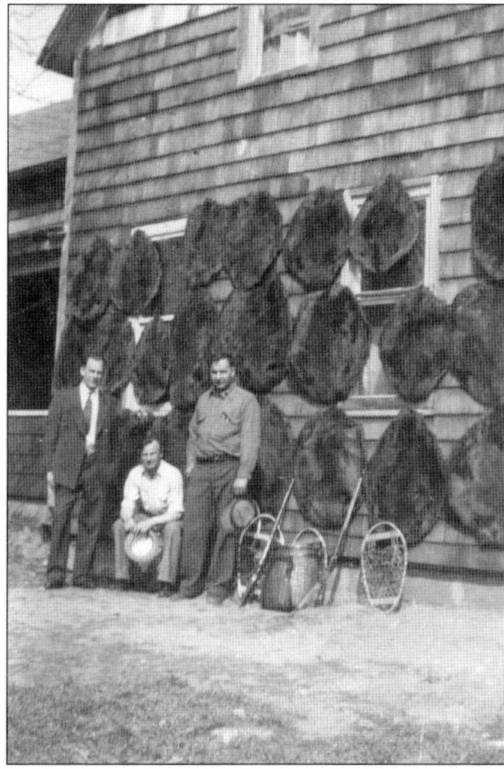

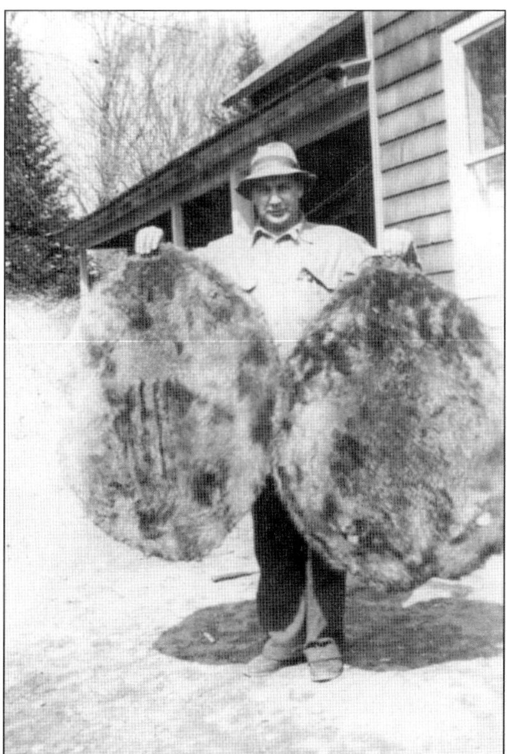

Old Bill Plete is holding up two beaver pelts from his trapping season. He was an all-around sportsman; he hunted, fished, and trapped furbearers. (Author's collection.)

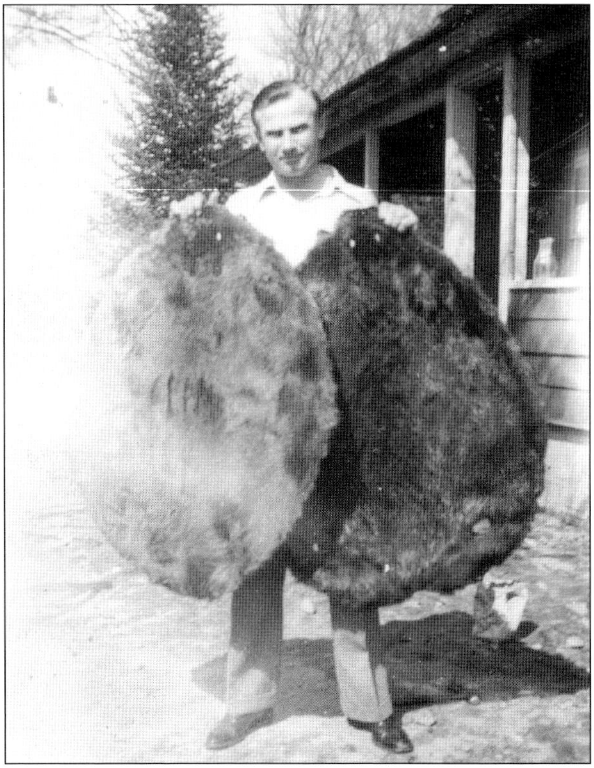

Joe Robenski takes a turn holding the beavers up for the camera. He was probably Plete's trapping partner for the season. Many people team up with other trappers to bring in twice the fur. (Author's collection.)

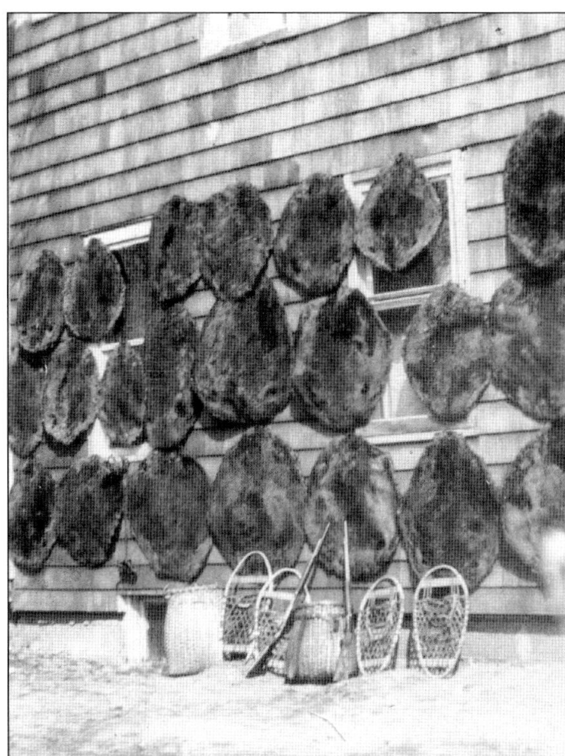

There are many reasons why people participate in trapping. The sport is uniquely challenging and can be very frustrating; there is a high sense of achievement when a trapper is successful. Preparation for the trapping season takes a lot of time and work. Checking traps is physically intense and time-consuming. Processing the fur is another step. This all adds up to a hobby fueled by passion. (Author's collection.)

Trappers have been catching furbearers in these mountains for hundreds of years. Before the state began passing and enforcing game laws, wildlife populations had decreased. Trappers in New York now must complete a trapper education course before they can buy their license and legally trap. Trapping is very structured, and trappers should adhere to best management practices. Equipment and techniques are guided by rules. Despite heavy enforcement coupled with low fur prices, there are still thousands of trappers in New York State. The map image above shows the Herkimer and Hamilton County lines. The image below shows the wilderness area around North Lake. (Both, author's collection.)

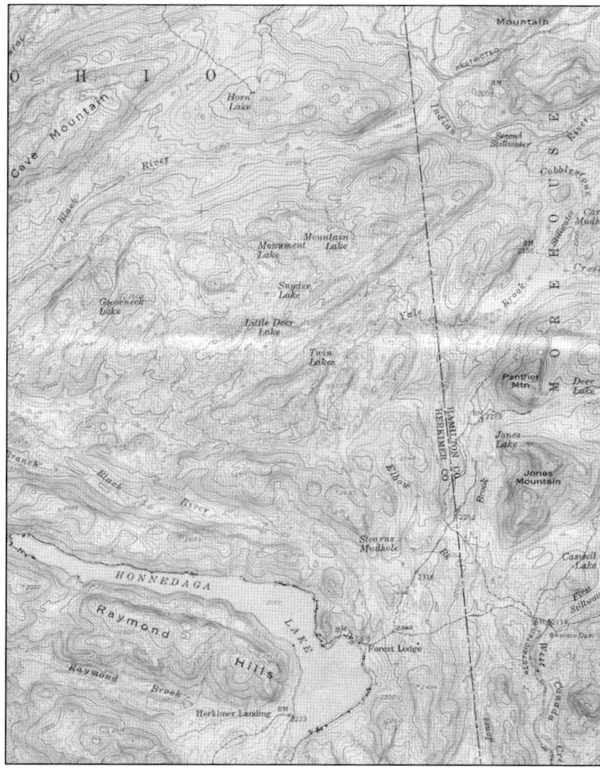

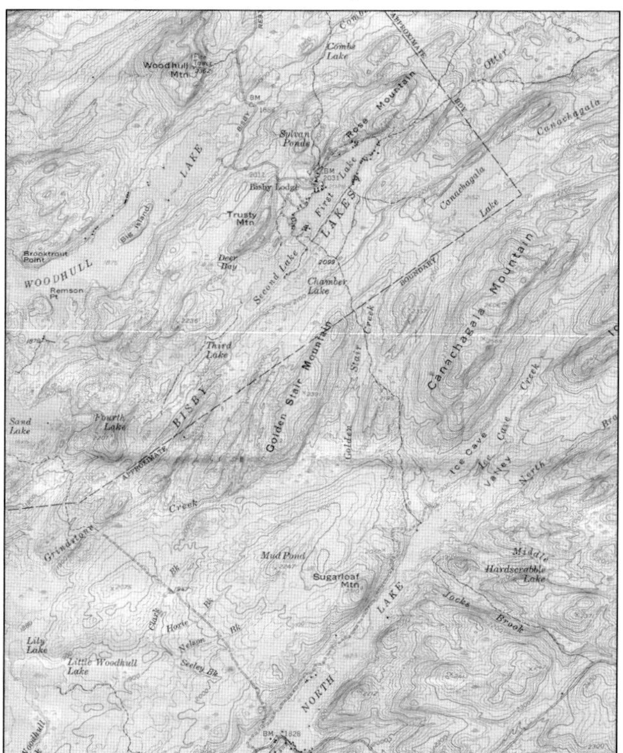

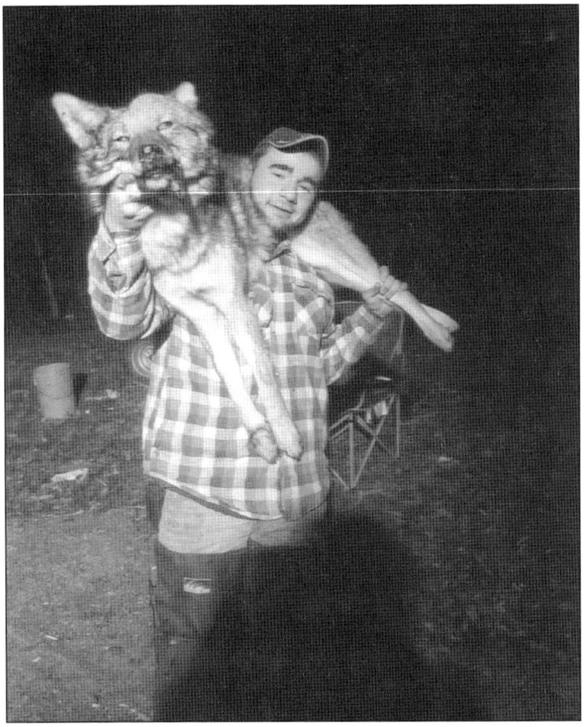

Bill Plete caught this huge coyote in a foothold trap in the Adirondack Foothills in 2013. It was very broad and long-legged. To date, it is one of his favorite catches. (Both, courtesy of Bill Plete.)

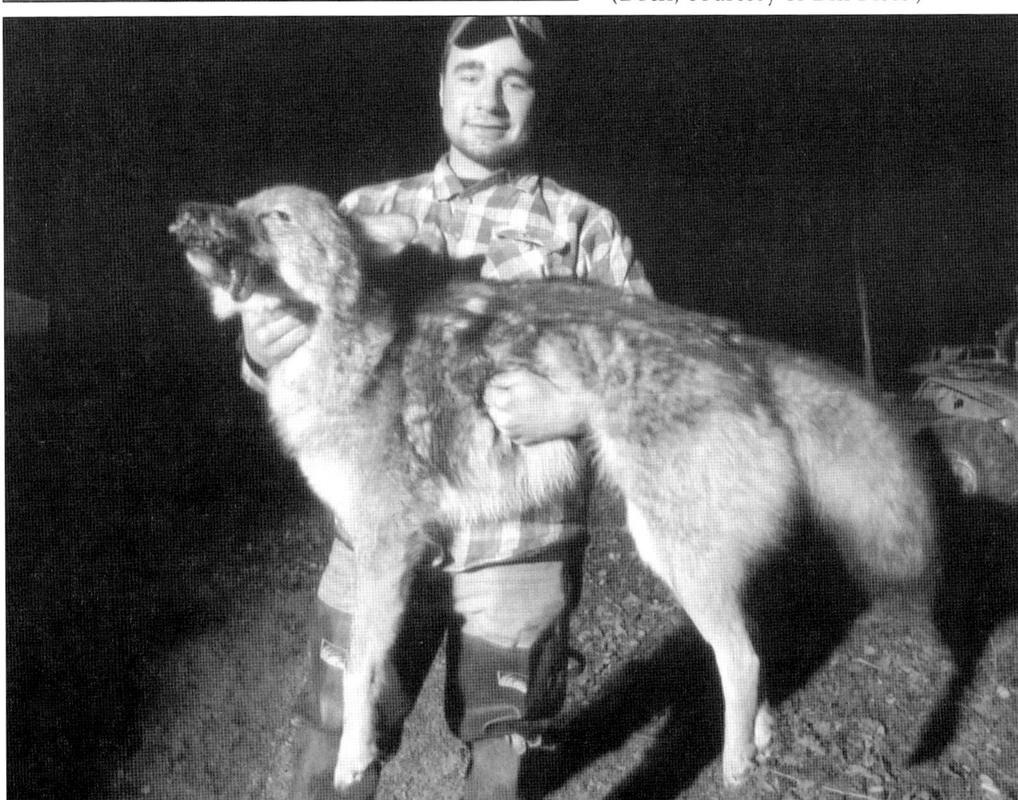

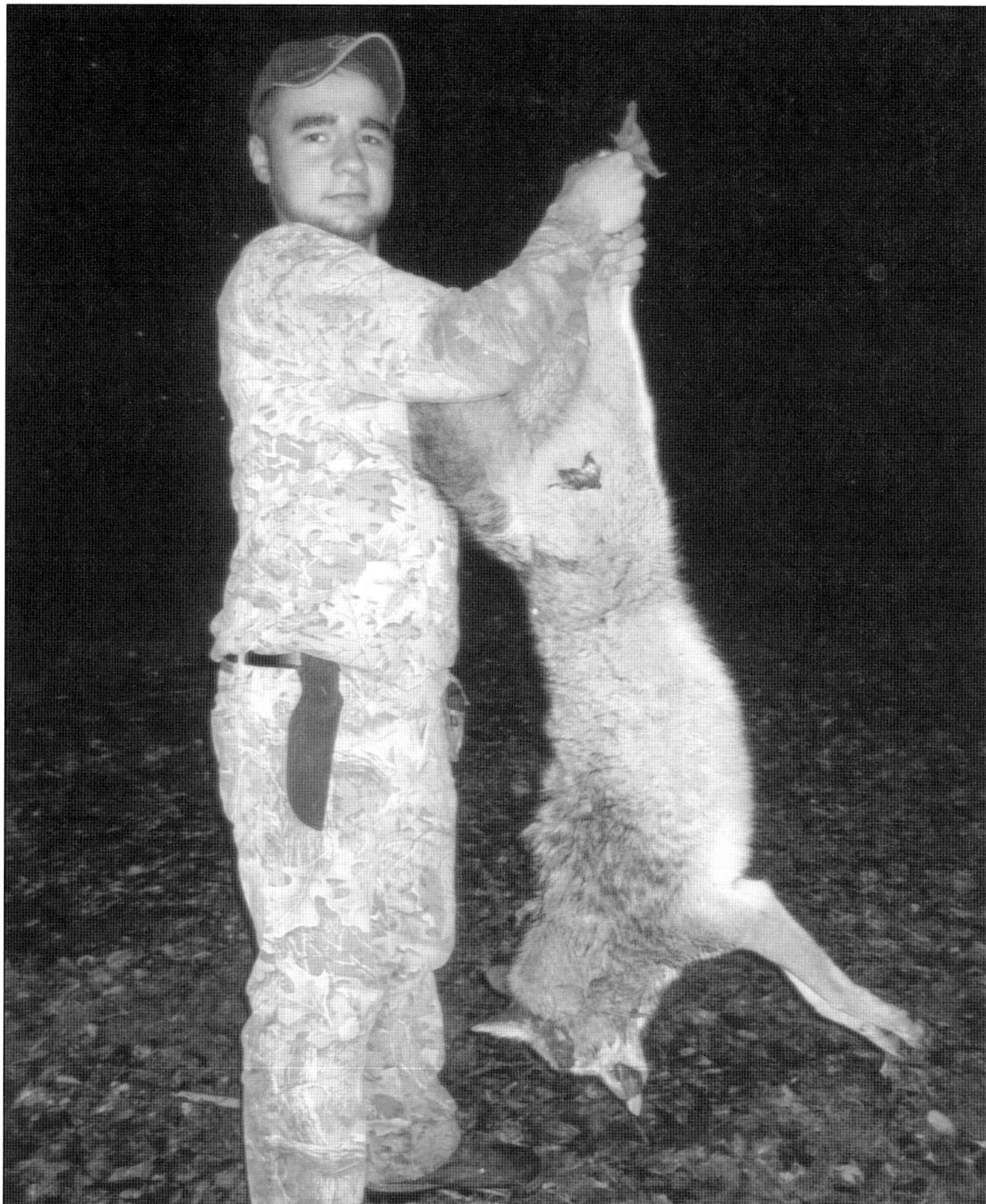

Bill Plete also caught this average size coyote in 2013. He started trapping as a preteen. His father and grandfather did not trap, but he knew that his great-grandfather had. Bill owned a few old books to learn from, but he had to learn most of it himself. Along the way, once in a while, an old-timer would give him a tip or two. The first animal he ever caught in a trap was a coyote. He had put a set out at the beginning of the season and checked it for nearly three weeks, and it was always empty. He had become discouraged and considered yanking all his sets and giving up when he finally caught his first coyote. He changed his mind about giving it up after that. For Bill, he said it is the anticipation that keeps him trapping. "You never know what you're going to get, and it's a tradition," he said. "It feels good to keep that tradition alive." (Author's collection.)

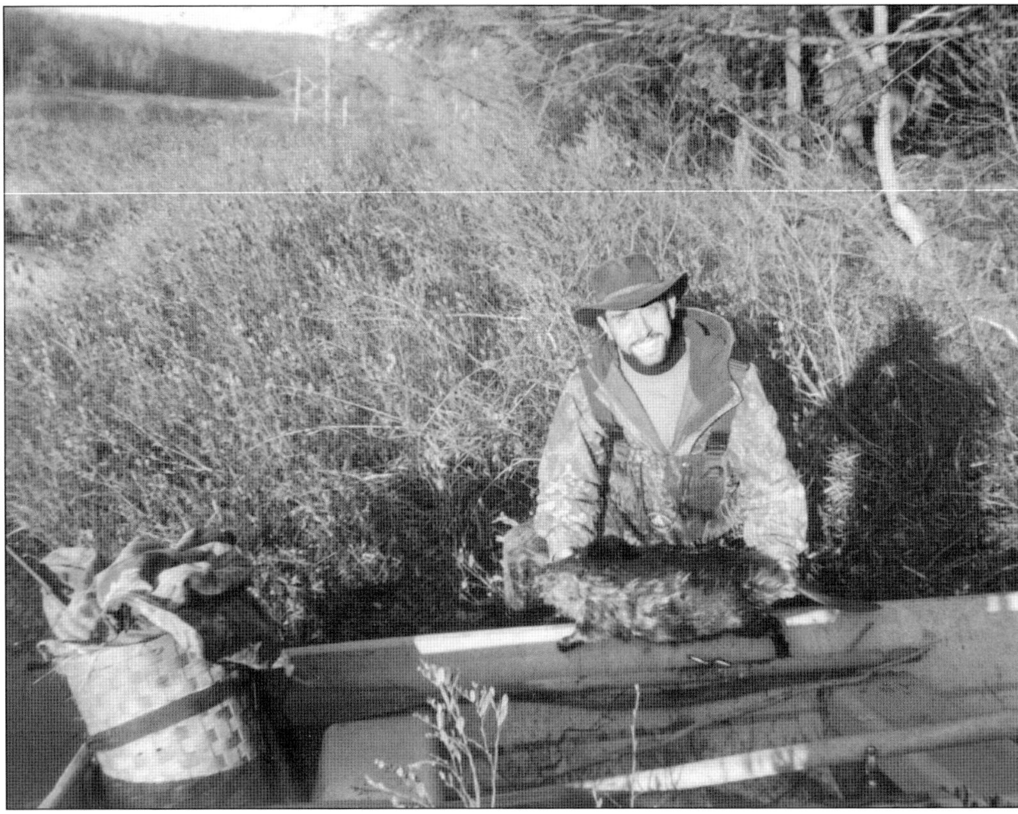

Greg Baker grew up around trapping, hunting, and fishing. His grandfather Ellsworth "Bud" Worden played a big role in exposing him to the outdoors. "My grandfather grew up trapping for income," Baker said. "That was a big staple of their livelihood. They not only sold the fur, but sometimes ate what they caught too. My grandfather always had a bunch of traps around when I was growing up. My father also trapped. My father trapped pretty big during the fur boom, mostly water animals. I learned quite a bit from my dad, too." (Both, courtesy of Greg Baker.)

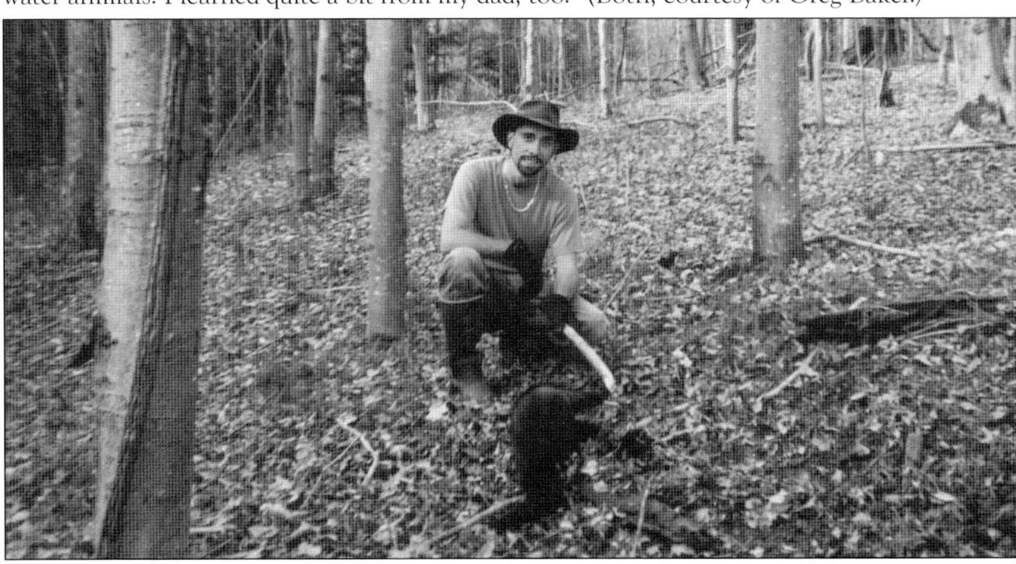

His first season with a real line, Greg Baker's line brought in about 100 animals. The fur prices were comparatively higher then than they currently are (in 2017–2018). The first animal that he trapped on a line was a muskrat, a popular beginner catch. He quickly surpassed those numbers in the years that followed. (Courtesy of Greg Baker.)

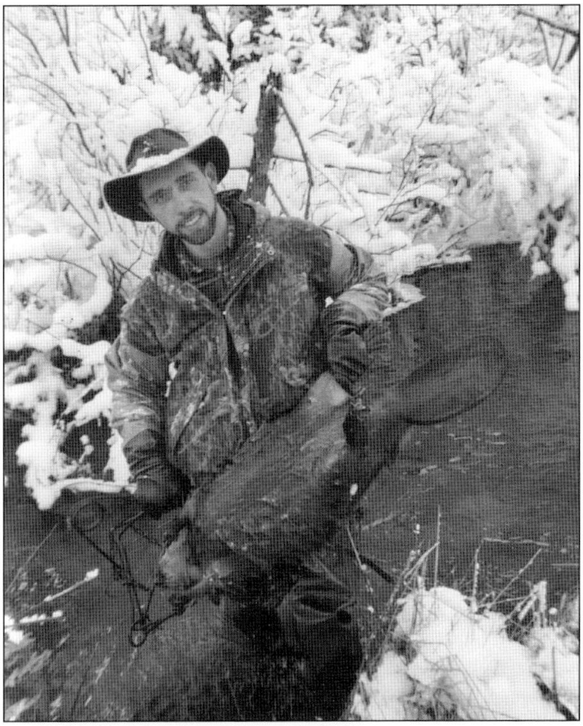

For about a year prior to this catch, people living in the vicinity of Lite Road in Remsen near Forestport had been reporting mountain lion sightings. As soon as this coyote was caught, those sightings ceased. This coyote had a black tip on its tail and could have been the culprit behind the "Lite Road Mountain Lion." (Courtesy of Greg Baker.)

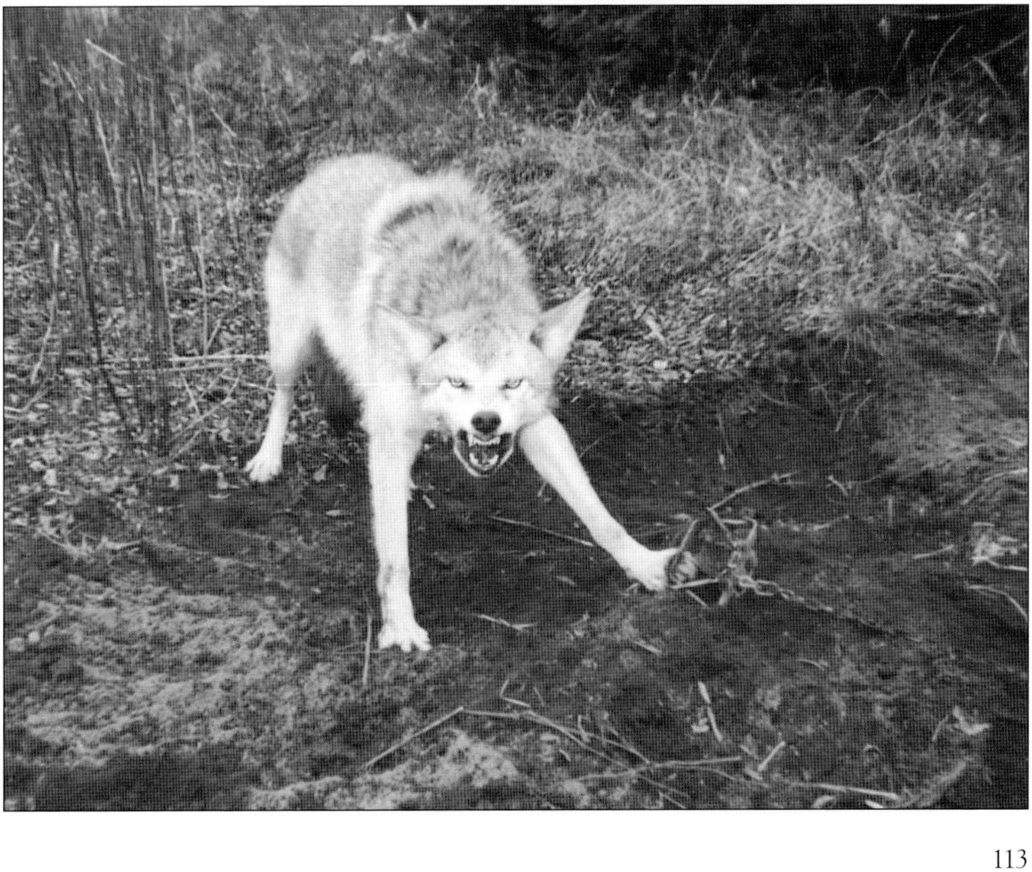

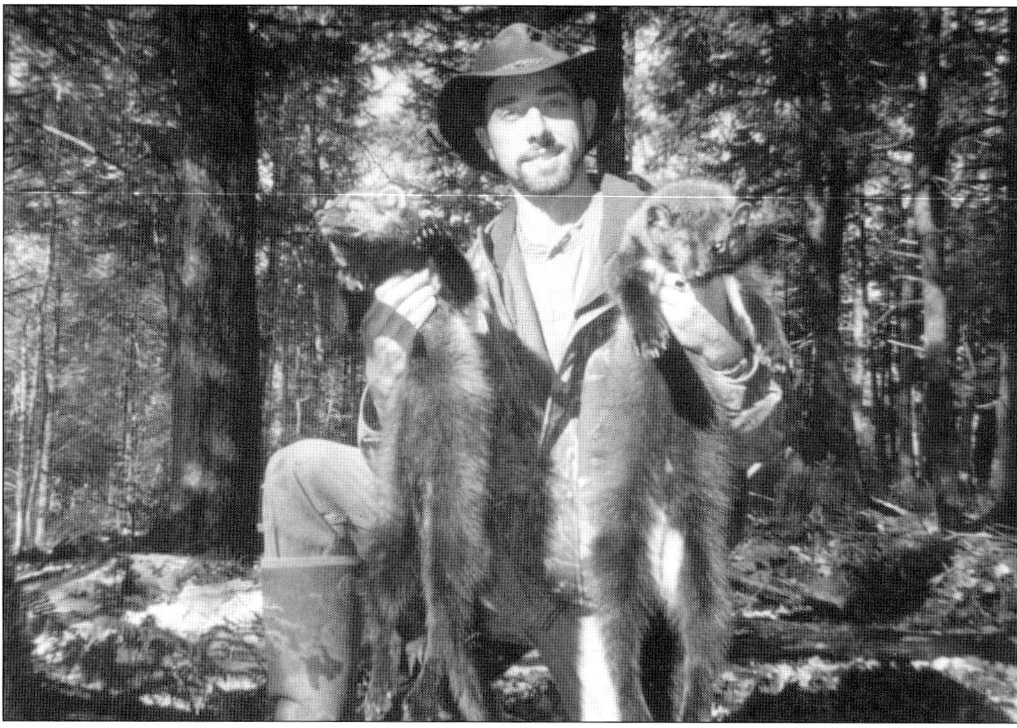

Trappers have the reputation of being notoriously tight-lipped about their techniques and tricks. Greg Baker (pictured): "An old-timer once said, 'You'd be willing to teach 300 guys that lived 300 miles away everything you knew, but you wouldn't teach 3 guys that lived 3 miles away anything you knew." That sums up the "learn it yourself" philosophy that many trappers operate from. The veterans usually give the rookies hints, but leave it up to them to learn most of it by trial and error. In the image above, Baker shows off two fishers he trapped. He is pictured below with a red fox he caught in a foothold on a small sandy knoll. (Both, courtesy of Greg Baker.)

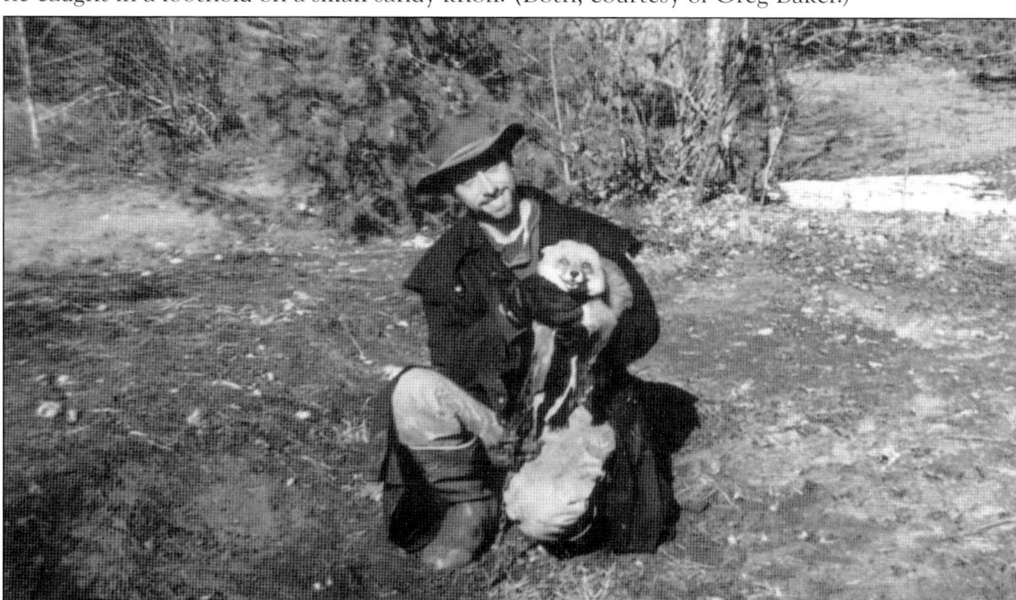

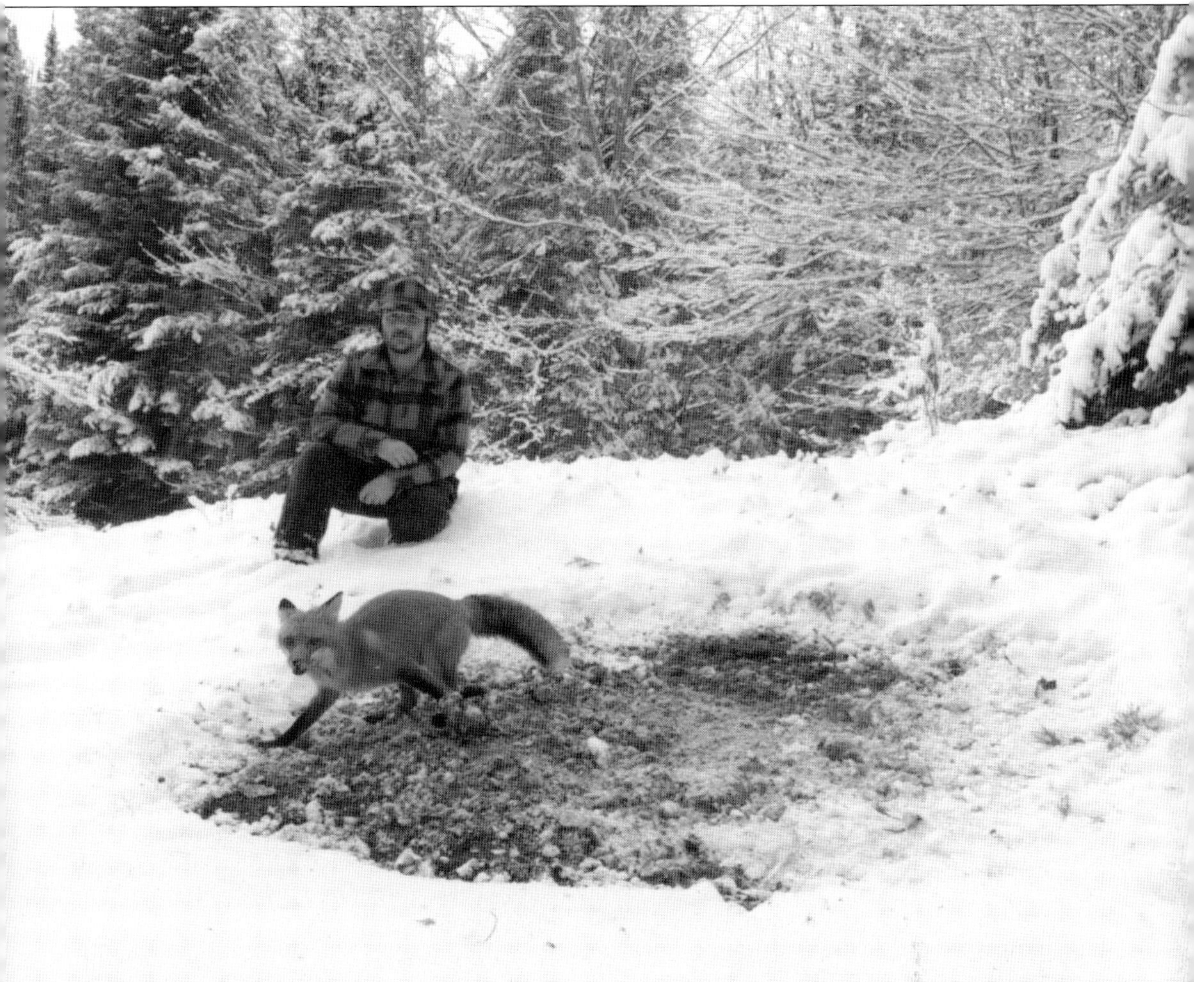

Bill Plete caught this red fox at a dirt hole set during one of the first snowfalls of the season. The fox's full, prime fur made a pretty contrast to the fresh, clean snow. (Author's collection.)

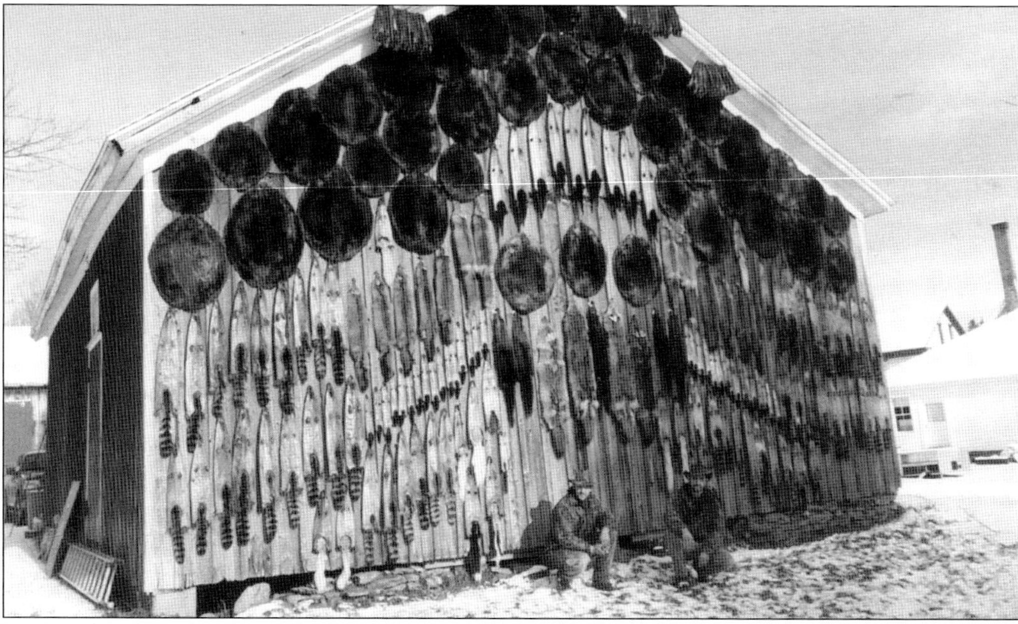

In the photograph above, the back wall of the barn is covered in Eric Horn and Greg Baker's 2006 season's catch of fur. Between opening day and December 31, they harvested 39 beaver, nine otters, 54 raccoons, four coyotes, five fishers, two opossums, four red foxes, nine grey fox, 122 muskrat, 35 mink, 15 skunks, and four squirrels. In the photograph below, Eric Horn is on the left, and Greg Baker is on the right. The two did a lot of trapping together throughout the years. (Both, courtesy of Greg Baker.)

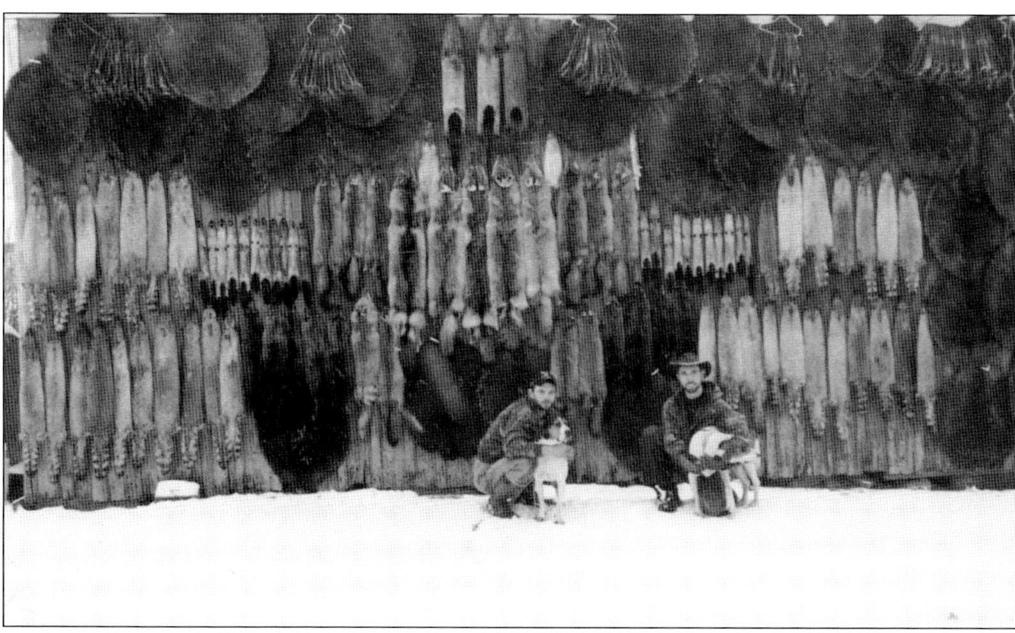

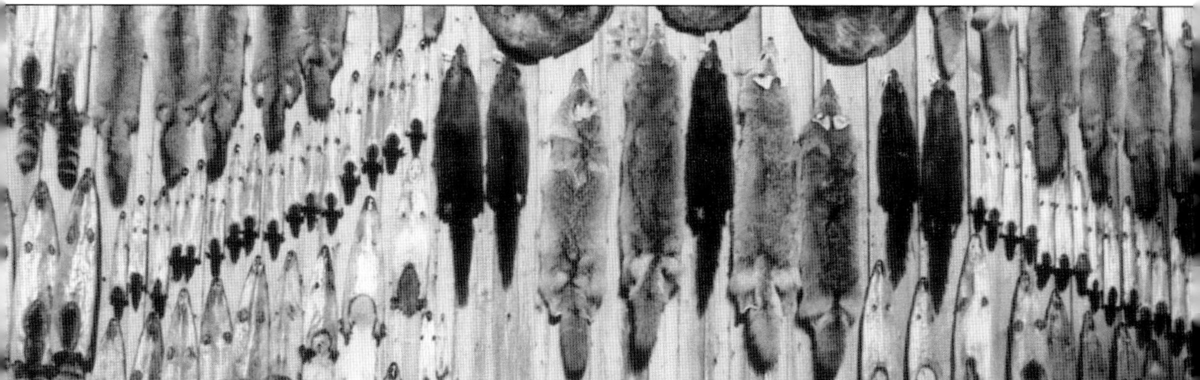

Fur trapping is an ethical form of conservation. Most people who adamantly oppose the practice do not understand wildlife management. Many wildlife biologists and conservation professionals support the use of regulated trapping for sustained harvest of some species of furbearers. Studies have shown that trapping is an effective method of managing furbearers, controlling damage caused by furbearers, and reducing the spread of diseases. These studies have shown that regulated trapping is a safe, practical, and moral means of capturing individual animals without impairing the survival of overall furbearer populations or damaging the environment. From left to right are Dave Horn, Eric Horn, and Greg Baker. (Courtesy of Greg Baker.)

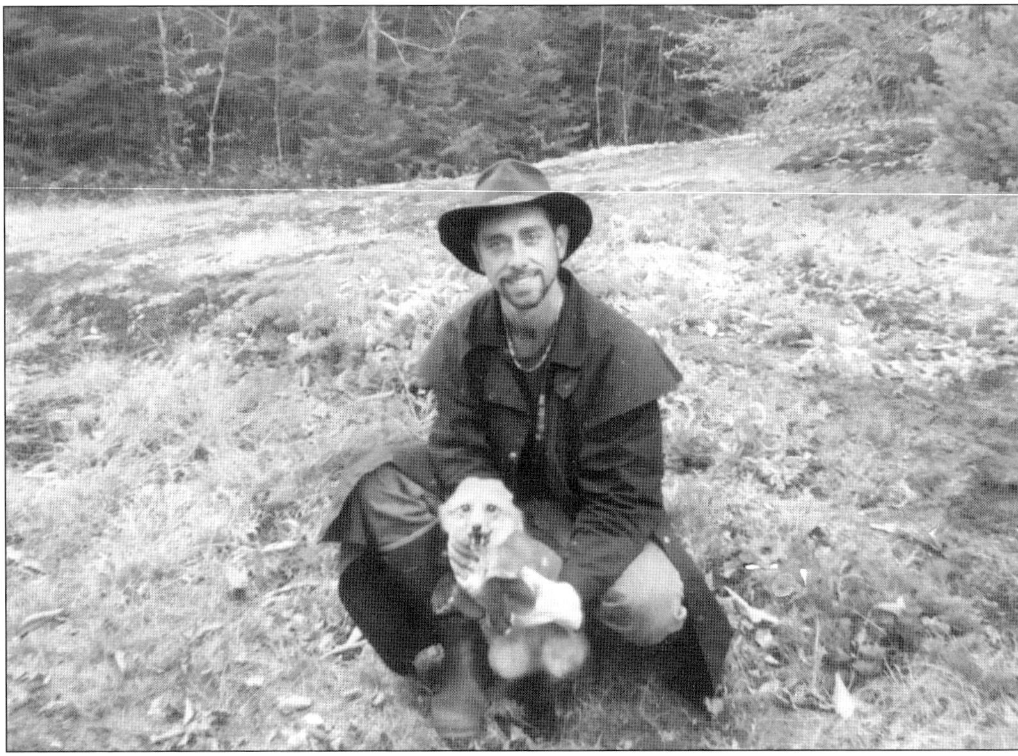

Greg Baker poses with a fox he caught in a foothold trap. (Courtesy of Greg Baker.)

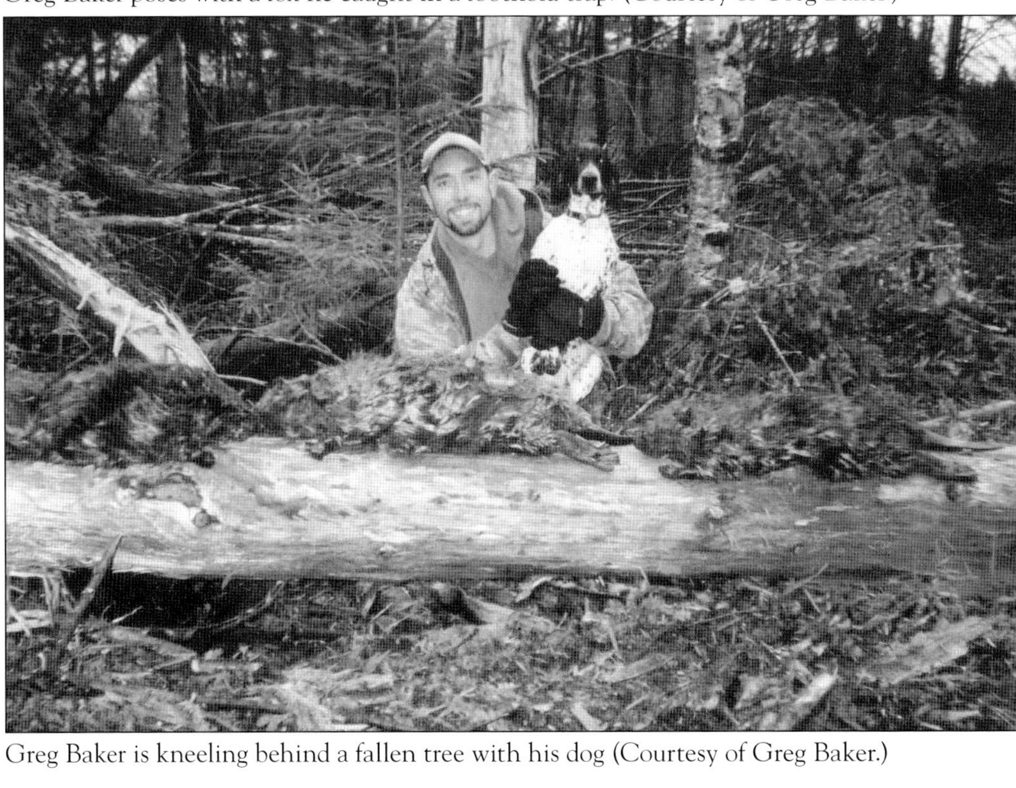

Greg Baker is kneeling behind a fallen tree with his dog (Courtesy of Greg Baker.)

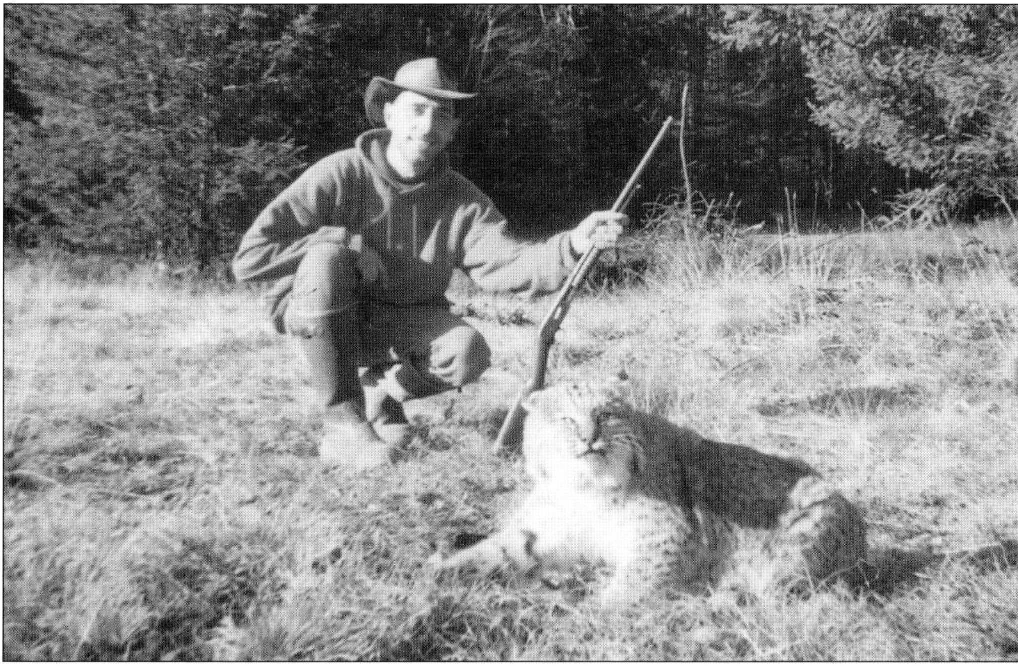

This large bobcat weighed about 40 pounds and was exceptionally light colored. It was a catch Greg Baker was proud of. The bobcat was trapped in the Wheelertown area of the Adirondack foothills. The forest is vast and dense in that area, and a lot of furbearers pass through. (Courtesy of Greg Baker.)

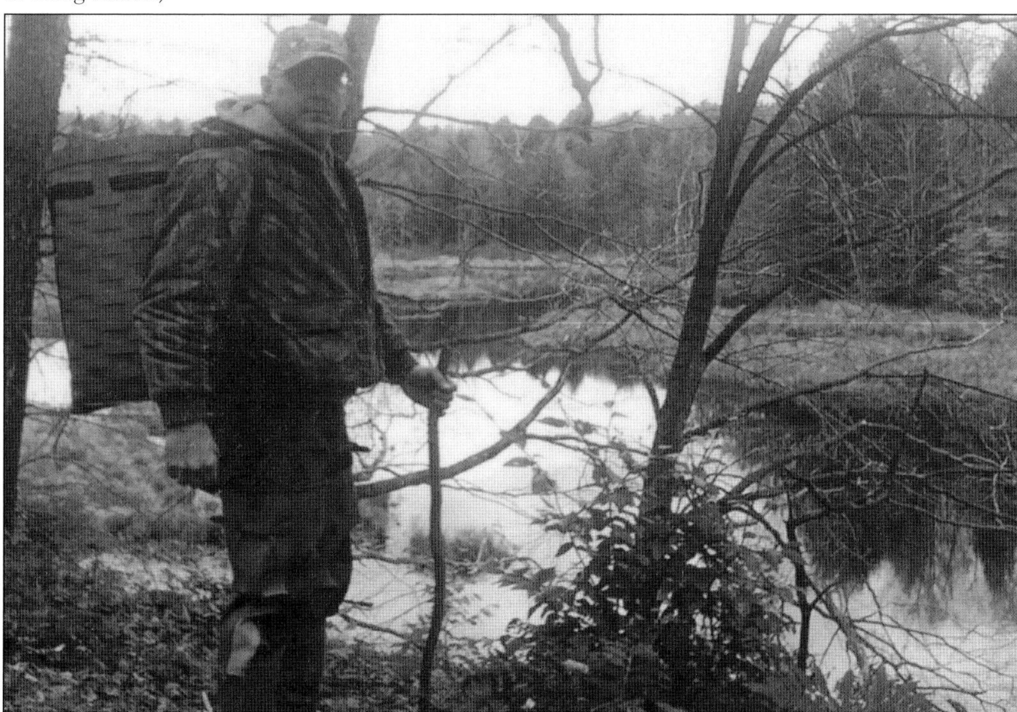

Tom Murphy pauses for a photograph on his Farr Road trapline. (Courtesy of Tom Murphy.)

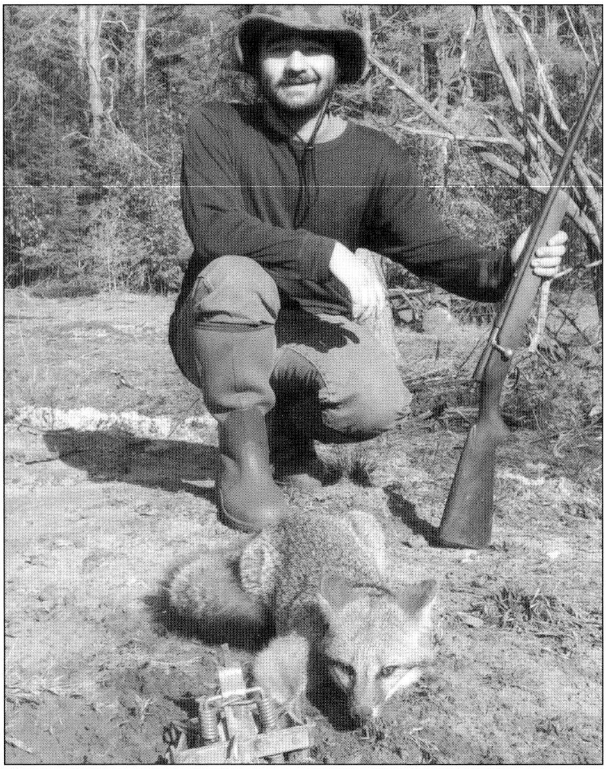

Bill Plete kneels behind the first grey fox of the season. He had missed him the first check, and then he missed him again for the second night. He then tweaked his set to a buried bait set. "I like to use that on slick fox," he said. "The next morning, I came to check the set, and there he was." (Courtesy of Bill Plete.)

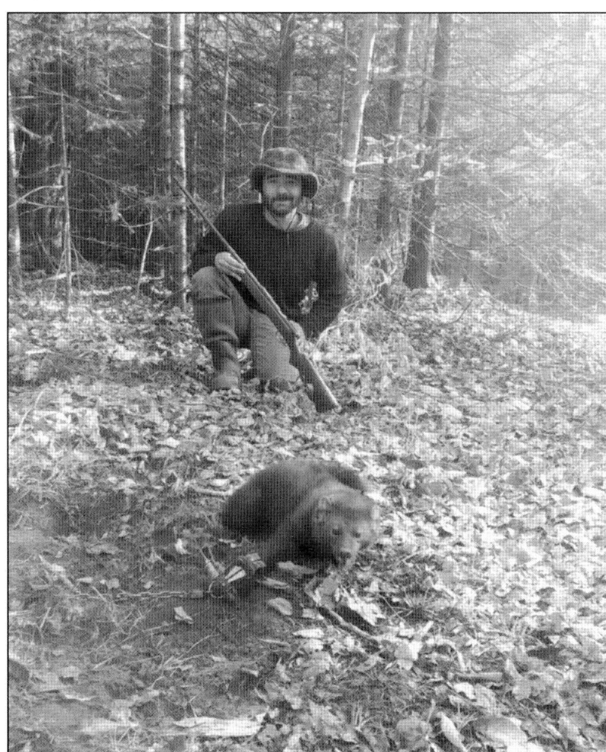

Bill Plete poses for a photograph with a fisher he caught in a foothold. Fishers are fearless predators. They eat rabbits, squirrels, mice, birds, and other critters. They also eat some nuts and berries. The physical characteristics of a fisher include its broad head with a narrow muzzle and the long, bushy tail. They also have very sharp teeth and retractable claws. (Courtesy of Bill Plete.)

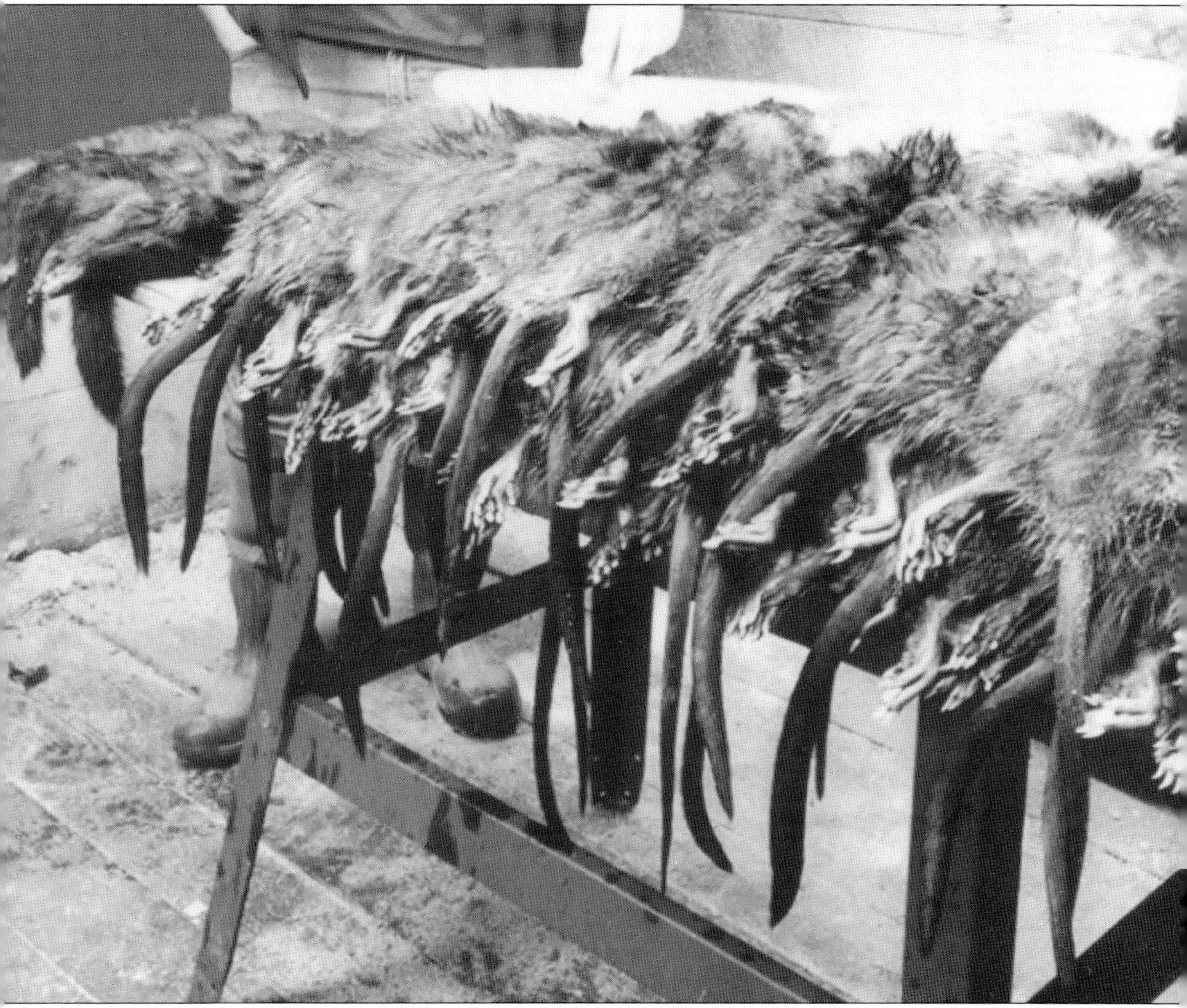

Here is another good day's catch for Shawn Horstman, consisting of 18 muskrats and three mink, piled up here. These critters were trapped in Boonville. (Courtesy of Shawn Horstman.)

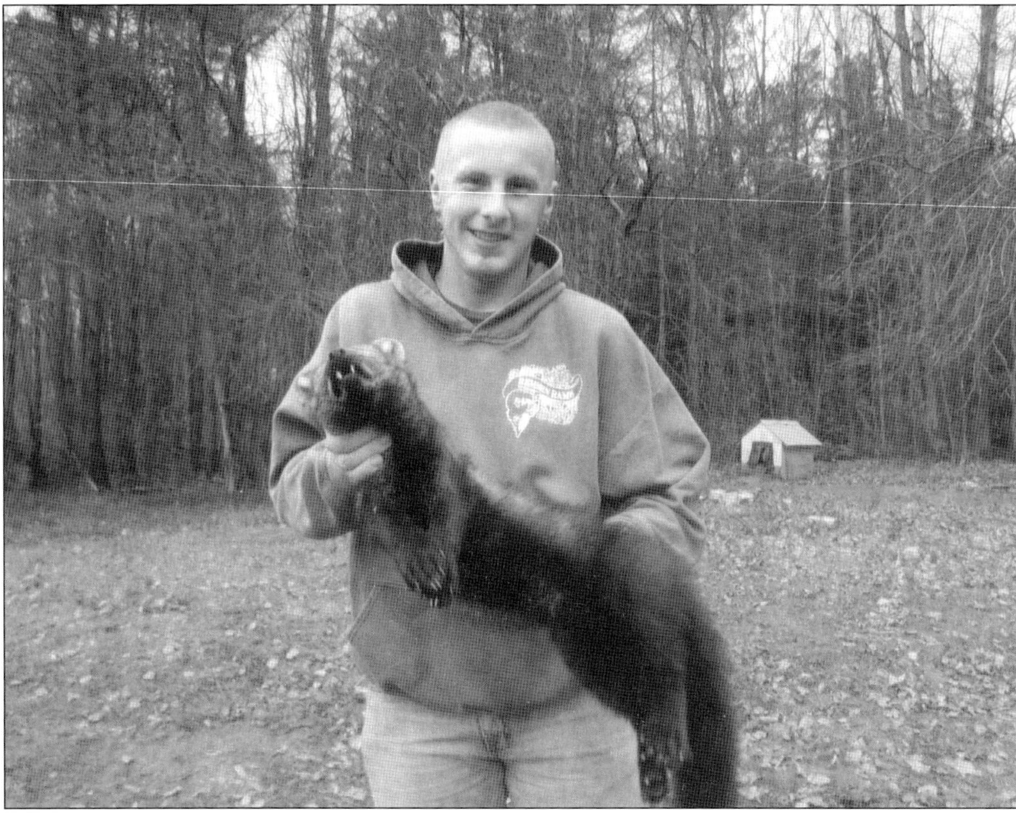

Shawn Horstman is seen with a fisher he trapped while he was in high school. Fisher trapping is heavily regulated. Every fisher must be tagged and reported. In recent years, the New York State Department of Environmental Conservation reduced the fisher- and marten-trapping season from 46 days to 30 days in select Adirondack Wildlife Management Units. (Author's collection.)

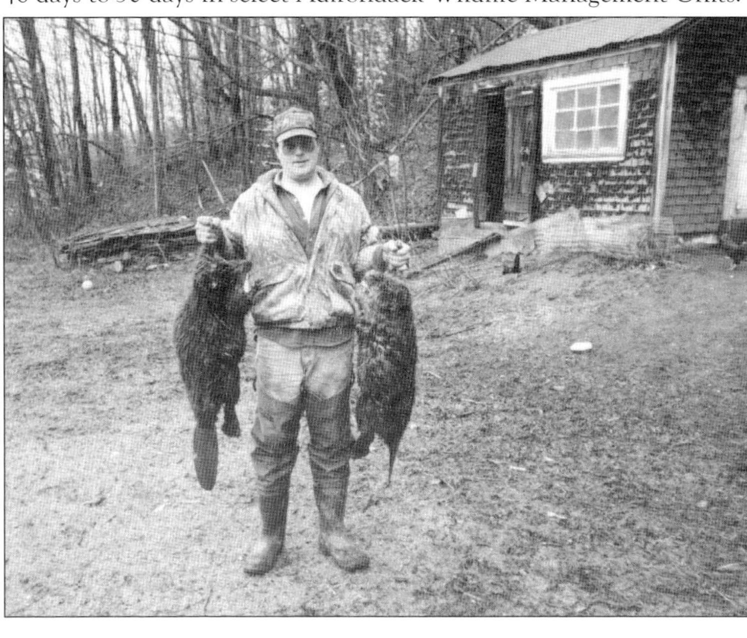

Chris Graves used to run a trap line from Remsen into the Adirondacks. He mostly focused on water trapping. His first catch on the line was a raccoon. In this photograph, he holds up two beaver he trapped. This image was captured somewhere around 1995. (Courtesy of Chris Graves.)

Michael Schauer trapped his first muskrat in 1978 when he was 12 years old in the Tug Hill region, on the west edge of the Adirondacks. He used a No. 1 Victor stop-loss with a homemade lure set in a small stream. "I was so proud," he said. "I carried that muskrat everywhere I went for two days, even into stores to show people!" (Courtesy of Michael Schauer.)

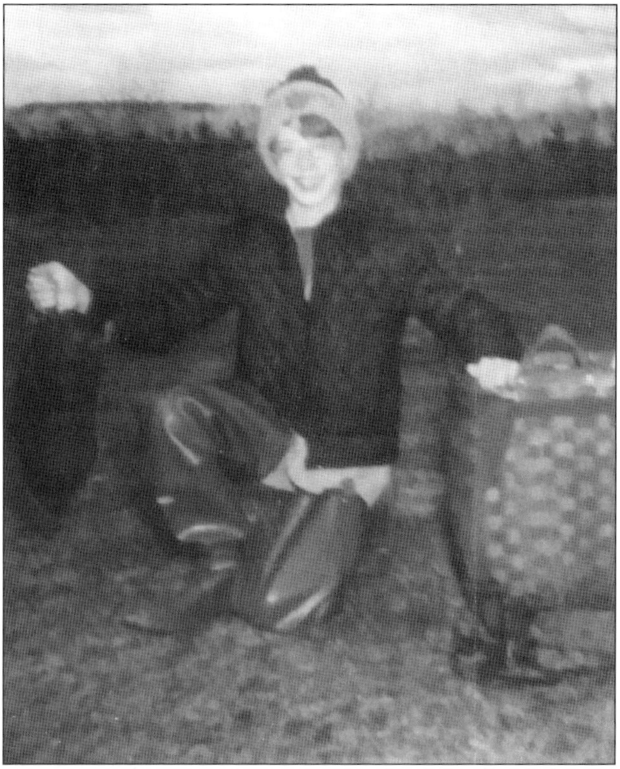

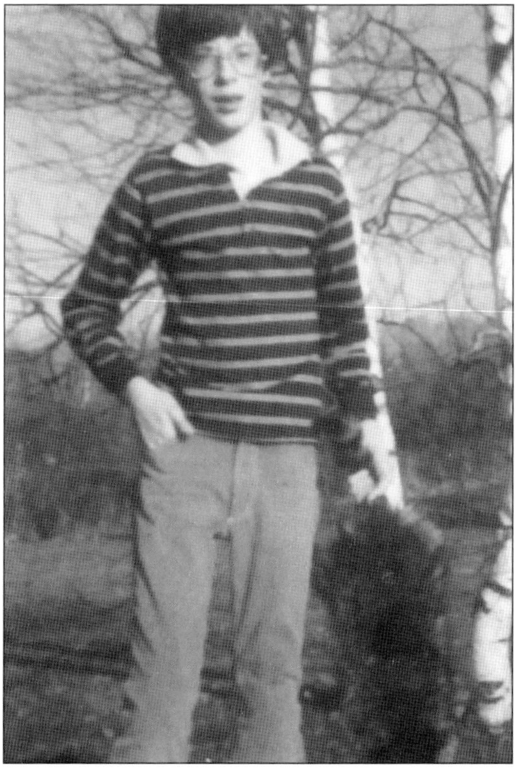

In October 1979, Michael Schauer caught his first raccoon with the same homemade lure he used to get his first muskrat. He used a No. 1 Victor stop-loss for this set as well. (Courtesy of Michael Schauer.)

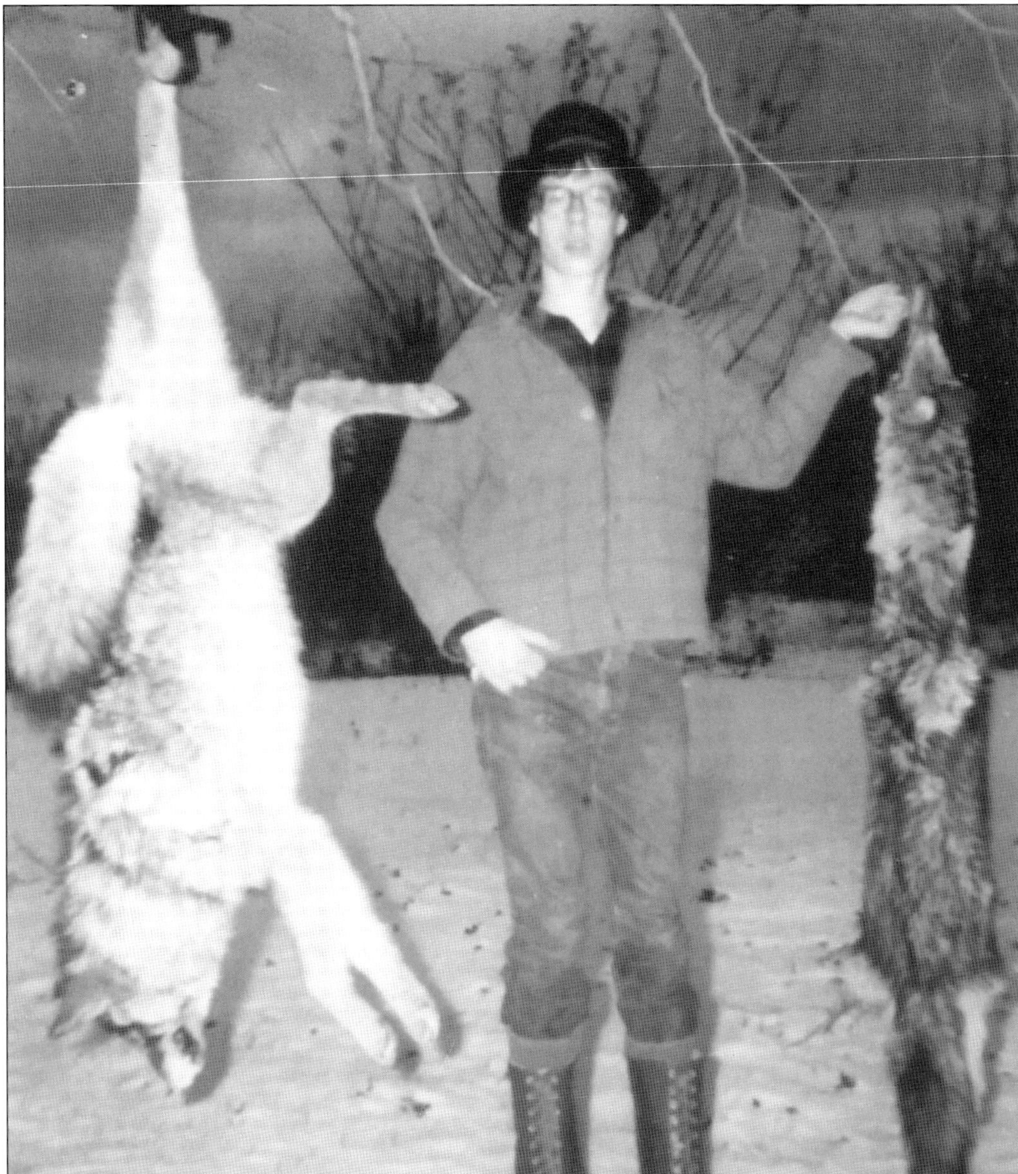

In November 1981, Michael Schauer was attempting to check his set, which was located in a pasture. That day, a bull that was grazing in the pasture decided to charge him from the top of the hill. He had just enough time to scramble up the lone tree in the pasture before the bull got to him. "I was scared and shaking uncontrollably when I happened to look across the field and saw a circle of cows all facing in," he said. "It took me a minute to realize that was where my fox set was. The bull was underneath the tree snorting and tearing stuff up. The bull eventually got bored with it and wandered back over the hill where he had come from. When the coast was clear I climbed down and made my way to the circle of cows. There was something in the trap and it was my first coyote! After shooting it I quickly took the coyote out of the set and ran as fast as I could to the fence." In the photograph, the one on the right that is skinned out is the coyote from the cow field. The one on the left was caught the next day in a different set. (Courtesy of Michael Schauer.)

Michael Schauer had a double otter catch in a water-set Conibear around 2009. Otters are social creatures who frequently travel in pairs. Males are generally larger than females, at around 44 inches in total length, and females at around 38-inches total length. Otter's weights range from 10 to 30 pounds. (Courtesy of Michael Schauer.)

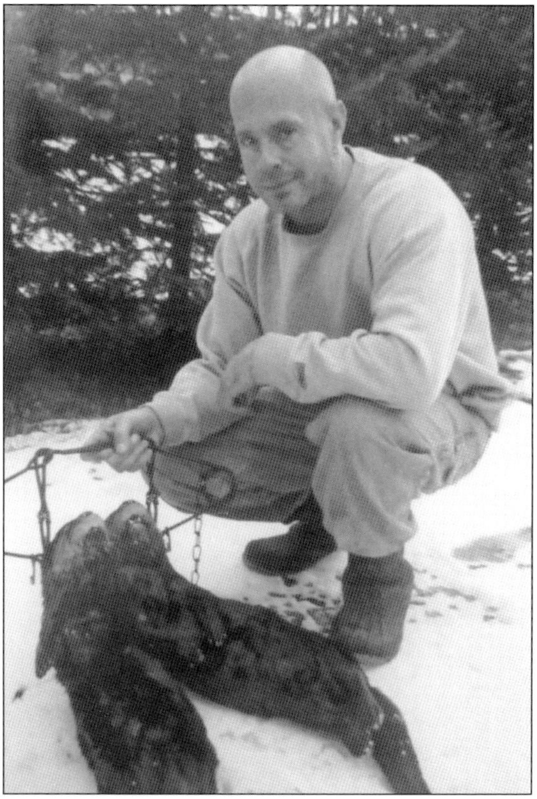

Pelts are sold in an elaborate chain that begins with local country buyers and travels to the overseas fur market. Fur buyers judge fur for size, color, quality, and primeness, which is the seasonal thickening of an animal's fur as it prepares for the colder winter season. (Courtesy of Greg Baker.)

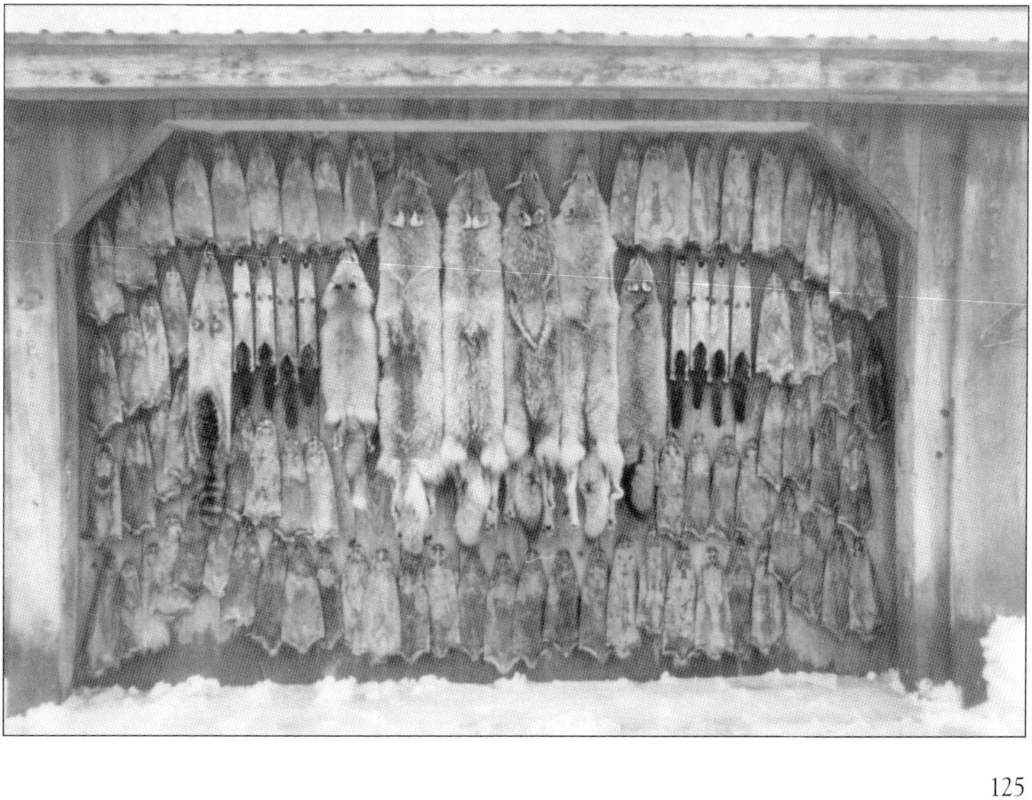

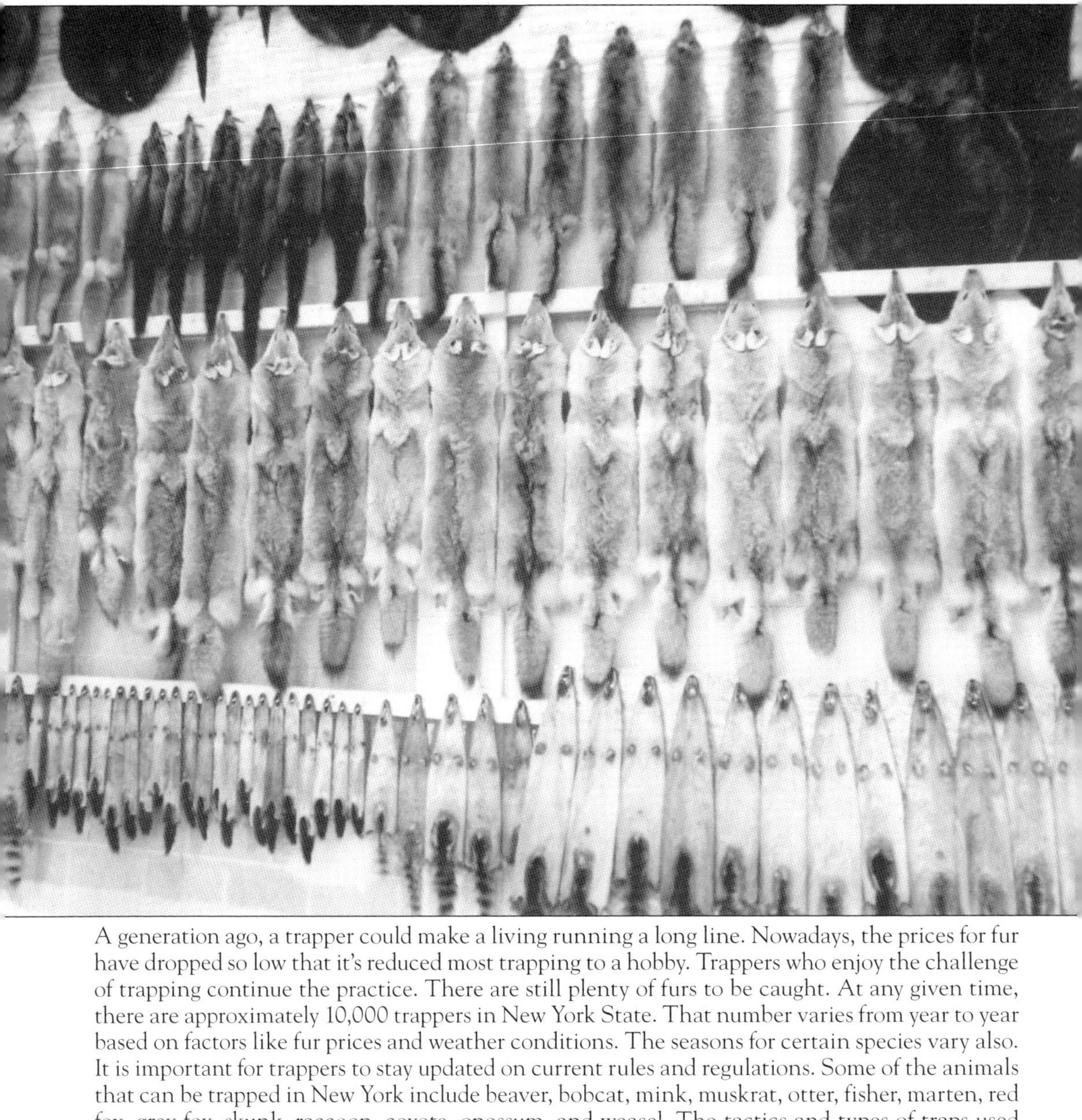

A generation ago, a trapper could make a living running a long line. Nowadays, the prices for fur have dropped so low that it's reduced most trapping to a hobby. Trappers who enjoy the challenge of trapping continue the practice. There are still plenty of furs to be caught. At any given time, there are approximately 10,000 trappers in New York State. That number varies from year to year based on factors like fur prices and weather conditions. The seasons for certain species vary also. It is important for trappers to stay updated on current rules and regulations. Some of the animals that can be trapped in New York include beaver, bobcat, mink, muskrat, otter, fisher, marten, red fox, grey fox, skunk, raccoon, coyote, opossum, and weasel. The tactics and types of traps used are tailored specifically to the target animal. (Courtesy of Greg Baker.)

Bibliography

Bogdan, Robert. *Adirondack Vernacular: The Photography of Henry M. Beach.* Syracuse, NY: Syracuse University Press, 2003.

Dunham, Harvey. *Adirondack French Louie.* Utica, NY: 1953.

Lyons, Nick. *The Quotable Fisherman.* New York: Skyhorse Publishing, 2010.

O'Hern, William J. *Adirondack Characters and Campfire Yarns.* Cleveland, NY: Forager Press, 2005.

Podskoch, Martin, David Hayden, and Sam Glanzman. *Adirondack Stories: Historical Sketches.* Colchester, CT: Podskoch Press, 2007.

Reehil, Roy E. & O'Hern, *William J. Adirondack Adventures: Bon Gillespie & Harvey Dunham on French Louie's Trail.* Cleveland, NY: Forager Press, 2012.

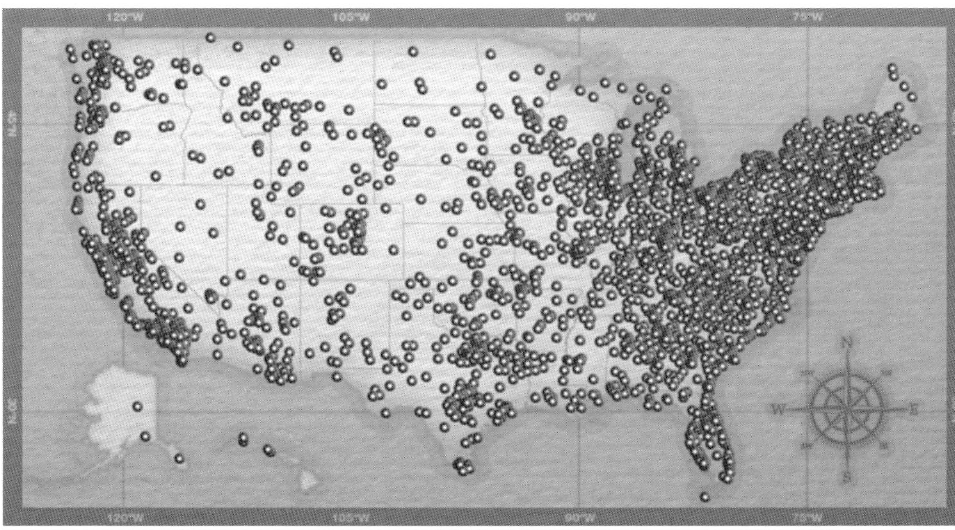

Consistent with our mission to preserve history on a local level, this book was printed in South Carolina on American-made paper and manufactured entirely in the United States. Products carrying the accredited Forest Stewardship Council (FSC) label are printed on 100 percent FSC-certified paper.